THE MAKING OF AN ASSASSIN

THE MAKING OF AN ASSASSIN

WHY SIRHAN SIRHAN MURDERED ROBERT KENNEDY

BY MEL AYTON

FRONTLINE BOOKS

First published in Great Britain in 2025
by Frontline Books
An imprint of
Pen & Sword Books Ltd
Yorkshire - Philadelphia

ISBN 9 781 39903 279 7

A CIP catalogue record for this book is available from the British Library

Typeset by Lapiz Digital
Printed and bound in the UK by CPI Group (UK) Ltd, Croydon, CR0 4YY.

Printed on paper from a sustainable source by CPI Group (UK) Ltd, Croydon, CR0 4YY

FSC
www.fsc.org
MIX
Paper | Supporting responsible forestry
FSC® C013604

The Publisher's authorised representative in the EU for product safety is Authorised Rep Compliance Ltd., Ground Floor, 71 Lower Baggot Street, Dublin D02 P593, Ireland.
www.arccompliance.com

For a complete list of Pen & Sword titles please contact
PEN & SWORD BOOKS LTD
47 Church Street, Barnsley, South Yorkshire, S70 2AS, England
E-mail: enquiries@pen-and-sword.co.uk
Website: www.pen-and-sword.co.uk
or
PEN & SWORD BOOKS
1950 Lawrence Rd, Havertown, PA 19083, USA
E-mail: uspen-and-sword@casematepublishers.com

CONTENTS

This book is dedicated to the investigative journalist Dan Moldea, whose work in seeking out the truth about the Robert Kennedy assassination is unsurpassed.

FOREWORD

By John Douglas and Mark Olshaker

As rational human beings, we are always trying to make sense of things. And as our long experience in criminal investigative analysis and behavioural profiling has shown us, this understandable trait applies just as powerfully to the realm of murder, particularly political murder. If a disenfranchised nobody can cut down the president of the United States, or even his presidential candidate brother five years later, then the universe is without meaning, and the foundations of history are built on chance. Far more logical and, in its peculiar way, emotionally sustaining, for the crime to be the result of a sophisticated conspiracy equal to the significance of the victim himself. As Norman Mailer put it in his examination of the JFK assassination, *Oswald's Tale*, "Tragedy is vastly preferable to absurdity."

In recent times the controversy surrounding the assassination of Senator Robert F. Kennedy has once again surfaced within the American media, including interviews with Robert Kennedy's son, Robert Kennedy Jr. The 2024 presidential candidate, and coronavirus vaccine conspiracist, has stated that he did not believe Sirhan Bishara Sirhan, the then-24-year-old man who was convicted, sentenced to death, later commuted to life in prison, for shooting and mortally wounding his father with a .22 calibre handgun on the night of June 5, 1968 in the Ambassador Hotel in Los Angeles, shortly after RFK declared victory in the California primary, was not responsible for the senator's death. He laid the blame for the assassination at the door of the CIA.

Motive is a tricky topic when it comes to political assassination. Some assassins and would-be assassins like President Abraham Lincoln's killer John Wilkes Booth, seem genuinely to have believed in a cause; in Booth's case the misbegotten notion that he could change the course of the American Civil War. Far more often, these men—and they are almost always men—have a subconscious or semi-conscious desire to make themselves as important as the object of their murderous obsession. John Lennon's killer and former fan, Mark David Chapman, initially claimed he murdered Lennon because he came to realize he was a 'phony'. John Douglas' prison interview with Chapman and our behavioral analysis showed a more straightforward motive: if he could take out a world-famous and beloved celebrity, then in a twisted way, Chapman was as powerful and significant as Lennon, and the two names would be forever intertwined. Arthur Bremer, who shot and permanently paralyzed Alabama governor and presidential candidate George Wallace at a Maryland shopping centre in 1972, originally set his sights on President Richard Nixon, but found his security too tight to get close enough.

The point is, whatever the titular motive for the crime, virtually all assassins (and here we might except the attempt in Operation Valkyrie late in the Second World War to try to assassinate Adolf Hitler), including Booth, share certain basic traits: a deep-seated sense of inadequacy and insignificance, coupled with a resentment about the way the world has treated them, triangulated with a resentment that they have not been recognized for their own significance and worth. At the same time, we cannot ignore the assassins' self-proclaimed motive, because that is the driving force and proximate cause of the often history-altering crime. How might the American sixties, seventies and beyond have been radically different had neither John Lennon nor Robert Kennedy fallen to an assassin's bullet?

Robert Kennedy's assassination came five years after his brother Jack's and two months after Martin Luther King was gunned down in Memphis. It occurred amidst youth rioting, soaring crime, Blacks protesting, and Americans disheartened by the fact there was 'no light at the end of the tunnel' of the Vietnam War. Americans began to believe yet another crazy misfit had slain one of their best and brightest leaders. However, throughout the 1970s and 1980s and fuelled by a recognition of the many anomalies that arose in the original police investigation, many American conspiracy writers alleged that Sirhan may have been an innocent dupe.

As concerns the RFK assassination, like Robert Kennedy Jr., conspiracy advocates have continued to promote the notion that the conflict in the Middle East was not the root cause of the assassination. Instead, they insist, Sirhan was controlled by elements of American Intelligence who brainwashed him to act as a decoy in order to allow another purported conspirator to carry out the murderous act. Robert Kennedy was thus killed because of right-wing dark forces within the nation.

In his previous book, *The Forgotten Terrorist,* Mel Ayton examined how these conspiracy theories developed and looked at the way in which their promulgators succeeded in persuading a substantial number of Americans that Robert Kennedy's assassin was either an innocent 'patsy' or had acted in conjunction with others to assassinate the senator. In an examination of the modus operandi of conspiracy writers, Mel discovered how the public was manipulated into accepting their conspiracy allegations and of how their theories were built around nothing more than misinterpretation and misrepresentation of the evidence, combined with crude speculation. In his latest book on the subject, Mel describes how the confusion about Sirhan's motive led many writers to assume he had displayed no real reason to assassinate the senator. To counter this, he meticulously and cogently demonstrates that the picture of the assassin painted by Robert F. Kennedy Jr. and the conspiracists is in direct contradiction to the real circumstances and the real character and motives of the assassin. Even Sirhan's diary-keeping with its notorious phrase, "RFK must die, die, RFK must die," is an almost universally common trait of the assassin personality.

It was our friend and colleague, investigative journalist Dan Moldea, who first took on the formidable task of sorting fact from fiction, and evidence from supposition, with his landmark 1995 book, *The Killing of Robert Kennedy*. With a clear and honest eye, Dan elucidated how many of the conspiracy theories arose out of mistakes by the Los Angeles Police Department in investigating the crime, especially surrounding the collection and collation of evidence. He pointed out how controversies about the assassination related to human error, including misplacing files, a mixing up Sirhan's firearm with a test gun, and misidentifying purported bullet holes in the hotel kitchen pantry by police officers and FBI agents who were not trained in ballistics. Some police investigators, Dan discovered, had made statements they later came to regret. All this added to the natural reticence to accept that one displaced and angry emigrant from the Middle East had been able to change our history and why conspiracy advocates were able to plant so much doubt in the minds of the American public and translate any mistakes in the investigation into conspiratorial intrigue.

However, *The Making of an Assassin* is not about the perceived conspiracies surrounding the assassination of Robert F. Kennedy. Those ideas, particularly the view that fourteen shots had been fired in the Ambassador Hotel's kitchen pantry, the assertion that Sirhan had acted as a hypnotised assassin, and the insistence by Robert F. Kennedy Jr. that Sirhan was never in a position to fire the fatal shot, have already been conclusively debunked by Moldea and Ayton.

While we do not go nearly as far as Mel in declaring that the Kennedy assassination was the first major act of Palestinian terrorism targeting the United States (we would classify it as a personal cause / individual extremist homicide), it is true that in many ways Sirhan's personal anger, grievances and inadequacies conform to the terrorist profile as well as the assassin's.

Although most Americans quickly became aware after the assassination that Sirhan was an Arab (he was referred to as a 'Jordanian citizen'), the source of his rage was not clearly explained in most news stories. In those days few people even knew what a 'Palestinian' was—Israeli Prime Minister Golda Meir said shortly after the assassination that there was 'no such thing' as a Palestinian people and that 'they did not exist'—and even fewer understood their grievances. At the time, the Palestine Liberation Organization would not be taken over by Yasser Arafat until a year after the assassination. The hijackings and killings that would bring the Palestinians to the centre of the world stage had not yet begun. And many Americans appeared to obfuscate the political motivation for the assassination by focusing on what American leaders insisted were broader cultural reasons for the crime, including a lack of gun control and how the assassin appeared to be 'deranged'. While we would argue that the vast majority of murderers have some degree of mental illness, they know exactly what they are doing, are mission-oriented within their own paranoid and obsessive world view and believe their 'principles' justify their actions. Sirhan also expressed a desire to eliminate President Lyndon B. Johnson and Vice President and candidate Hubert Humphrey. This is not the ideation of a deranged killer or an unwitting patsy. This is the obsession of someone who is, at the same time, a mentally unstable and angry nobody and a driven, mission-oriented idealogue.

In this book, Mel delves deeply into Sirhan's background, from the time of his birth in war-torn Palestine to his decades-long struggle to secure his freedom. He writes of how "the mumbo-jumbo of Sirhan's mirror-gazing, purported amnesiac episodes and trance-like states as an explanation for the Robert Kennedy assassination has succeeded in obscuring just how explicit his motive was." And the answer to the question of conscious motive, Mel reveals, "lies not in purported conspiratorial intrigue but in the story of how Sirhan's life developed from an innocent 12-year-old Arab immigrant into a committed and fanatical supporter of the Palestinian cause who embraced virulent anti-American sentiments." It is this crucial examination of Sirhan's self-identified motives—his hatred of Jews and his fanatical desire to eliminate a pro-Israel presidential candidate—which has often been ignored or overlooked by the American mainstream media.

Using FBI and LAPD reports and investigative files—including police 'Special Unit Senator' files—and examining seldom seen materials, Mel has managed to unearth neglected witness accounts and overlooked forensic evidence, including interviews with family members, work colleagues and friends. He constructs a compelling review of Sirhan's life, providing the reader with rational analysis of Sirhan's state of mind leading up to and following the assassination.

Like two of Mel's previous books, *The Forgotten Terrorist* and *Dark Soul of the South, The Making of an Assassin* represents a substantial contribution to the record and history of a horrendous crime, as well as the literature of the assassin personality and motive.

INTRODUCTION

"The deepest sin against the human mind is to believe things without evidence." Aldous Huxley

Most Americans today place the first act of terrorism on American soil to the day in 1993 when the first attempt to bring down New York's World Trade Centre was carried out. The terrorist act left six people dead and more than 1,000 wounded. However, in reality, the first act of modern terrorism in the United States actually occurred fifty-five years ago when Sirhan Sirhan assassinated Senator Robert F. Kennedy—an act that subverted the American electoral process and altered the history of the United States.

Kennedy had just won the California presidential primary on the night of June 5, 1968, when he thanked a huge crowd of enthusiastic supporters at the Ambassador Hotel in Los Angeles and made his way out through the kitchen. Waiting for him there was Sirhan, 24 years old, holding a .22 calibre revolver. The Palestinian Arab shot the presidential candidate three times, twice in the back and once behind his ear. It was the last shot that proved fatal. Kennedy died twenty-six hours later at the young age of 42. Five other people in the crowd were wounded but survived. Sirhan—who emigrated with his family to America when he was 12 years old—cited Kennedy's support for Israel as the reason for the assassination.

Kennedy had appeared on a path to the Democratic nomination with support from a broad coalition of voting demographics, while his youth and liberal ideology energized the Democratic base. Following his assassination, Democrats instead nominated then Vice President Hubert Humphrey at a chaotic 1968 convention, where Humphrey—a moderate who supported the Vietnam War—fended off a challenge from anti-war progressive Eugene McCarthy. Humphrey went on to lose the general election to Republican Richard Nixon by a margin of more than 100 electoral votes.

In March 1969 Sirhan was convicted of the murder and sentenced to death. Three years later, when the California supreme court invalidated all pending death sentences issued before 1972, the conviction was commuted to life imprisonment with the possibility of parole.

Sirhan never denied that he went to the Ambassador Hotel with a gun, waited in the pantry, approached Senator Kennedy with his gun drawn, and fired it eight times. Nor would his numerous appeals over the years deny he obtained a gun, purchased ammunition, and practiced at a target range on the day before the murder. He never denied he had on his possession when he was arrested newspaper clippings about Senator Kennedy's support for Israel.

In court Sirhan said he had been 'politically motivated'. He said he admired RFK but felt betrayed by his staunch support of Israel and his intention to send it fifty bombers. His lawyers argued 'diminished capacity', meaning Sirhan was likely insane at the time of the shooting. However, the idea of diminished capacity was too novel a concept in 1968. Furthermore, many Americans did not understand Sirhan's Palestinian identity, since many newspapers simply identified him as Jordanian. Most Americans did not know what a 'Palestinian' was. Additionally, few realised how the conflict between Arabs and Jews created bitter resentments within Arab American communities within the United States. This defense was discounted.

As time passed a coterie of conspiracy writers, many of whom became lawyers and advocates for the assassin, began to place in Sirhan's mind the idea that he could secure his freedom if he could convince the American public that he was simply a tool in the hands of others. In other words, he had acted as a hypnotized assassin. Because he claimed he could not remember the actual shooting, he must have been a controlled patsy and therefore innocent of the crime. Sirhan went along with this suggestion and it became central to his appeals procedures and parole hearings over the years.

Because the assassination came just over four years after Robert Kennedy's brother, President John F. Kennedy, was murdered in Dallas, and just two months after Martin Luther King Jr. was gunned down in Memphis, the nation focused on gun violence and hatred of the Kennedy family as motives for the assassination.

To this day the subject of the assassination of Senator Robert F. Kennedy has remained in the news as conspiracy writers, assisted by the ruminations of Hollywood celebrities, have continued to pour scorn on the official investigations into the murder without so much as providing *any* credible evidence to back up their claims.[1]

It is no mystery why some Hollywood celebrities support the notion of an innocent Palestinian refugee railroaded into a notorious murder case. Many in Hollywood have endorsed and embraced the Palestinian cause mimicking the American left's decades-old support for Palestinian Arabs. Unable to gauge Sirhan's true character by reading recent conspiracy books, they would naturally assume Sirhan mysteriously acted without a motive.

Most recently, Robert Kennedy's son, Robert F. Kennedy Jr., has joined the fray, and repeated the decades-old, debunked story that Ace Security guard, Thane Eugene Cesar, who accompanied his father to the pantry of the Los Angeles Ambassador Hotel at the time of the assassination, was the real shooter. However, RFK Jr. did not provide any substantial and credible evidence whatsoever.

RFK Jr. and the conspiracists have deployed theories of alleged amnesia and mental fog to excuse Sirhan's behavior at the scene of the crime and posited unproven and unprovable theories of hypnosis.[2] And the falsehoods promoted by conspiracists: a 'girl in a polka dot dress' controlled Sirhan; conspiratorial interference with the ballistics evidence; the creation of suspicion around LAPD crime scene mistakes; multiple teams of CIA-controlled assassins skulking around the Los Angeles Ambassador Hotel; allegations that Sirhan was never close enough to RFK to fire the fatal shot, allegations of Sirhan firing 'blanks'; accusations against an innocent security guard Thane Eugene Cesar, have all been addressed and debunked over the years.[3]

In 2018, on the fiftieth anniversary of the assassination, Sirhan's brother Munir said, "From the start, I doubted the charges because Sirhan couldn't hurt a fly. He wasn't capable of it, running at someone and shooting them." Munir and many others believe this notion forms the key to the mystery of how his ostensibly peace-loving brother wound up convicted of killing Robert Kennedy. Sirhan Sirhan was a 'hypnotised CIA assassin', they say.[4]

They all characterized Sirhan as an apolitical, non-anti-Semitic and a non-violent 'hypnotized patsy' who, at best, had only a minor role in the killing of the senator. Over the decades Munir, conspiracy advocates and Sirhan's lawyers have one thing in common.

They have all attempted to present the assassin to the public as a misunderstood soul who had no real animus towards Kennedy because, in reality, he had been used by others, particularly agents of the CIA, to kill the senator.

As this book demonstrates, the picture of the assassin painted by Munir Sirhan and conspiracy writers is in direct contradiction to the real character and motives of Sirhan Sirhan. The mumbo-jumbo of

Sirhan's 'mirror-gazing', 'amnesiac episodes' and 'trance-like states' as an explanation for the assassination has succeeded in obscuring just how explicit the motive of Robert Kennedy's assassin was. And the answer to the question of motive lies not in conspiratorial intrigue but in the story of how Sirhan's life developed from an innocent 12-year-old Arab immigrant into a committed and fanatical supporter of the Palestinian cause, embracing virulent anti-American sentiments.

Using Los Angeles Police Department FBI investigative files and obscure material which has never before been fully examined—including parole hearing transcripts; recorded interviews with family members, work colleagues and friends; and the LAPD 'Special Unit Senator' files—a compelling review of Sirhan's life is constructed, providing the reader with an in-depth analysis of Sirhan's state of mind and behavior in the months and years before the assassination (as much as can be determined). The book also provides insights into how Sirhan has promoted his fight for freedom for the past fifty-six years.

This book does not pretend to address the many historical and disputed political issues between Palestinians and Israelis and the conflict between Arabs and Israelis during the time the Sirhans lived in their homeland before eventually settling in the United States. It does, however, examine how the Sirhans interpreted the Arab–Israeli conflict and of how the conflict made deep and abiding impressions on the character of the assassin.

Additionally, this book is not about the claims made by conspiracy writers, although the issue of Sirhan's acceptance of their claims, which have been utilized by him in his many attempts to secure his freedom, is discussed. Those conspiracy issues have already been debunked time and time again with books like Dan Moldea's *The Killing of Robert Kennedy: An Investigation of Motive, Means, and Opportunity* (Norton, 1995), and my books, *The Forgotten Terrorist: Sirhan Sirhan and the Assassination of Robert Kennedy* (Potomac Books Inc., Second Edition, 2019) and *The Kennedy Assassinations: Debunking The Conspiracy Theories* (Frontline Books, 2022). For readers who are interested in the multiple (and false) conspiracy theories surrounding this case, I have provided an appendix which provides readers with links to articles, books and podcasts about the Robert Kennedy assassination myths.

Author's Note

In May 2023 I wrote to Sirhan Sirhan via the Richard J. Donovan Correctional Facility (RJD), 480 Alta Road, San Diego, CA 92179. My letter was sent by Royal Mail (UK) recorded delivery. I provided him with the opportunity to write to me and answer questions I would put to him, thus allowing him to say what he wanted to say . . . and to say it the way he wanted to say it. I also gave him the opportunity to amend and/or correct any answers he had provided before I published anything.

Sirhan did not reply to my letter.

1

JERUSALEM

The Arabic name Sirhan means 'wolf'

Haldor Lillenas, a native of Norway, whose first wife had died during the Second World War, was a noted protestant hymnologist in the Nazarene Publishing House and a music editor for years before he retired and moved to Pasadena with his second wife, Lola Lillenas. Following his retirement in the mid-1950s, Haldor continued to be an ordained minister of the Church of the Nazarene and he and his wife began making frequent trips to Europe, including visits to Scandinavian countries, shipping their car by the boat on which they were passengers. In 1955 they travelled into central and southern Europe, driving down from Denmark through France and Spain and across southern France and into Italy. While on the trip the committed Christian couple decided to visit the Holy Land and took a ferry across the Mediterranean.

During the Lillenas' visit to Jerusalem, they spoke to a 'Jordanian' who spoke 'broken English'. His name was Bishara Sirhan. He told them he was an ardent Christian, interested in the work of a small Christian oriented orphanage. According to Haldor's daughter, Evangeline, Bishara attached himself to them as a 'sort of guide'. The couple appreciated Bishara's assistance and said he "added to the pleasure of the trip."

Bishara thought America was "...a wonderful country where one could always find work and make money..." He had first noticed Haldor when one of his friends was "talking to a foreigner." Bishara, "stopped to greet him" he said, "and he introduced me to the person he was talking to. From his accent I knew he was an American so I said to him directly, 'You are an American, I want to go to your country, will you sponsor my family?' And the American said that he would try to help and later he did arrange to sponsor us."[5]

Bishara had tried to emigrate to the United States since 1951 without success. Now he saw an opportunity to succeed in that endeavor. When Haldor returned to the United States after his visit to the Holy Land, he agreed to help Bishara but not until he had received letters from him which he could use to solicit support from the US government and church institutions. In the next few months Bishara wrote to Lillenas, with each letter containing a plea to help his family "escape their plight by sponsoring their application to enter the United States" and how the family were 'good Christians', refugees of the Arab–Israeli War and forced to live under terrifying conditions in a perpetual wartime no-man's land.

In one letter Bishara wrote, "If you sponsor us, you will be delivering a Christian family from absolute darkness and hopelessness. I assure you that I will be willing to perform any type of service or job in whatsoever nature—garden, servant, sweeper—humbly and mildly. I have a sincere purpose to become a US countryman with a willingness and readiness to do any kind of work to the satisfaction of any employer."[6] It had the desired result. Haldor told Bishara he would find him a job in the United States. However, he refused to sponsor the two oldest sons as they were of legal age, and they made their own arrangements to emigrate to the United States, arriving there in June 1960 after receiving sponsorship from the Church World Service in New York.[7]

Working through the Church World Service and the Department of Immigration and Naturalization, Haldor provided a guarantee to the US Immigration authorities that Bishara and his family would not become public charges. He also promised he would allow the Sirhans to stay in their Pasadena home when they arrived in the US and would assist Bishara in seeking employment. The request was processed during the latter months of 1956.[8]

After the Sirhans arrived in the United States, Haldor told his daughter he may have made a mistake in sponsoring Bishara. He said the newly arrived immigrant found it difficult in finding and holding down jobs and disliked every job he had arranged for him. After Bishara quit one job, he told Haldor it was "too hard and the hours too long." Haldor's wife Lola noticed Bishara seemed to "enjoy the comfortable living" in their home. Haldor expressed the fear to her that he might have "a sort of 'man who came to dinner' situation on his hands."

Although Mary Sirhan and the children were very happy to be immigrants, Bishara became sullen and dissatisfied. After around ten months of living in Pasadena, he had failed to live up to the promises he made in his original letter to Haldor. Nor did Bishara like the customs of his new country or the laws of the United States, complaining that his strict control of his family, as practised in his homeland, was weakening. According to Lola, he believed that living in the United States did not allow him to control his family as in the past and consequently wanted to return to Jordan.[9]

In 1958 Bishara returned to his home in Ramallah, Jordan (later named Ramallah, West Bank, Occupied Palestinian Territory). He wrote letters to his wife requesting her to join him and that if she refused, he would divorce her. She did refuse and told her husband that since she was a member of the Greek Orthodox Church, no divorce would be granted.

In a letter to the Immigration and Naturalization Service in August 1957, Haldor wrote of his regrets in sponsoring the Sirhan family's emigration to the United States. He told immigration officials of how he had been fooled by Bishara's willingness to work hard if he was allowed into the country. "[Bishara Sirhan] failed to live up to these statements," he wrote.[10]

Bishara Salameh Ghattas Sirhan was born on March 17, 1913. He was originally from Taybeh, a small town with a Greek Orthodox and Roman Catholic population, situated near Jerusalem in what is now a West Bank village just outside Ramallah and controlled by Israel. It is one of a dozen majority-Christian villages in the West Bank.

According to local tradition, Saladin met a delegation of its inhabitants during his wars against the Crusaders. Impressed by the hospitality of the locals, he renamed the village Taybeh, or 'the goodly' in Arabic. The village is built on several hills about 30 miles north of Jerusalem; on a clear day the Jordan Valley and the Dead Sea are visible. Three stone churches - Greek Orthodox, Greek Catholic and Roman Catholic Orthodox - stood on three of the hills surrounding the village. The majority of villagers were Christian living in 200 or so houses, and the vast majority were also members of these three churches. When Bishara lived in the village it had a population of around 1,000. The village holds fast to its memory of Jesus seeking refuge there shortly before his crucifixion, with the gospel of John saying Jesus went to Taybeh—then called Ephraim—after he raised Lazarus to life and the Jewish authorities planned to put Jesus to death.

Bishara's father, Salameh Ghattas Sirhan, owned land in Taybeh that was rich with olive trees and wheat fields, bought from savings he had accumulated while working in South America. The family were unpopular with the townspeople, partly because they always kept to themselves and also because Bishara's father was a money lender.[11] Bishara's mother was Nasra Salameh Ghattas Sirhan (89 years old in 1968), and he also had two brothers and a sister.

Bishara Sirhan was a small, strong-boned man who lived in the village of Taybeh from his birth until 1916, when he moved to Jerusalem. He prided himself on his knowledge of the *Bible*, particularly the Old Testament. He was a mechanic by profession but had the intelligence to turn his hand at many engineering jobs including building his own house in the years after he returned to Taybeh. He married Sirhan's mother, Mary Muzher, in 1930 and moved to Jerusalem, where Mary had been born and raised, when they were both 17. Mary had been born in Jerusalem on January 13, 1913, although her family originated from Bethlehem. She had seven years of formal education and spoke Arabic and English. When she married Bishara the couple had $4,000 in savings.[12]

Jerusalem was the capital of the British Mandate of Palestine and had been governed by the British since 1922. Palestine had been part of the Ottoman Empire and ruled by the Turks until the end of the First World War in which Turkey, having sided with the Axis powers, was defeated. When the Ottoman Empire was dismembered at the end of the war, the Allies assumed power over Turkey's control of large swathes of the Middle East and the responsibility for Palestine was given over to the British.

Bishara became a mechanic working for the British government. He repaired water pipelines, particularly ones that had been blown up by the Palestinian Arab population during the campaign of rebellion between 1936 and 1939. By the time of the 1948 war, he had attained the position of foreman and held testimonials as a good worker from the British Mandatory Authorities, including praise for repairing pipelines "in circumstances of danger" during the 1936 outbreak of violence, when water pipelines were blown up by Palestinian Arabs in the three-year uprising beginning that year between Arabs and Jews. He had been one of many Arabs during the Mandatory Period who were loyal to the British authorities, and believed the British government had brought "fairness and justice" and "the regularity of good administrative order to the country".[13]

During the 1930s and 1940s the Sirhan family increased to six children, including five boys and a sister, Aida*, who was born in 1936. Four boys had died natural deaths before and after Sirhan was born in 1944. It was difficult for Bishara to maintain his large family, even though he was paid relatively well by the British authorities and received what was considered a generous wage compared to most of the Arab population.

In 1968 Bishara's son Sharif was 38, Saidallah 36, Adel 30, Sirhan 24 and Munir was the youngest at 19. The Sirhans would have had thirteen children had it not been for the babies who had died shortly after birth. The children were all born in Jerusalem and while Aida survived into adulthood, she had died of leukemia in 1965. In 1946 the family's oldest child, Munir, was run over by a car and killed in Jerusalem; Bishara received 500 dinars compensation as a result of the accident and they later named another son after him.[14]

At the time of Sirhan Sirhan's birth on March 19, 1944, the family lived in West Jerusalem, known as the 'New City', in a comfortable five-roomed apartment. No clashes between Arabs and Jews were reported during their first few years there. Between 1946 and the birth of the State of Israel on May 14, 1948, the family lived in three locations, the last time being in the Musrara quarter, at 82 Shivtei Yisrael ('the tribes of Israel' in Hebrew).

Musrara was founded by upper class Christian residents during the late nineteenth century as a part of the 'departure from the walls', during which people began living outside the Old City. The upper portion of St George Street was called St Paul's Road, because of the Anglican (Episcopalian) church that was constructed there in 1873. Before 1948 it was a mixed Arab-Jew area and one of the many streets in Jerusalem dividing the Jewish and Arab sections of the city. Later, it became the ceasefire line.

The apartment house on St Paul's Street had an internal courtyard and was a stone's throw from the Damascus Gate, the main entrance of the walled Old City of Jerusalem. The home was rented but the Sirhans lived comparatively well in five rooms on the ground floor in the three-storied house. It had red-roofed tiles, a courtyard, and elegant arched windows set in thick stone walls. The house had electricity and a garden that grew eucalyptus trees, although water was drawn from a cistern. The Sirhans lived in this ground-floor apartment for

* Saidallah said her name was spelt A-i-d-a-i, although her death certificate names her as 'Aida'.

seven years. A British radio station, positioned above the Sirhan home, would later become a strategic point during the Arab/Jew conflict.[15]

The young Sirhan Sirhan, together with his brothers and sister, would play in the streets outside their home. Favorite games were 'aseer', a form of tag using a ball, and hopscotch. Being too poor to purchase their own, the family would sometimes hire a bicycle or tricycle. From accounts of those who knew the family at the time, the young Sirhan would prefer reading to outdoor activities. His parents were also anxious that violence could erupt in the streets at any time and may have discouraged their son from playing outdoors.[16]

Although Musrara was subjected to frequent shooting and mortar attacks, it was relatively safe before conflict between Arabs and Jews intensified after 1947, leading to the British handing over the administration of the former mandatory territory to the United Nations and then leaving before the proclamation of Israel in mid-May 1948.

Until the war, Musrara had been a decent place to live and the family lived comfortably. However, in 1947 Palestine was close to anarchy and violence had grown between Arabs and Jews.

The creation of Israel was a result of the First World War, which enabled Britain and France to establish mandates over areas previously controlled by the now-defunct Ottoman Empire, an ally of the defeated Germany. While France was rewarded with Syria and Lebanon, Britain got Iraq, Jordan and the poisoned chalice of Palestine, where Jews had already begun settling in the expectation of once again, after 2,000 years, the establishment of a Jewish homeland.

Arabs and Jews thereafter struggled for control over Palestine throughout the first half of the twentieth century. Violence had been a common occurrence during the 1920s and 1930s but the more pressing concerns of the Second World War brought it to a hiatus. European Jews had called for the implementation of a Jewish state within the borders of Palestine throughout this period, especially German Jews who were being persecuted by Hitler's Third Reich, but Britain and France were too concerned with the stability of Europe to concentrate on a small Middle Eastern colony.

The call for a homeland for the Jews was called Zionism and its religious roots lay in the Old Testament prophecies that the Jewish people should 'return' to Zion (Jerusalem). The Zionist political agenda was first articulated by Theodore Herzl, an Austro-Hungarian Jew, in his book, *The Jewish State*, published in 1896. Initially, many Zionists, especially Russian Jews seeking refuge from the Tsar's pogroms, were prepared to consider a number of proposed sites for the Jewish nation. However, the religious elements of Zionism began to predominate and the movement sought to persuade western nations that Palestine was their homeland.

As Jews began to immigrate to Palestine from Europe, violence erupted. Arabs resented the new Jewish settlements, which were growing during the First World War. However, the British government decided to support the Jews and issued the Balfour Declaration of 1917 that committed it to a 'Jewish National Home'. The effort was two-pronged: firstly, Britain would support the institution of a Jewish state once enough Jews had entered Palestine. Secondly, after the First World War had ended, Zionists would then be responsible for trying to secure for Britain the mandate for Palestine from the League of Nations rather than it going to the US, France or other European states. In a world of geo-political bargains, Britain was aware that an Israeli state would be important in helping to protect British imperial interests in the Middle East and the Suez Canal.

However, throughout the 1920s Jewish immigration into Palestine was not increasing as Zionists had forecast. It was not until Hitler began his program of solving 'the Jewish Question' within Germany that immigration took off. By 1942 the Jewish population in Palestine had increased to 30 percent of the population. In order to deal with the growing resentments of the Arab population and especially following the 'Arab Rebellion' of 1936-1939, Britain sent over 100,000 troops to keep the peace. Concomitant to this action, the British government began to curb Jewish immigration. However, Jewish opposition to this policy was muted because of the outbreak of the Second World War in 1939. That year, a document later known as the British 'White Paper' established Palestine as an independent state to be governed by both Arabs and Jews.

The first part of the 1948 Arab–Israeli War began in late 1947 as a civil war between Arabs and Jews. After the British government announced it would end its mandate on May 15, 1948, and would not be responsible for order, the conflict between Arabs and Jews increased incrementally. A scramble for strategic positions, which were important for both sides in the inevitable war, continued unabated. From December 1947 to May 1, 1948, 5,000 casualties, both Arab and Jew, were reported.

The British government asked the United Nations to study the Palestinian problem and submit their recommendations. On November 26, 1947, the United Nations General Assembly approved the recommendations of the special committee on Palestine, which called for the partition of Palestine into separate Jewish and Arab states. The Jerusalem area, including Bethlehem, because of its great importance, was to be internationalized and placed under the direct administration of the United Nations. The Jewish Agency accepted the 1947 United Nation's plan for the partition of Palestine, but the Arab states and Palestinian leaders rejected it.[17]

On Sunday, 30 November 1947, armed Arabs attacked a Jewish bus at Kfar Sirkin during its journey from Netanya to Jerusalem. Five passengers were killed. Later in the day, another bus was attacked killing one Jew and was followed by a succession of attacks by both Arabs and Jews. The incidents occurred only hours after the United Nations voted for the partition of Palestine and is considered by most historians to be the beginning of Israel's War of Independence and which Palestinians call the Nakba (catastrophe).[18]

In December 1947 Arabs in Jerusalem "went over to the offensive" according to the *Palestinian Post.* Jewish houses near the Jaffa Gate were stoned, Jewish transport was fired on and Palestinians burned and looted the Jewish Commercial Centre. Three Jews were wounded when Arabs fired on the Jewish Quarter in the Old City and Arabs crossed rooftops to storm it. In four incidents, two Jews were killed and four injured.

The Jews responded with reprisal attacks on December 13 and 29 and on January 7, killing thirty-five Arabs. During the attack on December 13, a black car occupied by members of the militant Zionist group, Irgun, stopped outside the Damascus Gate. According to historian Ian Black, "the occupants rolled two cylinders with burning wicks into the milling crowd" killing twenty people.[19]

The Sirhans found themselves caught up in the attack on December 29. The Irgun targeted crowds standing at bus stations: the first two at the Old City's Damascus Gate and the third at the Jaffa Gate. They were hit and run attacks using sticks of dynamite thrown from a vehicle.

Around four o'clock in the afternoon, when Bishara finished work, the infant Sirhan had accompanied him on a trip to the Post Office and, on returning home, dynamite was thrown from a speeding car, exploding as the father and son approached the Damascus Gate. They had been about to go through when the bomb exploded. Two British constables and eleven Arabs were killed and another thirty-two wounded. "I was going to the store to buy coffee and a few other things for the house and took Sirhan with me," Bishara said.

> "We were just about to go into the Gate when I heard people shouting. I looked back and saw something black being thrown out of a car. It began to roll down the slope and then it exploded with a great bang. I picked up Sirhan and ran into the gate and then to the left. He seemed to have fainted. I was mad with anger. I laid Sirhan down on a shelf. He wasn't hurt anywhere but his eyes were shut. I rubbed his face and his hands. After a few minutes his eyes opened and I asked him, 'Sirhan, do you feel any pain?' And he answered, 'No, Daddy'. I kept on rubbing his hands and his body. Then he got up and asked 'Why do the Jews do this thing? Don't they believe in Christ?'"[20]

As the young Sirhan gradually recovered his ability to walk, father and son exited though the gate after the dead and wounded had been taken away. Bishara witnessed the carnage that had just happened as he passed bones, blood and flesh laying in the road. Shocked survivors mingled with the crowd as they looked for family members. Sirhan and his father had narrowly escaped injury.[21] When father and son arrived home, Sirhan told his mother, "Mama, the bomb came down and made the people's blood run down there at the Damascus Gate."[22] Sirhan remained in bed for two days and stayed in the house for two weeks.

According to his parents, the 4-year-old witnessed five other separate incidents of violence and death during the rest of the family's stay in Musrara. A family friend, Joseph Tabello, who lived across the street from the Sirhans, reported that he heard Sirhan had witnessed an Israeli soldier kill an Arab in front of his home when he was a small child. After one violent incident, Sirhan's mother said, "[Sirhan]...was pale for some time. Wouldn't move for some time. Couldn't move. Fainted. After a truck full of dynamite exploded near our home Sirhan wouldn't go out of the house for days... Sometimes he would talk in his sleep...one night, living in Old Jerusalem, I felt him and he was cold like a stick. More than any of his brothers, he had less blood and more fear." She also said Sirhan would go into 'trance-like' states.[23]

Later in 1947, another violent incident occurred during the time the Sirhans lived on St Paul's Street. Sirhan and his 8-year-old brother, Munir, were playing in front of their home when a British Army lorry that had come under fire veered off the street trying to avoid a sniper and struck Munir, killing him. Sirhan returned home and, according to Mary, said, "Munir is killed! That's the same bomb, Mama." Mary further added, "that is what he has seen before. He never forgot that Damascus Gate thing… Sirhan never forgot his brother. Every now and then he used to cry and ask me, 'Mama, why did he take so long? Can't he come and play with me?'"[24]

Following the violent confrontations between Jews and Arabs between late 1947 and the end of the British Mandatory period in May 1948, the Arab armies of Syria, Egypt, Lebanon, Iraq and Jordan—collectively called 'The Arab Legion'—launched a united offensive, with many of its citizens, both Arab and Jew, enduring untold suffering.

The conflict had severe ramifications for the residents of Jerusalem because the most intense fighting was in the Jerusalem area. Artillery bombardment and firing incidents continued between Arab and Jewish sectors. By 1948 the Tel-Aviv – Jerusalem road was closed because of Arab ambushes, while Arab artillery shelled the Jewish part of Jerusalem and the Jews returned fire.

When the Second World War broke out in 1939, several Arab leaders had expressed support for Hitler's policy of exterminating Jews. This came to be seen as a crucial mistake after the western allies had defeated the fascist dictator and became appalled at the atrocities committed against European Jews. During the Second World War one of the Arab leaders in Palestine, Al-Husseini, the Grand Mufti of Jerusalem, spent time in Berlin urging Hitler to quickly facilitate his plans for the Jews. According to Harvard law professor Alan Dershowitz, "The Palestinian leadership, with the acquiescence of most of the Palestinian Arabs, actively supported and assisted the Holocaust and Nazi Germany and bears considerable moral, political...culpability for the murder of many Jews."[25]

At the outset of the 1948 Arab-Israeli War, the Sirhans were among 30,000 Palestinians who took refuge in Jerusalem's eastern section. It was cut off from the western side of Jerusalem by a no man's land that was bordered by minefields and anti-sniper walls. There was one official crossing: the Mandelbaum Gate.

As a result of Jewish forces taking over the Musrara house in a raid on the radio station, situated on the roof of the Sirhans' building, the family fled to the Old City taking as many possessions as they could muster. The Sirhans also fled because of their fear of what life would be like under Jewish rule. Mary said they left because, "You know it was the shooting, bombing, and the terrorism of the Zionist—we couldn't take it so we had to—when we left was really a moment of shooting very hard. Wherever you could see a person there is a shot at him. So, we couldn't stay. And we couldn't open, even dare to open the windows or the door because the shooting will come right into us, and we got out of there because we wanted to save, to protect our lives."[26] Even though he was only 4 years old, Sirhan recalled in later years how the family had to flee Musrara.

> I remember when my family was…compelled to pack up their belongings from [St Paul's Street] onto some kind of a cart, and then moving towards the Old Jerusalem. I remember that. It's the whole family. And it was, it wasn't just my family; it was the whole community. We were evicted from that, from, uh, from New Jerusalem area. And, uh, it was, it was quite traumatic because we had to make new friends. We had to make, you know, adjustments, lifestyle adjustments because we went from, from bad to worse, really, but we survived, and we managed as best we could. I remember distinctly with my mom when they were back and forth, you know...lobbing...bombs from between, between us and the Israelis that my mom used to stuff cotton in our ears so that we wouldn't hear the sound of the bombs. It was that intense at going on nights, some nights when the conflict was going on.[27]

For the next few weeks, the Sirhans lived in a 900-year-old convent, the Greek Orthodox Convent of St Nicholas, which had been converted to accommodate hundreds of Arab refugees and was now being used as a school and hospital. Mary said, "We didn't know really where to go, but there was a big building like a convent, so we had to go there. …There were hundreds of people in that building at that time."[28]

Within a short period of time the Sirhans were relocated to the Jewish Quarter, which had fallen into Jordanian hands. Their new home had been partly damaged by the fighting within the city walls and was a ground floor flat at the corner of Suq el Husroor and Al Malak Street, inside the Old City. The 1,200 Jews there had surrendered. Like the Sirhans, the occupants had fled. The synagogue and much of the area had been destroyed.[29] The Jews were barred from returning until 1967 when Israel regained control during the Six-Day War.

The old building was occupied by nine families, a total of fifty people in a two-story house. There was no adequate running water, so families had to wait for trucks delivering fresh supplies. There was no electricity and the families collected water from a cistern. The Sirhans lived in a single room measuring 15 by 30 feet and had the bare essentials of life, cooking on a tiny kerosene stove and relying on UN rations. The elder boys were forced to look for odd jobs after their father had lost his employment when the British withdrew from Palestine.

Bishara's father was a man of 'modest affluence' but may have been unable to help his son because it would have involved selling some of his land, which was never an option. Besides, Bishara said he was "a grown man with a family and I alone was responsible for them."[30] There was little contact between father and son except for the occasional visits by Bishara when he would collect olive oil from his father's farm.

A boyhood friend of Sirhan's, Ziad Hashimeh, who lived directly across the hall from Sirhan, said the nine families had grown up in the midst of murder, filth and terror. He described Sirhan as a 'sensitive' boy and related the story of how they were outside playing football when:

> Sirhan started…getting nervous…he was moving, shaking and he was a very good friend of mine so I had to go and ask him if there was anything wrong, that I could do something. He said, 'Leave me alone, leave me alone' and he wouldn't let me talk to him... He went to the house and he went inside the house and I didn't see him and you couldn't talk to him that morning. Nothing that I remember [provoked Sirhan's reactions].

Hashimeh also observed how Bishara struck not only his son but also his wife, "different times, different ways, you know, by hand; sometimes pushing her…" He claimed Bishara beat his son Sirhan "many times" and used to be "too emotional" and struck him using "all sorts of sticks and hands."[31] Mary said she once returned to the house to find Bishara hitting Sirhan. "What are you doing?" she shouted. Bishara replied that he was "making a real man out of him." Mary told him, "Not anymore. Sirhan is not like the others. Look at him. How pale and weak."[32]

Hashimeh also witnessed the effect the continuing conflict between Arabs and Jews had on the young Palestinian. He once heard Sirhan shouting for his mother, "So when you hear somebody shouting, somebody calling 'Mother, mother', the whole apartments, they go out and he was shaking, you know, like that, moving his body and he was crying, 'Hand, hand', so we had all to go to the well. We saw a hand in the well."[33]

Mary Sirhan was economical with the truth when she described the 'Deir Yassin massacre', which had been committed by the Irgun on April 9, 1948. Deir Yassin was situated west of Jerusalem above the road to Tel Aviv, making it an important strategic village for both Arab and Jewish fighters. Sirhan later said:

> I was told...that these two hundred and fifty some people, women and children... were slaughtered in cold blood by the Jews, the Zionists and by the military guards and the Haganah and they were dumped into wells and some of the women...were taken on a truck and paraded through the city to frighten the remaining villagers that refused to be evicted in order to push them out of their homes once and for all in order for the Zionists to take over.[34]

Mary said she actually witnessed the aftermath of the 'massacre', citing open trucks along her Musrara street filled with Palestinian girls who had their 'breasts cut'. "They were naked," she said, "and the Zionists were laughing and clapping hands…and saying, 'See what will happens to your girls'…Sirhan was with me."[35]

The Deir Yassin massacre did happen, but it is rarely seen in the context of the other 'massacres' by Arab fighters of the time at Hebron, Kfar Eyzion, Hadassah Hospital, Safed and Mount Scopus University. In Haddasah, for example, Arab fighters murdered a convoy of doctors, nurses and patients on their way to the hospital, killing seventy, then setting the convoy of buses and cars on fire.

Most historians, including Arab experts, believe there are no historical accounts of the massacre, which include women being naked or having been mutilated, and the only humiliation the captives experienced was that "prisoners were paraded through the centre of Jerusalem before being released."[36]

Alan Dershowitz wrote, "Some Palestinian leaders actually circulated false rumours that women had been raped." When confronted with the reality that no rapes had taken place, Hussein Khalidi, a Palestinian leader said, "We have to say this, so the Arab armies will come to liberate us from the Jews." (Arab journalist) Hazam Nuseibeh told the BBC years later that the deliberate fabrication of the rape charge, "was our biggest mistake…as soon as they heard that women had been raped at Deir Yassin, Palestinians fled in terror."[37]

On July 11, 1948, the Arab League forces in Jerusalem subjected the Jewish sector of the Old City to its first air bombardment. The Jews retaliated by bombing the Arab sector. Joseph Tabello said his house was among the first destroyed by these raids.[38]

Following the move from the New Jerusalem to the Old Jerusalem, the Sirhans were now occupying property that had once belonged to the Jews who had also been forced to flee as the Arab legion soldiers pushed the Israeli Haganah forces westward (Haganah was the military organization representing the majority of the Jews in Palestine from 1920 to 1948). In total, 830,000 Jews had been expelled during the 1948

Arab–Israeli War from the Arab countries of Egypt, Iraq, Yemen and North African countries. Like the Sirhans, they also became refugees. The war also resulted in a significant displacement and upheaval for many of the Sirhans' fellow Palestinians: 700,000 to 750,000 Palestinian Arabs were expelled in 225 localities or fled in fear resulting in what Arabs call the Nakba (catastrophe).[39]

After seven months of fighting, the Arabs had lost their best and last chance to have a state of their own. When Israel's War of Independence drew to a close in 1948 and ceasefire lines divided Jerusalem in two, St Paul's was cut off from its Arab congregation. The Jordanian annexation of the West Bank formally occurred on April 24, 1950.

The Sirhan family had now been reduced to the misery of refugee status. For most of the years between 1948 and 1956 Bishara was unemployed, receiving small jobs and financial assistance from relief organizations. The family was registered as refugees with the United Nations Relief and Works Agency for Palestine Refugees, UNRWA.

In the Old City, Mary Sirhan ran a crèche and Sunday school whilst Bishara was unemployed. They sent their children to the Jerusalem Evangelical Lutheran School in the Old City of Jerusalem. The school was attached to the Lutheran Church of the Savior that stood facing the door leading to the courtyard of the Church of the Holy Sepulcher. Bishara Sirhan's decision to send the children there was also based on the fact there were no Greek Orthodox schools in the Old City and because the Lutherans gave the Sirhans a lot of help. The children did not have to pay tuition fees and second-hand clothes were passed on to them. The church also provided employment for Mary and the elder sons.

It is likely that the Lutherans wanted the Sirhans to change from their adherence to the Greek Orthodox Church, and for as long as the Sirhans received aid from the Lutherans, they gave them their loyalty and were regular attendees at its place of worship.

The school's headmaster said Sirhan had been a promising student, near the top of his class, but the headmaster also said the Sirhan home was deeply troubled and the parents had 'terrible fights'. He also noted that Bishara, who blamed the loss of his job on the Israelis, was a person who had become emotionally unstable and who beat his wife and children repeatedly.[40]

Nominally Christian, teachers at the school were mainly drawn from the Arab community, which was predominantly Muslim. Christian

Arabic children used Jordanian textbooks and from 1948 to 1967, Christian schools in East Jerusalem were required to teach the *Koran*.[41] The textbooks contained material that went beyond the worst excesses of Nazi Germany. Arab leaders compiled a curriculum of hatred for use by their children and the anti-Israeli and anti-Jewish teachings became a basic element in the study of history in the schools. Arab children were taught that Jews were the ultimate embodiment of evil and should be 'destroyed'. As an FBI report stated, "...in the textbooks used in connection with the teaching of grammar, the first two verbs to be conjugated were hate and kill and the object of these two words was 'Jews'."[42]

As the Arab world ignored the United Nations' call to legitimise the State of Israel, Arab Jordanian school textbooks continued to refer to Israel as foreign occupied Palestine. The texts called for Israel's destruction and made reference to the obligation Palestinians had to defend Islamic land. The textbooks used by Palestinian Arab schoolchildren also referred to Israel as a foreign colony that massacred and expelled Palestinians. They contained emotionally charged scenes of the stoning of Jews and Jewish property; the message being that killing Jews was a worthy and honorable act. Maps within the textbooks did not mention Israel and denied its existence, while history and geography books for grades 1-6 contained maps portraying all of Israel as Palestine and called on Palestinian children to liberate all of Palestine by taking up arms against the Jews.[43]

The majority of students at Sirhan's school were Palestinian Arabs who had been taught the principles of the Palestinian cause and Palestinian nationalism by Arab teachers. The students were constantly told about the great Arab warrior, Saladin, who had expelled the 'foreign crusaders' from Jerusalem.[44] Sirhan told of how he had been influenced by one particular teacher in his school, 'Mr Suheil', who indoctrinated his pupils in Arab nationalism and urged them to be like Saladin and fight for the Arab cause. Sirhan was so impressed by Mr Suheil he later decided upon a future career as a diplomat.[45]

One of Sirhan's contemporaries wrote of how he was educated in Jordan in the early 1960s and of how he remembered:

> ...the first song I learned in school...titled, 'Arabs our Beloved and Jews Our Dogs'... In an attempt to change the hearts of Palestinians the Israeli television stations would show Holocaust documentaries... I would sit and watch cheering the Germans while I chewed on food. It was impossible for me to change my heart and mind concerning the Jews... Hitler [was] my idol.[46]

Eventually, the Sirhans were offered Jordanian citizenship during the time they spent in the Jordanian-controlled sector of Jerusalem. They had little choice but to accept as they had nowhere else to go. Other Arab communities living in pre-war Israel had fled to Syria and Lebanon, amongst others, and the host nations made no attempt to give them citizenship or make any attempt to integrate them. This was one of the central reasons why Palestinian Arabs became refugees from one generation to the next, including the Sirhan family. And the Arab countries had a motive for doing so; they wanted to keep the Palestinian refugee status alive as a diplomatic and moral weapon against Israel. It was also the one issue that could unite the Arab world.

There can be little doubt that the experiences Sirhan suffered as a child in Jerusalem during the 1948 Arab-Israeli War and the frequent clashes between Palestinians and Israelis he witnessed as an infant and as a young boy produced some level of psychological trauma. As his father noted, "...Sirhan had seen Arabs in Jerusalem killed by Jewish terrorist gangs and had seen a woman neighbor stabbed by an Israeli soldier. Furthermore, he witnessed the death of one of his childhood friends when an Israeli bomb exploded in the school yard and the small boy died immediately."[47]

The newly formed state of Israel controlled 78 percent of Mandatory Palestine, 23 percent more than the land that had been allocated by the UN plan.[48] However, the cost of victory was steep. Many lives were lost, homes destroyed, and families torn apart. Arab and Jewish families mourned their fallen soldiers, paid tribute to their sacrifices, and faced the painful reality of the war's aftermath.

As the children grew, strains developed between Bishara Sirhan and his two elder sons, Saidallah and Sharif. According to neighbors who knew the family in Jerusalem, the boys were aloof, displayed weak characters and took money from the family finances to spend on themselves. They also took out debts in their father's name. Bishara's response was to throw the two eldest boys out of the family home. The elder sons still maintained contact with their mother, however, who would frequently send them food and money. After a while Bishara reconciled with his sons but did not allow them back into the family home. The two older boys remained in Jerusalem until 1960 when they, too, emigrated to America.[49]

For the remaining time the Sirhans spent in the city—1948 to 1957—Jerusalem remained split in two. Between 1951 and 1953, when Joseph Tabello did carpentry work with Adel Sirhan, he saw the Sirhan family as existing "in the lower socioeconomic class".[50]

According to his father, the 7-year-old Sirhan was very much interested in the 1951 assassination of King Abdullah of Jordan, which was organized by Amin al-Husseini. A friend of Hitler's, Husseini took an extreme view of how Jews should be treated in any proposed Palestinian state. He wanted to exterminate them. In fact, on his visits to Berlin during the Second World War, Husseini became influential with Hitler when the subject of Jews was discussed.

Following the 1948 War, Husseini rejected all proposals introduced by moderate Arabs that would solve the continuing Arab Jewish conflict and took all measures necessary to eliminate Arabs who opposed him, including assassination. His main opponent for the leadership of Palestinian Arabs was King Abdullah of Transjordan, who had granted citizenship to Palestinians on the West Bank after it had been conquered in 1948. On July 20, 1951, after the king attended Friday prayers at Jerusalem's Al-Aqsa Mosque, a ten-minute walk from the Sirhan home, a Husseini loyalist who had been a soldier in the Mufti's militia during the 1948 War shot him dead.[51]

The Arabs had been expelled from the western quarter and the Jews had been expelled from the eastern side. However, even though the war had ended, clashes between Israelis and Arabs continued, including thousands of clashes and acts of sabotage inside Israel. On April 22, 1953, firing broke out. On June 30, 1954, open hostilities began in Jerusalem and continued for four days. The sixty-one casualties on both sides were predominantly civilians, although heavy construction of buildings in the area was credited with alleviating a higher casualty rate. Between 1954 and 1955, the Jordanian controlled East Jerusalem saw more violence. In 1955 riots took place in Jerusalem and other Jordanian controlled cities. From 1953 to1956 more than 400 Israelis were killed, and during this time, Sirhan later remembered, he came upon an Arab military checkpoint at Jerusalem's Zion Gate, where the Arabs were in control of the city wall. An Arab soldier let him look through binoculars at the Jewish sector, telling him that "all the land he could see belonged to them."[52]

It took nearly 10 years for the family to find a sponsor in the US. After Haldor Lillenas agreed to support the Sirhans, the family applied for visas and met with American authorities. They had qualified for refugee status under a presidential decree allowing 2,000 Palestinian families to emigrate to the US. Bishara told the authorities the family lived in a 'refugee camp' in Jerusalem and had Jordanian nationality. The Sirhans also qualified for expense-free passage.

Although the family saw the move as beneficial, the young 12-year-old Sirhan Sirhan, became sullen and ran away from home. He was gone all day and spent his time in a park in Ramallah, 15 miles north of Jerusalem. When he returned to the family home later that evening, his father was angry and prepared to mete out punishment. However, Adel Sirhan stepped in and asked his father to show forgiveness. Over a meal of tabouleh, a cold mixture of cucumbers, tomatoes and grain, the family united in their desire for a new life in America and an escape from the Arab–Israeli conflict. According to Sirhan, "I didn't want to leave; I wanted to stay in my own country with my own people. I knew that the US was against the Arabs and was friendly with Israel, and a friend of my enemy is my enemy. I knew about US policy because I did a lot of listening on the radio to the Voice of America."[53]

In January 1957, the Sirhans moved to the US, travelling first through Amman to Beirut and then by ship to Naples before sailing to New York. They entered the US on a 'permanent resident status' and remained citizens of Jordan. On arrival, Sirhan was treated for a minor parasitic condition of the small intestine. They next travelled by train across America to Pasadena. Saidallah, who remained in Jerusalem with his brother Sharif when the family emigrated, was the only member of the family to apply for citizenship after their arrival in the United States in 1960.

2

PASADENA

[The Sirhans] *"...were a normal Christian, God-fearing family."* Munir Sirhan

"..the rest of the family was bitter because their father was over there and not with them." Church member J. Edward Burn

Bishara and his family arrived in the United States on January 12, 1957 on the *C. Columbo* ship, docking at New York. At the time they entered the United States Bishara and Mary were 44 years old; Aida was 20; Adel was 18; Sirhan was 12 and Munir was 9. Bishara immediately telephoned Haldor Lillenas then travelled by train to his home in Pasadena. The Sirhans stayed with their sponsoring family for three days and then, with the assistance of the church authorities, Lillenas was able to arrange a furnished house for them at 1321 N Mentor, Pasadena. From 1957 they stayed at 1647 Lake Avenue in Pasadena.[54]

Haldor Lillenas obtained two jobs for Bishara Sirhan, neither of which satisfied him, and he was fired from both. With the help of the Church, Mary obtained employment as a housekeeper at the Westminster Nursery School in Pasadena. Meanwhile, Aida enrolled as a student at Pasadena City College and Sirhan and Munir were enrolled in the Pasadena School system.

The Sirhans maintained contact with their sponsoring organization, The First Nazarene Church, for a year after their arrival. They continued to receive aid from the church and also continued to give it their loyalty.

Although assisted in their immigration to the United States by a member of the Church of the Nazarene, in 1958 the Sirhans were attracted to the First Baptist Church of Pasadena, run by Charles Bell. Only Mary and Munir attended services regularly, but they never became official members. It is likely the Sirhans changed churches because Bell placed Sharif Sirhan in an accountancy job with the Southern California Baptist Convention in Los Angeles.

Bishara had already clashed with family members in Jerusalem and things were no better in America, declaring: "America may be good for young people. It is a country of go, go, go. A man over 40 cannot stand it."[55] He was especially disturbed at how his position as *pater familias*, or head of the family, had been eroded by the newly acquired western attitudes his wife and sons displayed. The socio-political divide was too much for him. He became disturbed that American women had a great deal of independence and was afraid his wife was adopting their ways. Bishara and Mary became temperamentally unsuited to one another and he argued frequently with her. Mary and her sons began to challenge Bishara's authority, and he was also upset that his wife had maintained contact with the two elder boys in Jerusalem, with whom he had fallen out, thus further undermining his authority. Sirhan said his father, "didn't bother [him] too much" and that "neither his father or mother had expressed affection with hugs and kisses as he was growing up."[56]

Following a family feud, whereby Mary sided with her sons, Bishara asked his wife to choose between him and the children. She chose the children. Bishara left, taking the family savings of approximately $500 with him. The young Sirhan Sirhan felt "no sense of loss" when his father abandoned the family and was "too preoccupied with getting along in America."[57]

During his seven months in Pasadena, Bishara made several trips to New York, where he worked as a maintenance mechanic, but was unable to hold down a job there. He returned to Jordan on a TWA flight on July 30, 1957. Mary Sirhan, embarrassed by her husband's departure, lied about his leaving, telling neighbors and friends Bishara had left to care for his 'critically ill' mother in Jerusalem.[58]

Following his arrival in Jordan, Bishara wrote to his wife demanding she and the children join him in East Jerusalem. However, Mary Sirhan had grown accustomed to her newly acquired 'freedom' and refused to return. "He writes to me…" she said:

> He goes to a court which is really where we belong to the church where we were married and he asks for divorce. He wants me to give him a divorce because he tried to divorce me before and he couldn't because he brought me to the United States and after he, like, brought me here, he went back and left me here so he couldn't. But he goes there because he wants me to go back to him and there is no way but to go to the court,

> that court, and ask for, to have a divorce, so he could have, ah, either have me there or I don't know what was in his mind and I answered the court.[59]

Haldor Lillenas sided with Mary and wrote to the Department of Immigration, describing Bishara Sirhan as an "undesirable alien" and informing them Bishara had left the country under "false pretenses". Concerned about Mary's welfare, he asked the immigration service to prevent her husband from returning to America.[60]

However, Bishara was allowed to return to the United States on May 14, 1959. He moved to 156 Allen Street, New York City, and found work as a 'driller' using various hand tools and machinery for a construction firm, Well-built Corporation. He remained with the company for three years before leaving the US once more to return to Jordan in May 1963 on a TWA flight out of New York. When he returned to the United States in May 1964, he was re-employed by Well-built, staying at his former Allen Street lodgings. On March 11, 1966 he returned to Jordan via a BOAC flight, settling in his ancestral village of Taybeh. In all, he had spent five years in the United States, having had no contact with his family in Pasadena.[61] He remained in the West Bank living off a "very small" retirement pension and working part time on his small farmland.[62]

Saidallah and Sharif moved in with their mother, sister and three sons after arriving in the United States in 1960. They were employed in various jobs between 1960 and 1968, and both moved to separate apartments in 1964 and 1965. Adel and Munir lived at home, along with Sirhan and their mother. However, the elder brothers visited the Sirhan family home frequently.

From 1957 until 1963, Mary and her family lived at 1647 Lake Avenue in Pasadena. By 1963 Mary Sirhan and her sons had moved into their new home at 696 E. Howard Street, Pasadena, a modest frame cottage, valued at $15,000 in 1968, with a large magnolia tree in the front yard. The area in which the Sirhans lived was a 'white' neighborhood; further east it became racially mixed and then African American. By then, Mary's annual income had risen to between $1,471 and $1,752 a year.

Mary and her daughter Aida had jobs; Munir and Sirhan were in school. Mary had secured a position as a housekeeper for the Westminster Presbyterian Church on Lake Avenue and Atchison for five mornings per week and also worked in the nursery. Aida worked as a secretary and Adel had part-time work as a painter. Sharif secured work in accountancy, having had experience working as an accountant for Mobil Oil in Amman, Jordan. The family pooled their money.[63]

The Sirhans stopped attending the church in January 1964 when Sharif, who had been employed for over a year, was dismissed after an arrest for felonious assault against his girlfriend. A church member, Mrs Clarence Robinson, said Sharif's leaving the church was a "blow-up" and "not a pleasant altercation".[64] Sharif's crime had repercussions on his family, and although his brothers were ridiculed by neighbors, the family's attitude was to unite behind Sharif. Mary became blind to her son's guilt and blamed Dr Bell for Sharif's dismissal.[65] For his part, Bell considered the family unstable and attributed this instability to the father's absence from the home.[66]

Church member J. Edward Burn was an associate pastor in charge of membership and, in 1962/3, lived down the street from the Sirhans. He had met Sirhan at St Nicholas Orthodox Church in Pasadena and both attended the church regularly while in Eliot Junior High School. They also had a similar ancestry: Burn's great grandparents had known Sirhan's relatives in Palestine. He was acquainted with the family after he was approached by Mary asking if he would talk to her son, Sirhan, about non-attendance at the church. He had 'several discussions' with Sirhan when the boy was a sophomore student at John Muir High School. Regarding Sirhan's belief in God, Burn said he, "...appeared to be a very intense atheist and could see no logic in God." Burn noticed the young Arab had been "... very close to one of the high school teachers who furnished him with a great deal of literature to substantiate his beliefs in atheism." The Associate Pastor said Sirhan considered his teacher to be "an authority on almost all subjects and perhaps associated with him as a substitute for his father." Burn also believed the Sirhan sons, "all seem[ed] to have a bitter attitude toward life, with the feeling the world owed them a living." This was due, he said, "in part, to the resentment they had for their father..."[67]

Another church member, Deborah D. Mokharian, had known the family since 1957 after she arrived in the United States as an immigrant. She lived a short distance away from the Sirhan home and regularly associated with them through the church and as neighbors. She said the Sirhans attended the First Baptist Church sporadically in 1957 and 1958 and believed they "were probably using [the church] to secure material things in the United States" and "what they could get out of it." [68]

A church member who wanted to remain anonymous said the Sirhans were intensely patriotic, but not towards their adoptive country. At a luncheon, she said, the family arrived with Jordanian food and a Jordanian flag, which they placed on their table. She was, "always struck by the fact that Sirhan was always extremely bitter, resentful and extremely unhappy." She could never recall him smiling and he constantly complained about the laws of the United States. Sirhan, she said, felt there was no justice in the educational system. She remembered him telling her he should be given a college degree in one year and that he should not have to work for it. When she asked Sirhan if he had become a citizen of the United States he replied, "No, never." She lost touch with the Sirhans in 1962.[69]

The Sirhan family's Arab roots and hatred of Israel ran deep. However, some neighbors were sympathetic, recognising that the family members had experienced the terror of the 1948 Arab–Israeli conflict. Mary told neighbors of how the intense feelings for Palestinians remained with the family, even after they were now far removed from the conflict. She told of how her family had lived in Jerusalem for "thousands of years" and also spoke of the bitterness towards and the hatred of the Israelis who had "taken their land." Neighbors reported the family often complained of their new status in American society; they had become part of a minority group, alienated and misunderstood within the larger community.

Linda Kamakian met the Sirhan family at a church picnic sponsored by the St Nicholas Greek Orthodox Church in 1960, when Sirhan was around 16 years old. She knew the whole family and felt sorry for them as they seemed "lonely and afraid in this new life that was foreign to them." She invited the family to her home, where Mary told her of "the oppression exerted on the Zionists towards her family and people in the old country."[70]

After the family moved to the United States, Mary's mother tongue remained Arabic and she had a poor command of English, often asking her sons to speak for her. Adel, Sirhan and Munir easily adapted to their new language. As he grew into his teens, Sirhan claimed to 'think' in English. However, the two older sons, Sharif and Saidallah, never became entirely proficient.

Arab culture and Arab pride remained central to the family's way of life. The Sirhans resisted acculturation; conversation at home was always in Arabic and they observed Arab customs. They listened to Arab music all day, especially the music of Egyptian singer Umm Kulthum, a supporter of Egyptian President Gamal Abdel Nasser, and read newspapers written in Arabic. Their way of thinking was always the 'Arab way'. All the brothers described themselves not as 'Christian Arabs' but as 'Palestinian Arabs' and were doubtless influenced by the opinions of both parents. Bishara and Mary taught them that Jews were evil and stole their home, and Bishara also taught his sons and daughter that all Palestinian Arabs had a legitimate cause and should live in hope that the family could one day return to live in Palestine.[71]

Lebanese American club owner Lou Shelby had graduated from UCLA with a Political Science degree and had completed a year and a half of graduate work at UC at Berkeley, specializing in International Relations and Middle East politics. He hired Adel Sirhan as a musician at his club the Fez. Shelby felt the family were 'strange'. He had visited them in Pasadena on several occasions for musical rehearsals and was able to see them in a social setting. "The Sirhans always struck me as being a weird family," he said.

> By that I mean something quite strange and unusual. Perhaps the best way to explain it is by saying that though they were Christians, the general quality, the atmosphere, of their family was that of a Muslim family. It was serious and heavy and lacking in the adaptability and quickness which most Arab Christian families here have. And there were their relations with their mother; the sons were fond of her, of course, but she had little influence on them and they didn't take her wishes or feelings into account.[72]

Aida Sirhan, small in stature with a pleasant disposition, was 20 years old when the family moved to the United States. She lived with the family until 1962 when she moved to Palm Springs to take a job as an accountant at the 'Fun in the Sun' candy shop on Palm Canyon Drive. It was here she fell in love with the owner of the shop, Herbert Mennell, and secretly married him. Knowing the family would disapprove of her marriage to an 'outsider', she kept it secret from her brothers. Mary likely knew about the marriage but never brought the subject up in conversation. Aida developed leukaemia in February 1965 and when her illness grew progressively worse, she moved back to the Sirhan home. The 21-year-old Sirhan remained home from Pasadena college for the next month and cared for her. She died at Huntington Memorial Hospital on March 20, 1965, aged 20, and was buried at Forest Lawn Park on March 23. The brothers only knew about her marriage when Herbert Mennell showed up at the funeral.[73]

Frederick Abbot and his wife knew the Sirhan family when they lived in Altadena in 1958 and were neighbors of the Sirhans until 1961, when they moved house. Frederick became a friend of Adel's and occasionally would play the oud at the Fez nightclub with him. Frederick described Sirhan as "quiet and polite" but rarely saw him. He said Saidallah and Mary Sirhan were "always talking anti-US" and would often speak about returning to Palestine. Saidallah, meanwhile, would frequently talk about Russia and "how the Russians were better." Frederick's wife said the Sirhans were a "nice" family, that is, until Saidallah and Sharif arrived from Jordan in 1960. "Some in the family preferred to return to the Middle East" she said, "and after the brothers arrived from Jordan the family would argue frequently."[74]

Mary said she had tried her best to raise her children properly and take care of them. However, she was now a single parent and had little or no effective control over them. Once Bishara left, the sons felt no inclination to obey her and a wall gradually grew up between the mother and her sons. The brothers had many disagreements with her and also amongst themselves, with Mary often asking Arab American friends to intervene in disputes. Mary's income was limited, rarely earning more than $2,000 a year, but that did not stop her sons from borrowing money from her, while at the same time providing no contributions to household expenses. All Mary's sons, with the exception of Adel, had found it difficult to assimilate into American society. They abhorred US culture, disliked the mores of the American people and, most importantly, hated the support Americans gave to the State of Israel.

Mary said Sirhan was a boy who kept to himself and did not talk to his brothers, other than Adel. Sirhan, she said, had not said "more than hello to his brothers [Saidallah and Sharif] in over three years." In early 1968, Sirhan and his brother Munir had a "violent argument and … were barely on speaking terms."[75]

The sons already had a difficult and strained relationship with their father, and Sharif and Saidallah had conflicted with him when they lived in Jerusalem. The estrangement began when the boys started taking money that had been set aside for household items and spending it on themselves.[76]

Sharif, who worked at ITT Cannon Electric, was described by one of his work colleagues, Ann Eustace, as being anti-Semitic and having strong political views. She sometimes had coffee with Sharif but only when she was with two other men she had become friends with, the brothers Abdul Saleh and Mustafa Ali. They worked at a nearby bakery and would often accompany Sharif to the racetrack on their days off. The three would discuss politics and their "hatred of Jews". She said Sharif believed "the United States owed him a living" and was a "heavy bettor at the track, taking racing forms to work with him to select horses for the next day." Ann thought Sharif was "creepy" and a "girl watcher" who always followed her around. Some employees believed a rumour that Ann and Sharif were having an affair, but she insisted there was "no truth to the story" and that she was "a happily married woman with children."[77]

Sharif had dated a student from the Pasadena City College and for him, at least, the relationship was serious. However, the girlfriend felt

Sharif and his brothers were sexist and she ended the relationship. Upset at the end of the affair, Sharif became desperate and made threatening phone calls. He also made two attempts at cutting the fuel lines to the girl's car and a third attempt at tampering with the brakes. Sharif had been put under surveillance by Pasadena police and, following his third attempt at sabotaging the car, was arrested on December 18, 1963, for attempted murder.[78] The charge was later reduced to four counts of breaking or removing vehicle parts. When news of his arrest was publicised by a Pasadena newspaper, Sharif, who had been released on bail, became angry and arrogant, believing the newspaper had no right to describe him as an "attempted murderer". After a jury trial in the Municipal Court of Pasadena, which lasted from December 19, 1963, to March 4, 1964, he was found not guilty on three counts and guilty of one count of breaking or removing vehicle parts without consent of the owner. The prosecutors in the case believed Sharif was a seriously disturbed young man, a decision which undoubtedly allowed him to escape imprisonment. He was sentenced to one year's probation and ordered to seek psychiatric treatment.[79]

Thereafter, Sharif's life took a downturn and things did not improve when he moved to 1711 Corson Street in Pasadena in 1967 and started his employment with the Southern Baptist Church as an accountant. After his dismissal, he failed to find another job and began to borrow money, spending his time gambling at the racetrack. Indeed, it was Sharif and his love of the racetrack that probably influenced his younger brother Sirhan to become a jockey.[80]

Saidallah, much older than Sirhan, liked Middle Eastern music, played the oud and was an admirer of the music of Ravi Shankar. Still, he was a surly and bitter young man who was virulently anti-Israeli, claiming the Jewish state "did not exist."[81] He made no effort to seek American citizenship and was self-conscious about his poorer English skills compared to those of his brothers.[82] "When we came to the United States," Saidallah said,

> I and Sharif, you know, my mother had been already in the United States for almost, I would say, three years or so. And she tried to tell us that this is the United States, and this is free country, and everybody on his own, and they do believe in individuality... So, what she meant by that, that there is no domination, you know, I cannot dominate no brother, nobody, you see, because this is free country and everybody is on their own. So, I realize what she means...and I try to calm down and not to bother them much, and that's why I move, so I said that's why this is for country. And I'm a person like discipline, you see, and your houses are small, and

> their conditions is not satisfactory so it's okay if I move on my own and mind my business...okay? Okay. So, I move. Then I didn't have much connection with the family...[83]

But Saidallah had been unsettled in America. He drank too much and argued with his brothers. He was arrested three times in 1962; twice for drink driving, in January and October, and once for drunkenness in November. By 1963 he had become a problem for the family.[84]

From 1963 Saidallah had no conversation with Sirhan during the times he visited his mother and siblings, other than to say 'hello'. His brother ignored his greetings.[85] Saidallah and Sirhan never got along because of their age differences; Saidallah was thirteen years older than Sirhan and believed that, as the older brother, Sirhan should defer to him. Saidallah also had nothing in common with his brother. "And I remember when I was his age," he said "...he indulged himself you know, in study and reading books and so forth...and which I was not too bother[ed] because I know that he more home studying and so forth...and I don't have much to talk to him." Sirhan was 18 years old when Saidallah reported him to the police for taking his car keys and running off with them, refusing to return them.[86]

On August 4, 1963, during an argument, Saidallah threatened his younger brother with a can opener after knocking Sirhan's chair from under him to gain access to the refrigerator. When their mother intervened in the dispute, Sirhan told her, "This drunken brother of mine. That's what's the matter. Either him or me. I'm tired of this."[87] The threat of violence was so serious Sirhan left the house and spoke to LAPD officer R.D. Cannow, who had been sitting in his police car nearby. Sirhan told him he was afraid to return home, but the officer persuaded him it was for the best. However, another argument occurred when the police officer and Sirhan arrived at the house. According to the official police report, "It was learned that [Sirhan] is at the stage where he does not want advice or will not listen to his elders, and when spoken to, he flies off the handle and an argument starts. The complainant [Sirhan] would not listen to the undersigned... And kept arguing with his family."[88]

Sirhan's mother wanted him out of the house for a short period so things could settle down. Sirhan obliged by leaving to live with his employer, William Beveridge, who had hired him as a gardening assistant. For a short time Sirhan lived in Beveridge's camper at the rear of the house.[89]

In May 1965, Saidallah moved to 308 Burton Court and opened his own painting business. In December that year he moved to 1080 N. Lake Avenue, Pasadena. When his business idea failed, he found employment as a machinist with Michael Ganguin Incorporated in April 1966, but terminated his employment on May 22, 1968, "Under conditions not subject to rehiring". Three months later he was arrested for being "drunk and disturbing the peace". During the period of November 1967 to February 1968, Saidallah purchased a total of $800-worth of foreign drafts made out to 'Bishara Sirhan'.[90]

A friend of Adel's, Robert E. Ritchey, had known the Sirhan family for approximately ten years, having first met Adel when he began working with him at the B and L Holding Supply Company, Pasadena, in 1958. According to Ritchey, Adel left the company in 1961 but still kept in touch, while Ritchey moved into an apartment with Saidallah and had joint tenancy with him from July to November 1967. After Ritchey left, Saidallah kept the apartment on.

Ritchey said he had seen Saidallah with a .38 calibre revolver with a 4-inch barrel, and a rifle in a closet. As an immigrant, it was illegal for Saidallah to own any firearm. Meanwhile, Linda Massri, a former girlfriend of Saidallah and a friend of the Sirhan family since they arrived in the United States, had also seen the rifle while helping move Saidallah from his Marengo Street address to the North Lake Street.[91] Another friend of Saidallah's, Abe Alex, also saw the pistol Saidallah owned.[92]

Before he shared the apartment with Saidallah, Ritchey received a threatening phone call from the ex-husband of a female friend who threatened to come to Pasadena and kill him. Ritchey phoned Saidallah and informed him of the incident. Saidallah came to his apartment, bringing the revolver and approximately fifteen rounds of ammunition, and stayed at the Ritchey apartment for two days to give his friend protection in case the ex-husband arrived to cause trouble. The ex-husband did not appear.

Ritchey did not get along with Sirhan Sirhan. Although he was close friends with Adel and Saidallah, he did not really know the younger brother but described him as a "loner type" with a great fondness for racehorses and often went to the Hollywood Park racetrack. Sirhan told Ritchey he was friendly with a well-known jockey there, Milo Valenzuela. He also attempted to engage Ritchey in political discussions without success and once told him, "Your country is against my country."[93]

The youngest son, Munir, was known as 'Joe' Sirhan. From 1966 he had been unemployed for around eighteen months, spending his time rebuilding and selling bicycles and raising parakeets before being hired as a stock clerk on 4 October 1967 at Nash's Department Store in Pasadena. He had a troubled history and conflicts with the law, was a disciplinary problem in school, and as early as 1959 a complaint had been made by a neighbor for malicious mischief. During October 1963 he was reported missing and later found sleeping in a neighbor's garage. In November 1963 he was involved in a high-speed pursuit with the California Highway Patrol, which resulted in his crashing Saidallah's car into a tree. Munir was knocked unconscious in the crash and the pursuing officers found several lewd photographs, precipitating a Pasadena Police Department juvenile investigation. This led to an allegation on March 26 that Munir had been involved in a "sex and homosexual party." However, no charges were proffered.[94]

On April 8, 1966, Munir became a suspect in a marijuana possession and sales case after the police had been tipped off by an informant, John O'Hanian. Munir had run away from home, was arrested for vagrancy in Flagstaff, Arizona on May 26 and served fifteen days in jail. Returning home, he began smoking marijuana and was arrested on June 10 for selling the drug to a state narcotics agent. He was tried as an adult and convicted of both charges on October 13, 1966. On December 1 he was placed on five years' probation with the first year to be served in County Jail.

On January 11, 1967, Munir Sirhan was ordered to show cause why he should not be deported as an undesirable alien and was ordered deported on July 11. On July 24, he filed a motion for reconsideration, which was denied on September 7. On March 27, 1968, the Board of Immigration Appeals remanded his case to a special inquiry officer to examine a motion to certify Munir to Juvenile Court. The deportation proceedings were eventually dropped.[95]

Many years later, Sirhan was to say of his brother:

> Had it not been for me...Munir would be out there in one of those [Palestinian refugee] camps. He would have been deported [for having a criminal conviction].... The whole world knows 'Sirhan' now. If they had deported his younger brother from America that would show an injustice on the part of America...But even without me, what's all the difference? Munir was just a good-for-nothing Aye-rab.[96]

Adel was a musician who loved music, made picture frames and played the oud at various Arab clubs around the Los Angeles area. At one time he worked as a barman at Shakers Bar, owned by Ali Kalla and Jesse Karadsheh, on Hollywood Boulevard. He was different from his brothers and was considered to have a "quiet nature and a polite, gentlemanly character" by most people who knew him.

Adel never got along with his brother Saidallah, however. They did not have a close relationship and Saidallah considered Adel to be,

> ...sort of childish, you know, he like [*sic*] fun and he don't care for responsibility, he I don't care for, you know, he's just a kid, you know... He can…fool around playing the lute, you know, dancing, entertaining people, and having fun joking, laughing, which these things do not appeal to me that much, you know. And once you talk to him of sort of advice, he won't even accept it. He thinks he must, you know, that he's the only one…[97]

Adel thought of himself as a "sort of the mediator in the whole family... I was like a father to (Sirhan)…in his early school years, especially in this country. I had to work, and I had to support…the whole family, just about, that is to say, after my father left..."[98] For his part Sirhan admired Adel, according to Sirhan's friend Patricia Strathman. "That's the only one he talked to us about," she said.[99]

Adel and Sirhan would sometimes play pool together at two pool halls on Colorado Street in Pasadena. According to Adel, "Once in a while we would go get something to eat, or go play some pool, or go to the races. One of the pool halls was…immediately across the street from PCC, and one...also on the same side of the street, just a little farther down from PCC."[100] Adel said that during the times they spent together, there were "...no indications at all where [Sirhan] would develop… hate…nothing at all."[101]

During 1963, Adel Sirhan found employment at the Fez nightclub in Hollywood as an oud player. When working he could earn up to $150 per week, but when not working there, he turned to picture framing. The family trait of gambling did not bypass Adel, although his game of choice was poker rather than betting on horses. He was no more successful than his brothers, however, and frequently borrowed money to pay off his debts.[102]

Adel's fiancée was an Australian woman named Myleen Kaye. Her real legal name was Eileen Norma Murphy, and she was employed as a dancer at the Fez during the time Adel was playing in the restaurant band. They met in 1966 and began to date in December of that year. They became engaged and planned to marry in June 1967 but called the wedding off when both families objected to the marriage. Fez owner Lou Shelby said the reason for the split between Adel and Myleen was because Adel felt he would be "looked down on" for marrying a girl who was a dancer.[103]

There were also other difficulties between the couple. Myleen had wanted Adel to get a job other than the one he had at the Fez, a job where he could 'settle down'. She visited England during this period and when she returned to Los Angeles, she quarrelled with him. It resulted in Myleen moving to San Diego to work at the Barefoot Bar in Vacation Village. Their estrangement, however, did not last long and they began dating once again.

Myleen thought Adel did not seem to know what Sirhan did most of the time and he didn't speak much about him. She resented the fact that "...all the family seemed to rely on handouts from their mother and all leaned on their mother." Following the 1967 Arab–Israeli War, she said that Adel did not seem concerned and showed no interest in politics, but that his mother was "greatly upset" about it. Myleen continued to see Adel every Monday for 'dates' up until the Monday before Robert Kennedy's assassination, when they had their "final, final breakup."[104]

According to Lou Shelby, Adel had been best placed by temperament to settle into American society. "It's true they retained their old nationality," Shelby said, "but Adel, at least, allowed his Jordanian passport to lapse, and I had quite a job getting it renewed in a hurry when he had an engagement in Mexico." Shelby said Adel never discussed politics and had "many girlfriends" while he worked at the restaurant. "He was not the serious type," Shelby said, "He believed in having a good time."[105]

However, Jordanian Simone E. Simann, who had known Adel since 1961 and considered himself to be a friend, said Adel had a definite opinion about Israel and the Arabs. Simann saw Adel at the Fez restaurant five days before the Robert Kennedy assassination. Adel was in the company of four or five Arabs, Simann said, and overheard him "bitterly complaining about the support for Israel Senator Kennedy had expressed during the Oregon primary". Simann added that he observed Adel was upset that Kennedy had been "cultivating the Jewish vote in the United States" and had been "exasperated with Senator Kennedy".[106]

Adel Sirhan terminated his employment at the Fez on June 28, 1967, and began playing the oud at the Shaker's Oasis Club in Hollywood. In January 1968 Adel began work at United Picture Frame Company in Pasadena as a part-time picture framer.[107]

3

SIRHAN'S 'AMERICAN DREAM'

"...school wasn't quick enough for him [he] *wanted success now... Sirhan thought that type of success lay in his idea of becoming a jockey because there was 'big money' to be made."* Sirhan Sirhan's friend, John Strathman

When the 12-year-old Sirhan arrived in the United States, he soon discovered he was 'different'. He asked his mother "...if we are Americans, are we going to be blond very soon?"[108]

In the spring of 1957, shortly after he arrived in Pasadena, Sirhan entered the sixth grade at Longfellow Grammar School and became known to his friends as 'Sol'. He was placed two grades below his actual age and his teacher, Mrs Floyd Fraley, would later say she could not remember anything outstanding about her pupil except for his alliterative name. Comments on his school record for January – June 1957 describe him as "trying hard" to overcome his language difficulties and "showing improvement". He was also described as "co-operative, well-mannered and well-liked". He achieved a C+ in his tests, barely above an average score.[109]

Terence Fell was one of Sirhan's classmates whom he first befriended. Sirhan was approximately four years older than the other boys in the class and he was "very much interested in the conflicts between the Arab and Israeli nations," Fell said. He was also "very pro-Arabic and often spoke of going back to his homeland and helping out in the conflict between Arabs and Jews." On one occasion when they were in either the sixth or seventh grade, they were playing a board game when Sirhan told him of how he disliked Jews. Fell also heard him tell a mutual friend he did not want to become an American citizen but instead return to his 'homeland'.[110]

After graduating Longfellow, Sirhan enrolled at Pasadena's Marshall Junior High School and was a student there from September 1957 to June 1958, completing General Shop classes, Basic English, Arithmetic, Music and Art with a grade average of C+. None of the teachers at Marshall during that year remembered him.[111] During his time there, Sirhan worked as a paper boy for Pasadena's *Independent Star News* for two months. John O'Hanian (known to his friends as 'John the Jew'), who emigrated from Jerusalem to the United States in the late 1950s with his parents, delivered newspapers with him. On one occasion, O'Hanian accused Sirhan of mistreating another newspaper boy, which resulted in a fist fight between them. Sirhan won after knocking O'Hanian down. When O'Hanian became acquainted with Sirhan's younger brother, Munir, he discovered he was selling heroin and pot. Seeking revenge for losing his fight with Sirhan, O'Hanian offered to work as an undercover agent for the Pasadena Police Department and was instrumental in facilitating Munir's arrest on a 'narcotics charge'.[112]

When Sirhan was in the seventh grade at Marshall Junior High, Munir was a student at Longfellow. The younger brother occasionally came to the attention of his teachers for fighting with other students, who teased him about his name and foreign birth. Sirhan told the school authorities that as his mother spoke very little English, he would take it upon himself to discuss Munir's difficulties. Sirhan told them about the honor of his family and the importance of preserving their good name. He considered Munir's misconduct as a threat to the family honor.[113]

At 13 Sirhan had taken general ability school tests, which showed he had low verbal and abstract reasoning. When he was nearly 15, his 'mental level' scores remained 'very low'. At the age of 17 he took the Stanford Binet IQ Test and scored 89, which was slightly below average.[114] Edward Beran said Sirhan belonged to a church group called Syrian Organisation for Youth and he attended showings of Arab movies that were hosted by the church. Although Sirhan had good grades in junior high, Beran said, there was still a language problem, but in Beran's eyes Sirhan appeared to be "very bright". He also noticed that Sirhan had been teased by other children about his "ethnic origin" which, he thought, made him "introverted". Sirhan had very few friends, Beran said, and was a loner who had "strong feelings for his nationality". He also described Sirhan as having an "extremely quick temper" and had "a few fights at the time that I knew him."[115]

During Sirhan's two years at Eliot Junior High, he began to make an impression on other members of the teaching staff and fellow students. Many students remembered how Sirhan spoke of his Palestinian origins and his dislike of the United States. Samuel Soghomonian, Sirhan's English and Social Studies teacher, described him as a boy who was bullied because he was "dark complected" and "a foreigner". He appeared to the teacher be a loner but also very obedient and well behaved. Soghomonian was Armenian, which led him to empathize with the young Palestinian, although he thought Sirhan had a "feeling of superiority over the average student".[116]

Carol Francis Neal, a fellow classmate of Sirhan's, described him as always arguing with Soghomonian and would wave his hands and snap his fingers to get the teacher's attention. She said the young Palestinian was "an odd person" who did not associate with other students, did not go on dates and did not attend school dances or games. She said Sirhan was always comparing "his country" with the United States and "gave the impression he did not care about the United States."[117]

In September 1960, Sirhan enrolled at John Muir High School after graduating from Elliot Junior High. His new school was a large establishment of 3,000 students; a mixture of socio-economic backgrounds representing the population of Pasadena. Students at John Muir were differentiated by social class, material possessions and social groupings, with students coming from wealthy backgrounds socializing amongst themselves.

His classes at John Muir High included three years of German, two years of Russian and one year of Algebra, History, Psychology and Social Studies. Although he was not an especially intelligent boy, his behavior and attitude in school gave his teachers the impression he was a slightly above average student. He seemed intelligent and articulate because he had a verbal IQ of 109, an above average score, although his reasoning level was far below.[118]

Sirhan's crafts teacher in 1960 recalled him as a quiet, mediocre student who did not associate with the other students in the school. Sirhan's German teacher remembered him as an extremely quiet, good-humoured, and 'proper' student. He believed Sirhan had gone to a British school because all his responses were either "Yes, Sir" or "No, Sir". Sirhan's Spanish teacher in 1960 said he was a polite and quiet student and very proud of being "an Arab" and had strong "nationalistic feelings". He said Sirhan engaged in intelligent discussions about the Middle East, but did not believe he was very "intelligent" or "bright".[119]

Sirhan took the California Cadet Corps course for three years at John Muir. A military science course similar to ROTC, it included military history, drill, rifle range practice, and firearm safety. Cadets on the rifle team practiced with the .22 calibre rifle, but as Sirhan was not a member of the team, he did not receive any training in the use of firearms. The possible exception was a trip once or twice a year to the National Guard Armoury, where all the cadets were permitted to fire a few rounds with a .22. None of the cadets received any training in the use of handguns. The Commander of the California Cadet Corps during Sirhan's participation remembered him as a better than average cadet who accepted discipline and showed "administrative ability". Sirhan's reports recorded him as getting along well with his fellow corps members and being "even tempered".[120]

A group of students at the school teased Sirhan because of his nationality and many avoided him. However, a student "of Armenian extraction" was quite friendly with Sirhan and understood his problems as he was also a "foreigner".[121] Michael Haggerty met Sirhan in 1963 at Muir High School and said that Sirhan frequently told jokes or made humorous remarks about his first and last names being the same, and that the only time he would see Sirhan in a serious mood was while discussing the Arab-Israeli situation. Sirhan often stated that Israel would still belong to the Arabs if it was not for the United States and Britain, Haggerty said. He recalled hearing Sirhan say that he did not care for the United States Constitution because it did not do much for the individual. It was the only statement he could recall Sirhan making about US politics.[122]

At school Sirhan began to develop strong feelings about social and racial discrimination and identified largely with Mexican Americans, African Americans and poor Americans, believing American ideals were becoming subverted by political leaders. His bond with alienated Americans was a result, Sirhan said, of Arabs being treated like second-class citizens in the United States. "Just because we're Arabs in this country," he said, "we have no power, no prestige, no influence, no money – nothing, really. We can be treated like dogs, like ants."[123] Fellow student David Stevens said he "bitterly opposed and hated Jews." He also said Sirhan listened to Radio Havana and believed him to be pro-Castro.[124]

Sirhan became interested in politics and often expressed his political views. Once he gave a talk to the John Muir High School's Foreign Relations Club. Arriving at the venue Sirhan became disgusted at the audience, which he believed was made up mostly of Jews. Asked if Arabs should accept the status quo and also accept peace between Arabs and Jews, Sirhan became inflamed. He berated his questioner and asked, rhetorically, "Give up our own houses? You want us to give up our own houses?"[125] He began to underline passages in his school textbooks that referred to assassination. In *A History of the American People,* Sirhan underlined:

> It was his last public utterance. The next day, as he was holding a reception in the Temple of Music, he was shot by a young Polish anarchist named Czolgosz, whose brain had been inflamed by reading the tirades of the yellow press against 'Czar McKinley'. After a week of patient suffering the president died – the third victim of an assassin's bullet since the Civil War.

Below the passage Sirhan had written, "And many more will come." He made no other marks in the book.[126]

Sirhan continued to describe himself as a 'Palestinian Arab' and by the time he finished high school, was beginning to show signs that his Arab heritage was becoming central to his life—on graduation, he signed his name in Arabic.[127]

Sirhan had read Victor Hugo's *Les Misérables* and was impressed with a passage he said meant something to him: "Teach the ignorant as much as you can; society is culpable in not providing instruction for all and it must answer for the night which it produces. If the soul is left in darkness, sins will be committed. The guilty one is not he who commits the sin, but he who causes the darkness."[128] Amongst Sirhan's collection of books, some stolen from his local library, was Louis Fischer's biography of Mohandas Ghandi. Although the passage he underlined was about the colonial situation in India, it was clearly analogous to the situation in the Middle East viewed from the perspective of a Palestinian Arab. Fischer wrote, "The British were masters in somebody else's home. Their very presence was a humiliation… Even if the British had converted India into a land flowing with milk and honey, they would have been disliked. Imperialism, like dictatorship, fears the soul, degrades the spirit and makes individuals small, the better to rule them. Fear and cowardice are its allies." Sirhan had underlined a passage and wrote "profound" in the margin.[129]

In a textbook Sirhan purchased on January 30, 1964, entitled *Readings for College Writers,* he underlined the following passage: "The enemy is not necessarily a bad man. Indeed, he may be a man of high character and considerable good will."[130]

On May 19, 1963, shortly before his graduation in June, Sirhan made an application to Pasadena City College. He was accepted as a student and attended the college from September 1963, first as a full-time student and then later part-time. He supported his schooling by working part-time as a gas station attendant, waiter and gardener. After

March 1964 he became a part-time student due to the heavy workload of his part time jobs. As Sirhan had a poor attendance record and was either barely passing or failing academically, he was dismissed on May 18, 1965.[131] He graduated 558 in a graduating class of 829.

In November 1962, aged 18, Sirhan had begun working part-time as an assistant to William Beveridge, a self-employed Pasadena gardener. In August 1963, after quarrelling with his mother and brother Saidallah, he had left his home and moved into a camper truck owned by Beveridge. He lived in the camper for seven months and in March 1964, he moved into a vacant house owned by Beveridge at 234 North Camello Street, Pasadena. Sirhan lived there for two weeks before returning to his mother's home. From 1963 to the beginning of the 1964 school year, Sirhan also worked part time as a waiter and short order cook at Peak's Hamburger Bar. The manager witnessed Sirhan losing his temper on three occasions and said Sirhan was "...quite visibly disturbed because of his anger..." Overall, however, manager Rene Juarez said Sirhan was a good worker.[132]

Beveridge was the caretaker of the Theodore Von Karman Estate in Pasadena and Sirhan was placed there by his employer to work as a full-time gardener beginning in February 1964. Sirhan hated working on the estate of a "Jew". In fact, he came to hate all the Jews whose gardens he tended. He referred to them as those "fucking Jews," "the goddamn Zionists" and the "fucking Zionists."

Sirhan once took a girl to the estate. He had met her at Pasadena City College and had admired her for some time. Their first date was driving around in his old Cadillac taking the Colorado Boulevard to San Marino route and stopping off at the estate where he worked. The couple were about to make love on the lawn when he blurted out that he wished he owned the house instead of "this goddamn Jew." The girl replied that she, too, was a Jew. Sirhan said he abruptly ended their lovemaking, apologized, and drove the girl back to the college after saying, "I'm sorry."[133]

On August 31, 1964, T. Edward Beehan, executive for Von Karman Estate, told Beveridge that Sirhan was not doing his job properly. On two separate occasions, Beehan said, he had found Sirhan sleeping in his car while the water from the sprinkler system was running off the lawn and onto the street. Beveridge fired Sirhan the same day. As well as being fired from his daytime gardening job, Sirhan also quit his second job as a short order cook.[134]

Sirhan had already started working for the Clarence Copping Elite Motor Service at East Foothill Boulevard, Pasadena whilst working for Beveridge. He began work there on March 10, 1964, earning a maximum weekly wage of $80. In September 1964 the station changed hands and on the 28th he was re-employed by the newly named Richfield Gas Station, managed by Jack Davies. He attended the gas pumps and cleaned the station and the rest rooms, working the night shift from 8 pm to 4 am. When Davies decided to close at midnight, Sirhan worked the 4 pm to midnight shift.

According to Davies, his new employee was a good worker, always polite, courteous and hard-working. However, Sirhan's boss said he enjoyed horse races and got the impression he bet most of his salary at the racetrack. Sirhan worked there until June 7, 1965, when he resigned after a fellow employee, a "superior" he said, began "needling him".[135] A fellow employee, Keith Young, said he had many conversations with Sirhan, who told him he came from Jordan and that it was one of the "best places in the world." Sirhan asked Young if he thought the USA was the best place in the world and when Young answered in the affirmative, Sirhan replied, "Like hell it is." From that date on, Young said he never had any conversations with Sirhan again.[136]

Sirhan made a few friends among the students at Pasadena College, including Janet Neilson, who met him in 1964 in a biology class and thought him to be a quiet, well-mannered person. She also thought he was intelligent, well-spoken and courteous. Another friend at college, Ivan Garcia, a native of Guatemala, described him as a sensitive and thoughtful person who was generous and unselfish toward his friends. Sirhan and Garcia did not discuss political affairs or political candidates. He visited Sirhan's home for dinner on two occasions.[137]

Nina Tihomirov, who taught Russian to Sirhan in the fall of 1964 and the spring of 1965, said Sirhan was "not a very good student" but acknowledged he was "good at languages." Tihomirov said Sirhan was frequently absent from class, citing his part time jobs or his sister's illness as excuses. She eventually dismissed him from class for lack of attendance.[138]

Sirhan became increasingly sensitive about his 'foreigner' status and believed he stood out on campus because "Just my name gave me away." When the issue of Palestine came up in one class discussion, Sirhan thought he now had the chance to "clobber this fellow [a teacher], this blonde son of a bitch... I really wanted to. I put him where he really belonged." Sirhan talked for an hour and as there were "two or three colored people in the class," he knew he had a sympathetic part of the audience who would applaud him. Sirhan argued, "If the US was really as benevolent as it claimed to be, why did it send Hitler's Jews to Palestine? Why not to the Mojave Desert? Then see how much milk and honey they could produce!"[139]

Sirhan also said he once attended a speech given at the college by diplomat Ralph Bunche. "Ralph Bunche?" Sirhan said, "Yeah, he made it in diplomacy, but he has a manufactured eminence. After that [speech] I realized that being an Arab is worse than being a Negro." Alluding to the purported racism of his fellow students, Sirhan added, "...the Jews were behind the scenes wherever you go. You tell them your name and they freeze. SUR-HAN?" He felt slighted every time someone mentioned his alliterative name.[140]

It was at Jack Davies' service station, according to Sirhan, where he had his first real sexual experience. There, Sirhan met a young woman who told him she had been training to be an air stewardess. They met up "three or four" times at the station, Sirhan said. One night she came late when there was little business. He tried to stall her by checking her car oil and when he opened the bonnet of her car, he saw a note which read "I trade ass for gas". It had been put there by her friends. Her embarrassment broke the ice and the next time she visited he took her to the rear of the garage and they made love. As Sirhan worked until four in the morning, he often took her out for breakfast. On one occasion they made love in the rear of his 1949 Cadillac as they watched a Burt Lancaster movie at a drive-in theatre. Sirhan confessed he had not experienced "sex with love too much…only sex for sex's sake."[141]

Sirhan's story about his love life may be true, but his experiences jar with reports from many of his college friends. According to them, Sirhan was not at all successful when it came to attracting young women, with most friends and acquaintances saying he did not date any of the co-eds from the campus.

In 1964, student Gwendalee Gumm was a contestant for Carnival Queen at Pasadena College when she first met Sirhan. She was sitting in a booth collecting donations for the carnival and votes for the contest, which were counted as a penny donation equal to one vote. Sirhan approached the booth and donated a ten-dollar bill. He proceeded to ask her for a date on several occasions but she declined.[142]

Robert Comfort, a fellow student of Sirhan in the spring of 1964 through 1965, was the publisher of a small campus periodical and was "acquainted" with him. "We weren't fast friends," Comfort said. He described Sirhan as "articulate without being pushy" and wanted very much to be "liked", but was an "introvert and loner". He thought his Palestinian friend was friendly, and "eager enough for acceptance that he'd buy coffee for everybody at the table." However, Comfort thought Sirhan was "lonely... a little guy with the top button on his shirt undone so the hair on his chest stuck out." Although Sirhan tried hard to be accepted by his fellow students and no one disliked him, "no one... liked him well enough to be his friend."

Because Sirhan was from a refugee background he was considered "unfit company by the rest of the Arab students, most of whom were the offspring of monied Middle East establishment parents." According to Comfort, Sirhan "disliked them for their smugness [and] they rejected him". However, he remembered that Sirhan asked a few girls for dates but "none accepted." In fact, Comfort said, the few girls he was friends with told him they thought he was a "nice guy" but were uncomfortable in his company and said they would not go out with him if he asked them. Of the few girls Sirhan asked out for dates, none accepted. The typical reaction of the girls, Comfort said, "would be, 'He is a nice guy, but I'd feel funny if I went out with him'."[143]

Sirhan's attitude towards women may have had something to do with his mother's influence. Mary said she "did not allow girls in the house because they were…different… If we don't want to marry a girl, we won't walk with a girl. It's against our, we're different. And my sons, you can see them all unmarried because it's [a] different way. I don't know, it's not different."[144]

When Sirhan had coffee with his fellow students they would engage in general conversation, Robert Comfort said. Sirhan was "not at a loss to express his belief in Arab nationalism [and] hated the idea of Israel." Sirhan thought Egyptian leader Abdel Nasser was "great" and the only time he raised his voice "were the times the Middle Fast situation was the topic of discussion."[145] Another acquaintance, Morris Flaster, said Sirhan idolized Nasser and believed Nasser's 'socialist state' was a success. Sirhan once brought in a magazine in Arabic which contained pictures of Nassar and various industries in Egypt. Sirhan would point to pictures of the industries and state what a wonderful job was being done under a socialistic government. Sirhan told Flaster he was against King Hussein of Jordan because he felt Hussein was "too moderate."[146]

Fellow student Bruce Edward Fulton met Sirhan in September 1964. Fulton did not socialize with Sirhan off campus, but he got to know him well. His conversations with Sirhan were usually held in the campus coffee shop during breaks or between or after classes. On "one or two occasions" he rode with Sirhan in an "old Cadillac". The last time Fulton saw Sirhan was "prior to December 1965." Fulton said that during the course of his year-long conversations with Sirhan, they often discussed the Arab–Israeli conflict. He said Sirhan was displeased with the US government's pro-Israeli position and was dissatisfied with the Johnson administration and US newspapers because he believed they sided with Israel. He was very devoted to Jordan and was loyal to "his country". It was Fulton's opinion that Sirhan wanted to return there someday.[147] James L. Fleming, who knew Sirhan in 1963 and 1964, concurred and said that Sirhan was very pro-Arab and critical of the United States' support of Israel.[148]

John and his wife Patricia Strathman,* a couple in their mid-twenties, were good friends with Sirhan. John had known Sirhan since junior high and high school and had formed a close association with him, before meeting him again at Pasadena College. He was a language instructor at Southwestern Military Academy at the time and was also studying for his degree at Pasadena College. Both men studied languages and the couple lived close to him on Maple Street, where they would see each other quite a bit and "talk on the street and everything." Patricia said John and Sirhan would meet each other at school or see each other on the street and drop into a coffee shop and talk as both were interested in languages. "That's probably how they got to know each other," Patricia said.[149]

The couple visited Sirhan at his home on numerous occasions in 1964 and 1965 and he visited the Strathman home "maybe twenty times" as a frequent house guest. The couple described him as an ideal guest. Sirhan would bring John tapes of Adel playing the oud, an Arabic stringed instrument, and with languages as a common interest, they would study together, John helping Sirhan with Russian while Sirhan helped John with Arabic.[150]

Patricia said Sirhan was more her husband's friend than hers. She listened to their conversations but did not get involved as she was not versed on the topics they discussed. She did, however, talk at length with Sirhan about mysticism as she had an interest in it. One of her recollections was of Sirhan at a dance when he refused to join in and he gave the impression he was "withdrawn". She wondered why he did not have a girlfriend. "I don't know why," she said, "but he never talked about girls. Never brought one over..."[151] She believed Sirhan was a "helpful person" and if he knew and liked someone he would do "anything for them" and he "seemed to have a desire to please." She recalled situations where he had been nice to her children. However, Patricia also described Sirhan as being "intense and stubborn". Her observations were corroborated by Sirhan's brother Munir, who also described his brother as stubborn and prone to "tantrums".[152] William A. Spaniard, who knew Sirhan before he joined the military and who

* FBI and SUS files alternatively spell the Strathman surname as 'Strathmann' and 'Strathman'.

fought in Vietnam, described Sirhan as a "...taciturn individual who did not say very much. Friendly, really, but hard to get to know."[153]

"He always looked as though he were thinking about something," Patricia said, who saw him "...several times walking in town...alone and with a thoughtful expression on his face." However, Patricia said that although he rarely displayed a temper, he would get "extremely angry" when they discussed the Arab–Israeli conflict. She said he did not like the fact that the United States was aiding Israel and became "emotional" when discussing the conflict.[154]

By 1964 John Strathman saw that Sirhan's interests had changed and his friend had become interested in mysticism and the powers of the mind which, John admitted, was beyond him. When he asked Sirhan about his studies at college, Sirhan told him that "...school wasn't quick enough for him" and he "wanted success now." Sirhan thought that type of success lay in his idea of becoming a jockey because there was "big money" to be made.[155]

During his time at Pasadena College Sirhan had been asked numerous times by friends and acquaintances why he had not taken American citizenship. He always replied it was because he was an 'Arab' and because he felt there was no freedom in the United States. He believed there was more freedom in Russia and China and that stories of refugees fleeing from those countries was a product of American propaganda. He also resisted American citizenship because of the United States' support of Israel. When it came to political discussions, Sirhan adopted a closed-minded attitude. No one could convince him his arguments were wrong and he always stubbornly resisted any attempt to argue that his position might be incorrect.

Margaret Lojeski was a student at Pasadena College and knew Sirhan from the fall of 1964 to spring 1966. During 'free study' periods she and Sirhan would sit and talk together, becoming "fairly well acquainted". She recalled one argument that Sirhan got into with a foreign exchange student who was either "Jewish or from Israel". Although she could not recall the nature of the argument, she remembered it was 'political' and Sirhan "got quite mad and stormed out of the room". Sirhan later told her, "The foreign exchange student had a high opinion of himself and thought he was 'so good'."[156]

Lowell J. Bean was an assistant Professor of Anthropology at California State College, Hayward, California and taught Cultural Anthropology at Pasadena College. He taught a class in the spring of 1964 and witnessed two emotional outbursts from Sirhan with other students during discussions about the Arab–Israeli conflict. Bean had requested Sirhan give an informal report to the class on Arab culture, specifically Pan-Arabism and the idea that Arab nations should unite to become a major political power in the Middle East. When a Jewish student in the class asked a particular pointed and controversial question, Sirhan had "an almost uncontrollable temper in defense of Arab National Unity," Bean said. Sirhan became "very emotional, almost to the point of violence in his defense of the Arabs." The "eruption" almost became a "fist fight" before Bean stopped it. A short time later Sirhan again became involved in a "very heated discussion" with a student in the hallway outside the class.[157]

There were two Arab groups active on campus: 'The International Club' and the 'Organization of Arab Students in the United States and Canada' (OAS). The OAS had been formed in 1952 to assist Arab students in adjusting to academic life away from home, but it was more politically active than its mission statement professed. According to writer James H. Sheldon in an article entitled 'Anti-Israeli Forces on Campus', the OAS was dangerously active in spreading extremist and violent ideas during this period. The organisation was not recognized by the college authorities, nor was it recognized as a formal local organization by its parent organization in New York City, because Pasadena City College did not give the group formal status on campus. Additionally, the college did not give it authorization to operate.[158]

Terry Fell, who knew Sirhan when he was a Pasadena College student, said Sirhan was member of a "banned foreign political group" at the college and was "resentful of the Shah of Iran" and the Shah's visit to the United States. According to Fell, Sirhan participated in a demonstration against the Shah held at the UCLA campus.[159]

Fawwaz H. Zedan, a former chairman of the Pasadena chapter of the OAS, described it as a social group largely composed of Arab graduates from Pasadena City College. He confirmed the chapter was not recognized or affiliated with the college. Zedan said Sirhan was not a member of the Pasadena chapter. However, Zedan did say Sirhan had a close association with OAS students and became a 'de facto member', even though he did not pay dues to the parent organization in New York.[*160]

Around 1965, Sirhan met the president of the Pasadena branch of the organization at the time, Kanan Abdul Latif Hamzeh, which

---

* In her book, *The Rise of the Arab American Left*, Pamela Pennock contradicted herself when she wrote about this important fact. "It is under dispute whether Sirhan was involved in the OAS while at Pasadena City College...Ayton states that while it was not recognized as an official student organization, the OAS did operate a chapter there." She then adds, "Sirhan was active in it for a while." (p.260)

occurred after Sirhan's expulsion from college. Sharif Sirhan, who was also a student at Pasadena College and an OAS member, introduced his brother Sirhan to Hamzeh. He volunteered for some of the less desirous work in preparing meetings, setting up chairs, arranging for a tape recorder, and procuring various refreshments for the group. Hamzeh said that in spite of the "technicalities" concerning acceptance by the college, it operated as all organizations of its kind on other college campuses.

Hamzeh helped Sirhan with some math problems and Sirhan visited his apartment to tape some Arabian music. He said Sirhan was accompanied by one of his brothers and a sister. In conversations with several of the Sirhan brothers, Hamzeh learned that Sirhan had constant arguments with them as well as his mother. He was not told what the arguments were about, but surmised they were strictly of a family nature. He recalled that Sirhan and "one other brother" said they were unhappy living in the United States.[161] Hamzeh believed both brothers were unable to adjust to the social and political atmosphere in the country, and also said that Sirhan could easily have been influenced "by any Arab Nationalist cause" since he had "intense feelings against the Israelis."[162]

Sirhan continued to maintain contacts with his Arab friends after he left Pasadena College. Faz'l Inayat'Khan first met Sirhan in the fall of 1966 at a private residence rented by Omar Ramzi, who lived in Los Angeles. Ramzi was an officer in the "Arab Students Association." The small group of students participated in discussions of current topics during the 1966 school year including various political situations in the United States and Middle East. Inayat'Khan said that during one group discussion at Ramzi's home, the topic of conversation "centred around various committees of the United States Senate and the United States House of Representatives and the key positions certain members had in influencing policies...in such areas as foreign aid, etc." He said Sirhan became quite agitated during this discussion and "indicated how unfair and undemocratic the committee system of our form of government is and can be if the wrong people control the power."

Khan said Sirhan and others in this group were supporters of the Ba'ath Party, a Middle-Eastern political party that was "composed of members that support any government that is pro-Jordan, Syrian, etc., in philosophy and ideology." Gamal Abdel Nasser, a heroic figure to Sirhan, was the dominant supporter of Ba'athism, which called for the creation of a single Arab state. In 1954 Ba'athists came to power in Syria, later in Iraq, and Nasser merged Egypt and Syria to form the United

Arab Republic. Palestinians were amongst Nasser's most enthusiastic supporters and their best hope for defeating Israel. Sirhan and other members of the group, Khan said, "...did not believe the rulers in their native lands were fighting with enough determination to regain their rightful land from the Israeli people." He described Sirhan as "a young immature individual that was very impressionable."[163]

Faizullah Khan met Sirhan in the fall of 1966 and early spring 1967 at Ramzi's home and at several political functions held at California State College, Los Angeles. The political functions would involve professors and others from the college who would lecture to small groups of students about various political issues. Faizullah also said that Sirhan was a "very impressionable individual," adding that Saidallah and Sirhan were both "unhappy and unable to adjust to the social and political atmosphere of the United States."[164]

Mohan Goel met Sirhan at Pasadena City College in 1963 and would see him at Santa Anita racetrack during 1964 and 1965. Both students were from a foreign background and it was this familiarity that brought them together. Goel described Sirhan as "usually very quiet, he used no profanity, except sometimes he used to swear in Arabic. Once a man spilled some coffee on his brother in a restaurant in Hollywood and Sirhan called him a 'mother f.... r' in Arabic."

Goel contradicted other reports saying Sirhan had never been a member of the International Club at Pasadena College. "I had many conversations with Sirhan," Goel said, "We both belonged to the Pasadena College International Club. The club was composed of about 150 foreign students." Most of the time, Goel said, Sirhan was polite, helpful and quiet but was "very much against the Jewish people" and "hated" the Jews. Sirhan told him "many times" about how much he admired Hitler and how the dictator "handled the Jews". Goel said Sirhan used to say that he could not understand the Americans, and questioned why "...they let the Jews suck the blood of the nation and keep putting the money in the banks, and the Americans let them get away with it." Goel also described Sirhan as a heavy bettor, betting as much as $60 to $80 on one race.[165] Goel last saw Sirhan during January and February 1968.[166]

The entire length of Sirhan's stay at Pasadena City College was only one year and five months. In his fourth and last semester, he had five F grades. On May 12, 1965, he was recommended for dismissal for poor attendance and was dismissed on May 18. Sirhan begged the college authorities to keep him on, arguing he had missed classes because of his sister Aida's illness. The authorities were unrelenting after they had been advised Sirhan was using his sister's illness as an excuse.[167]

Embarrassed that he had once again failed in life, Sirhan lied about his dismissal from college, telling one acquaintance that the reason why he was asked to leave was because he was having an affair with a math teacher. Having lost the success attached to immigrant sons who acquire a college education, Sirhan became bitter. "The way they did things at [college] helped detach me from society, or at least campus society," he said.

> But for me that was society. I majored in political science, foreign languages. Diplomacy was my main interest. But soon I gave up on the idea of being a diplomat. When I figured the score, I saw that the odds were stacked against me. You gotta be rich to be a diplomat. You have to give big parties. You could blow your entire year's salary in three months.[168]

Sirhan had desperately wanted the life of a typical American citizen: a decent job, family, house, cars. He was not satisfied with a simple job and basic material possessions because his ambition demanded more. And he would have attained it, Sirhan thought, if he had been given "More acceptance on the part of American society," which could have altered his path. "Don't tell me America's the greatest," Sirhan said, "Show me, prove to me. Don't let me look at it. Let me feel it. We claim to live in a democracy. Poor, rich, white, all equal before the law, whose votes and opinions count. I never experienced this. Rather the contrary. I experienced the injustice that these people have committed against me."[169]

Sirhan had always felt that throughout his life:

> in this country and back there I always felt that I had no country, that I had no place that I could call really my own and I was just sick and tired of being a foreigner. It is as simple as that. I wanted a place of my own where the people would speak my own language, where they would eat my own food, where I could share my own politics and my own, something that I could identify as Arab, a Palestinian-Arab, and have my own country, my own city, my own land, my own business and my own everything..."[170]

4

THE JOCKEY

"...[I] *loved it... That was the most enjoyable experience of my life...horses... they're easy to be with. I love to be with them... It was nice to get up in the morning and go for a ride. Sitting on a horse, with the wind beating against you, you feel like you're something."* Sirhan Sirhan

In the summer of 1965, after he left Davies's employment, Sirhan moved to another service station a short distance away, managed by Ivan Milicic. However, he soon left after a win on the horses at Santa Anita racetrack. After showing his employer a "bundle of money", Milicic thought Sirhan's win on the horses was the reason he was leaving. He was unemployed for approximately one month after leaving.[171]

Sirhan said he could not afford to settle down as he did not have what American society demanded: "money and wealth". He said that 90 percent of American marriages broke up over money problems and he did not want that. He was frustrated he did not have what the Jews had—financial security—which was why he visited the races so much.[172]

Having nearly attained success at Pasadena College, Sirhan was brought down to earth by his inability to meet the demanding level of his studies. Unskilled in any career or profession, he dreamed of buying a Mustang because he equated it with success and the acquisition of wealth. He told his friend Walter Crowe that he wanted to make money, "lots of it".[173] Patricia Strathman said Sirhan's conversations always turned to horses and money. Sirhan wanted to make, "lots of money...fast."[174]

By the middle of 1965, following two years of low-income meager jobs, Sirhan set his sights on becoming a jockey as a way to achieve financial success. On October 15, 1965, aged 21, Sirhan obtained employment at Santa Anita racetrack, Arcadia, with horse owner and trainer Gordon

Bowsher. He was hired as a stable hand and 'hot walker / exercise boy', in addition to learning to ride, and earned $375 per month. The job entailed walking horses to cool them off following a race, but he spent most of his time in the stables mucking out and grooming the horses, so the job was not to his liking and he became frustrated at the lack of progress in becoming a jockey.[175] Bowsher once saw Sirhan mistreat a horse, "...kicking and hitting it with his fists." Sirhan, he said, "... was in a rage of temper." By way of explanation Sirhan told him the horse had 'provoked him'.[176] On January 1, 1966, Sirhan told Bowsher he had received his 'Hot Walkers' license from the California Horse Racing Board.

Sirhan's foreman, John Shear, said Sirhan, "worked hard and was kind." However, the stewards at Santa Anita said Sirhan was too old, at 22, and at 5'5" and 120 pounds, too big to be a jockey. On various occasions Shear loaned Sirhan books and horse equipment and allowed him to practice his riding on thoroughbred ponies. Unfortunately, because Sirhan was a poor horse rider, he was constantly being thrown or falling from horses he was working and would sometimes lose his temper with them. Shear was also witness to Sirhan's intense feelings about the Arab–Israeli conflict. The newly hired Sirhan once heard a co-worker read aloud a newspaper account of Robert Kennedy recommending the allocation of arms to Israel. "Sol just went crazy," Shear said. "He was normally very quiet, but he just went into a rage when he heard the story." Shear heard Sirhan say, "That man is killing my people. 'He should be dead.' 'He should be dead,' that's what he said."[177]

Walter 'Tom' Rathke, a stable groom for Gordon Bowsher, became friends with Sirhan. Rathke thought Sirhan had an "unusual personality" and told him he had a "calming effect" on the horses at the track by using his "thought waves". Rathke was a follower of Rosicrucianism, which he compared to Christianity, and believed the meditation which Rosicrucians practised was akin to praying in the Christian religion. He thought Sirhan should take the practice up and that it would improve his life, providing him with Rosicrucian literature consisting of a half-dozen pages on meditation. Sirhan had been impressed by Rathke and engaged in long conversations with him about mysticism. Sirhan also researched and experimented on related subjects like psychokinesis.[178]

'Mysticism' was not new to Sirhan. His mother had dabbled in it, and she had often read people's fortunes in tea leaves. Sirhan had also been fascinated with his Arab neighbor Linda Massri's fortune-telling and said he was attracted to the occult because

> It was a kind of meditation, silence and quiet. It's like the New Age movement toward tranquillity and peace of mind... I was trying to improve myself. I started to learn about the metaphysical occult after the death of my sister. I was hit hard when she died... A guy I knew [Tom Rathke] when I was down in Corona pushed me along the way to reading more. It was more intellectual and abstract. It was more about Theosophy, which is about the spiritual afterlife. It expanded my knowledge and horizons of life, as well as my own nature and spiritual being.[179]

Rathke also introduced Sirhan to the practice of self-hypnosis. One of the books he recommended to Sirhan was *Cyclomancy: The Secret of Psychic Power Control* (1967). In June 1966 he pursued his interest in the subject by answering an advertisement by the Rosicrucians, based in San Jose, the Ancient Mystical Branch of the Rose Cross, which advertised itself as an 'apolitical' and 'humanistic' sect pledged to the study of 'life and the universe'. Sirhan applied and mailed his $20 membership fee.[180] In his application, Sirhan stated he had been a student of Metaphysics, Psychology or Philosophy for three years and wrote, "By reading your book *Mastery of Life,* I have discovered how much I do not know about myself despite all the philosophical works that I have been reading. I sincerely want to better myself, and on that basis, I submit my application."[181]

John Strathman said he used to talk a lot about Tom Rathke. "I think he was the guy who introduced Sirhan to the occult," Strathman said.

> He seemed to have Sirhan sort of transfixed. From what Sirhan told me, I got a sinister picture of Sirhan and Rathke riding around in this old car. Rathke is driving and talking and Sirhan is listening and filling his head with all this junk on the occult. (Sirhan began saying he could see) mystical bodies (and started practicing) magic.[182]

Sirhan's real ambition was to be a jockey, but he became bitterly disappointed that he was not making the grade at Santa Anita and was destined to remain as a stable boy and hot walker. He left on March 31, 1966, and set his sights on a job opening at a horse-breeding ranch in Corona. Sirhan said he had "...seen a note on the bulletin board at Santa Anita, offering a position as an exercise boy. I responded and met Frank Donnorauma, who was the trainer... I didn't know that 'Frank Donnorauma' was an alias... I didn't know anything about criminals."

Donnorauma would later be used by conspiracy advocates to claim Sirhan had been connected to organized crime.*

On June 2, 1966, approximately two months after leaving his employment with Bowsher, Sirhan was hired as an exercise boy by Bert Altfillisch, the owner of the Granja Vista Del Rio Ranch, located about 8 miles west of Corona in a rural dairy and horse ranch area. The ranch had modern facilities, including a Spanish décor home, modern stables, racetrack and corrals. Sirhan would earn $350 per month. He showed Altfillisch his hotwalkers' license from the California Horse Racing Board and told him he had five months' experience at the Santa Anita racetrack. Altfillisch told him he would be doing 'everything', including working as an exercise boy.[183] During his time at the ranch, Sirhan met many celebrities including horse owners Desi Arnez (the husband of Hollywood star Lucille Ball), Dale Robertson (the star of the western series *Wells Fargo*), and Buddy Ebsen (of *The Beverly Hillbillies* fame).

Edward Van Antwerp, a self-confessed alcoholic who had a job working at Taylor Rents in Norco, California, said he had been sitting in the Merry Note Cafe in Norco having a few drinks when he first met Sirhan. The bar was located a half block from the motel where Van Antwerp was staying and he took pity on the young trainee jockey after learning of his financial plight. He offered to share his one-room Highlander Motel lodgings with him. Sirhan introduced himself as 'Sol' and was known by that nickname by his fellow employees and racetrack acquaintances. Van Antwerp characterised himself as a close friend of Sirhan, although they did not socialise too often as Sirhan always returned to his home in Pasadena on weekends.[184]

Van Antwerp's room had been rented by his sister, Genevieve Taylor, in May or June of 1966. He slept in the bedroom and Sirhan

---

* The FBI, LAPD and various authors spell the name Donnarumma differently. Donnorauma, alias Henry Ronald Ramistella, was a former jockey who had been involved in petty crime and had also had his licence revoked in New Jersey after providing false testimony to track stewards. Like many individuals who were connected to gambling, horse racing likewise attracted many characters with less than pristine backgrounds. Donnorauma certainly fitted that category. However, after he was investigated by the FBI it was found he had no criminal links to Sirhan. *RFK LAPD Microfilm, Volume 59 (Interviews, I-1930 thru I-2101) Current Section: Ramistella, Henry Ronald, April 4, 1969, https://www.maryferrell.org/showDoc.html?docId=99754#relPageId=7&search=Frank_Ramistella*

Sirhan said, "Frank always seemed to be having financial problems, which probably stemmed from his gambling. He was a heavy gambler… I knew nothing about [his criminal record]." Donnarumma was a heavy drinker and arrested for drunk driving. His later dismissal from the ranch was because of his drinking. *Moldea, 294.*

slept on the couch in the living room. Both lived at the motel together for approximately five months and later moved to Genevieve's house after she offered them lodgings. The two men shared a room there with twin beds for around three months. Van Antwerp said Sirhan was "very quiet and an avid reader of horse racing magazines" and had often expressed his wish to "make it big and [become] rich." He had the impression that his new friend, who drank a "lot of tea", felt that he was "getting an unfair deal in life mainly because he was economically poor."[185] According to Genevieve, Sirhan acted as a virtual housemaid for Van Antwerp and would take care of him during the times her brother would get drunk. Sirhan would also attend Alcoholics Anonymous meetings with him. He continued to live with his friend until December 1966.[186]

When Sirhan first arrived at the ranch he befriended a ranch watchman, John Abonyi. Sirhan did not have a car when he first started working at the ranch and Abonyi offered to give him a ride to and from work. Abonyi and Sirhan became very close and Sirhan visited his new friend's house many times for dinner or a social visit. The main basis for their relationship was the fact that they were both foreigners and could both converse in German. After work, Abonyi and Sirhan would stop off for drinks at 'The Huddle', a poolroom in Corona, and play pool. Abonyi would drink beer and Sirhan would always order a soft drink. He believed Sirhan was too old and did not have the skills to become a jockey, despite Sirhan's insistence to the contrary. Sirhan was a very hard worker, he said, but did "not make friends among fellow workers." He and Joe Tarjani, who lived with Abonyi, were the only friends Sirhan had, according to Abonyi.

During the latter part of Sirhan's employment at the ranch he bought a car, a 1961 Ford Galaxie, for approximately $500. After that Abonyi discontinued picking Sirhan up and taking him to work. Although Abonyi did not see Sirhan as often as before, they remained close friends.[187]

Sirhan was excited to have a job working on a ranch, saying he "... loved it... That was the most enjoyable experience of my life...horses... they're easy to be with. I love to be with them."[188] Sirhan said, "It was nice to get up in the morning and go for a ride. Sitting on a horse, with the wind beating against you, you feel like you're something."[189]

Terry Welch met Sirhan at the ranch in the summer of 1966 during their employment as exercise boys. Welch considered Sirhan to be his best friend and described him as a neat, clean, intelligent person who was both thrifty and generous with his friends. According to Welch, Sirhan did not drink but would accompany his co-employees to local bars and often purchase drinks for everyone present. Welch said Sirhan spoke English with little noticeable accent and was an "avid reader of law, frequently discussing cases which he had read about." During their free time Sirhan and Welch would often meet at 'The Huddle'. He said Sirhan would make friends at the bar by purchasing drinks for patrons while he waited to play pool.

In their conversations Sirhan repeated the lie of how he had been expelled from Pasadena City College when the administrators became aware of a romantic relationship between him and a math teacher. Welch was sceptical as he never saw or heard of Sirhan dating and thought he had made up the story for the benefit of co-employees, who used to rib him about his lack of girlfriends. Welch said that he and Sirhan had discussed wealthy people, especially Burt Altfillisch, and they both envied "people with money".[190]

A young woman, who wished to remain anonymous, was an exercise employee at the ranch. She worked there in the summer of 1966 and said Sirhan had no close friends at the ranch because he was "very argumentative and seemed to be sullen and sarcastic in most of his comments." She recalled he was teased quite often as being a "Mexican boy". He had made a good first impression, she said, as he was neat and clean, had a good vocabulary, and a good use of English but she soon learned that "he had a strong temper [and] could not control it around animals." She also said Sirhan was "egotistical in that he thought he was a good rider and was going to become a jockey, but he was not..." He was "not a hard worker and appeared lazy" and he used "foul language on many occasions...in the presence of both girls and men." She described Sirhan as "belligerent".[191] Another two exercise girls who worked at the ranch corroborated her observations and said Sirhan treated the horses "cruelly".[192]

Peggy Osterkamp, a 5'3", blonde haired and blue-eyed girl, was known as a notable beauty by the other ranch hands who worked for Bert Altfillisch. She was employed at the ranch from February 3 to June 1, 1966, and met Sirhan during her time there. Altfillisch said the young men at the ranch could not work when she was around as they were so taken with her. She knew Sirhan as 'Sol' and only had a short conversation with him about horses. The only other time she could remember meeting Sirhan was at a Corona restaurant. Sirhan picked up her check and paid it after she had lunch with a friend. He did not call or write to her and they did not date. Sirhan's friend Terry Welch said Sirhan had a "crush on her."[193]

In fact, Sirhan became obsessed with Peggy. Her name appeared in his notebooks numerous times and he fantasised about her; one of the entries identified her as 'Peggy Sirhan'. Although he admired her, he was unwilling or, more likely, unable to form a relationship with her. When he saw her at the ranch, he thought she looked "beautiful on a horse".[194] Peggy last saw Sirhan at Santa Anita racetrack sometime during the early part of 1967 or the last four or five days of 1966. Fellow workers knew that someone of Sirhan's physical stature and background simply had no hope in attracting her. They were poles apart.[195]

Despite Sirhan's claims to the contrary, there is very little evidence he had *ever* been successful with girls. A police report stated that he was so shy he used to drive around a girl's home for days at a time without stopping to say hello.[196] Sirhan's friend Walter Crowe said he loved to sit with girls at lunch breaks and "had a great time" but was never successful in his romantic pursuits.[197] In fact, according to his brothers, Sirhan was so shy around women he was rejected many times by female students with whom he tried to form a relationship.

Sy Norris. a horse trainer at the Granja Vista Del Rio started working there in October 1966 and also knew Sirhan as 'Sol'. Sirhan wanted to watch Norris work as he believed he could benefit from it. However, Norris did not have any discussions with him other than to give him instructions as an exercise boy. Sirhan told Norris he wanted to be a jockey and learn as much as he could about the job. However, Norris said he did not have the capabilities and was unsure around horses. He "seemed to be somewhat frightened of them and this certainly would not be a good disposition for a jockey," Norris said.[198] Another employee, Joseph (Chuy) Moreno, who often spoke with Sirhan and sometimes engaged in 'teasing' also said he "had a strong desire to become a jockey but [he] was a very poor rider and had trouble controlling the horses."[199]

Sirhan and Bert Altfillisch soon clashed. Sirhan had put himself forward as the spokesperson for an exercise boy strike and attempted to organize his fellow employees into going home at noon and doing only exercise boy work. When the employees met with their boss, they complained they were overworked. Sirhan approached him and, "using big words," articulated the exercise boys' grievances. Altfillisch refused to give in to their demands and was able to convince Sirhan and the others that if they did not do their work as directed, they would all be fired immediately. After this confrontation they all returned to work, including Sirhan, and no more was heard regarding the matter.[200]

On September 25, 1966, Sirhan had an accident that would put an end to his dreams of becoming a jockey. It was a foggy day as

Sirhan led a mare named Hy-Vera for a workout. The fog had the same effect on a horse as a blindfold. One trainer, Millard Sheets, was frightened enough about the fog to withdraw his horse from the workout, but trainer Larry Heinnemann told the owners, who had come all the way from Los Angeles to see their horses run, that the fog had lifted sufficiently to take the chance. At first the horses began to jog very slowly at an "almost canter" before the riders brought them into a gallop. As Sirhan took the lead, the fog returned.[201] Suddenly the owners heard a crash and a scream. Sirhan had been thrown against a metal post, where he lay crumpled, crying and bleeding. When onlookers arrived at the scene of the accident Sirhan was semi-conscious, blood trickling from his ear. He was covered in mud and blood and thought he had gone blind. It was believed the fall was the result of the saddle not being tight enough and that Sirhan probably pushed his weight to the inside portion of the saddle when he was thrown from the horse.

After fifteen minutes an ambulance arrived and took Sirhan to Corona Community Hospital. Trainer Larry Heinneman accompanied him in the ambulance and on the way there Sirhan wanted to know how it had happened. Heinneman explained it was the same mistake and bad habit he had of leaning instead of pulling up on the horse. Sirhan was treated by Dr Richard A. Nelson and although his injuries were diagnosed as minor, at Nelson's request, X-rays of the spine, skull, left shoulder and left hand were taken and were later analysed by Dr Paul H. Deeb, M.D., head radiologist at the hospital. The results of the X-rays were all negative, revealing no severe concussion, fractures or internal injuries. According to Nelson, "Sirhan questioned all of the medical applications and all the medicines administered to him and appeared unduly frightened of the various treatments. He was one of the most reluctant patients I ever had."[202]

On the day of the accident, Nurse Patricia Kramer administered medicine to Sirhan and had a conversation with him when she was on duty at the hospital. Kramer told him she had a friend who came from Lebanon. She was attempting to make Sirhan at home and asked him if he would like to speak with her. Sirhan asked, "Is she Jewish?" When Kramer said she was not, Sirhan told her he would like to meet her.[203]

Doctors wanted Sirhan to stay a few days, but he said no. On September 26 Heineman picked him from the hospital, and took him home to 5th Street, Norco. On September 27, one day after his release from the hospital, Heinneman visited Sirhan at his home. He looked well, Heinneman said, and did "not complain about any pain, injuries or problems of any kind."[204]

Sirhan returned to work on October 1, six days after the fall, and assumed his normal duties. Sy Norris said Sirhan told him he was only "scratched up painfully" and had no serious injuries.[205] Trainer Millard Sheets, who said he was the first person to reach Sirhan after his accident, saw him back at work two days later.[206]

On October 8, a week after his return to work, Sirhan again fell off his horse. Once more he was taken to the Corona Community Hospital where he was treated by Dr John Schnepper. Schnepper described Sirhan's injuries as 'minor' and said his patient had reopened an old cut in the area of the left eye, sustained from the first accident. A minor abrasion on Sirhan's nose was cleansed and medicated. No other damage was evident, and no X-rays were taken due to the minor nature of his injuries. Sirhan was lucky, but he did have a strong constitution, as many of his friends testified to. Many who knew Sirhan throughout his youth described him as a wiry young man who had great strength despite his small stature. Later, Sirhan's apologists would come to believe his great physical strength proved he was in some sort of 'disassociated state'.

On November 13, Sirhan quit his job at the Altfillisch Ranch. He gave no reason for leaving, but was aware that Altfillisch and the trainers did not think his horsemanship was good enough. His boss had lost confidence in Sirhan, whose skills were less than competent and he had fallen off his horse twice, with each accident requiring hospital treatment. Altfillisch believed the young rider had a lot of ambition, but the accident made him lose his nerve. Additionally, Sirhan did not like long hours of work, was too timid towards horses to ever become a good jockey and was not looked upon with favor after he had attempted to organize the exercise boys to strike action. He also felt he was above doing groom work since he was hired as an exercise boy.

Sirhan's ambitions to be a jockey were now lost. He blamed 'the Jews' who, he said, were the people he worked for and who hindered his advancement as a jockey because he was an Arab. He especially blamed his former boss, Bert Altfillisch, and wrote in his notebook, "I believe I can affect the death of Bert C. Altfillisch."[207]

A Corona High School senior who worked part time at the ranch said Sirhan referred to Jewish people as "dirty Jews", did not appear suitable to "handle horses", treated horses "in a cruel manner" and "seemed to be quite afraid of them". Sirhan, she told FBI agents, "...had a chip on his shoulder due to his small size, made comments that many great people in the world had been small, including Hitler and Napoleon, was very set in his ideas, and was "unyielding" in discussion.[208]

Robert Lynn Wheeler, a trainer at the Granja Vista Del Rio Ranch, recommended Sirhan to his father Robert Wheeler, a horse trainer at Del Mar and on November 16, 1966, Sirhan went to work for Wheeler as a free-lance exercise boy. He was paid according to the number of horses he worked each day.[209] Larry Peters, Sirhan's supervisor, recalled that on November 25, Sirhan again fell from a horse and on another occasion, a few days later, he almost fell again. Peters decided at that time it would be wiser not to continue using him on the track and told him he could not qualify as a rider. Peters had also seen Sirhan kick a horse in the belly and after he remonstrated with Sirhan, he was taken aback at the vitriol which emanated from the young employee. Peters said Sirhan's temper had been unusually violent when he was told he would never make a jockey. Sirhan insisted he could gallop horses as well as the other exercise boys, but Peters was still dissatisfied with his work and fired him on November 30, after an argument.[210]

On December 2, after his brief period of employment with Wheeler, Sirhan returned to the Granja Vista Del Rio Ranch and was given a second chance by Altfillisch. He exercised horses for ten days, but Sirhan was demoralised and still unhappy with his work. On December 12, he voluntarily submitted his resignation and left the ranch without giving a reason for his departure.

Sirhan had two follow-up check-ups after his accidents, on November 8 and December 20. He complained of pain, blurred vision and "extreme motion in his eyes". On December 20, he was examined by Dr Milton Miller, a Corona ophthalmologist, who concluded that Sirhan's vision was normal and that he had been exaggerating his ailments. It appeared to Miller that Sirhan was attempting to get the doctor to write a letter that could be used for a disability claim. After the doctor refused to give him the letter, Sirhan threatened him. Sirhan said he was "going to get me" and "[I] would be sorry", Miller said.[211]

On July 10, 1967, Sirhan filed a claim for his horse accident injuries and it was adjudicated on October 2, 1967 and February 7, 1968. Sirhan's doctor, Dr Maurice Nugent, and the insurance company's doctor, Albert Tashma, an ophthalmologist, reported Sirhan had 20/15 vision and did not have "any permanent disability as a result of the accident."[212] However, a consultant neurosurgeon said there was no way of checking a complaint of head injuries and advised the adjudicator to err on the side of caution. The amount awarded was $2,000. Sirhan bitterly complained the award was too small.[213] He also believed the claim had been delayed because he had mistakenly retained the services of a Jewish lawyer and because he was an 'Arab'.[214]

5

THE CATALYST

"I will be appreciated not now, but the next time the world goes to war, the next conflict comes up. That's when they're gonna think of Sirhan. Appreciate my own political views." Sirhan Sirhan

"The Jews are behind the scenes wherever you go. You tell them your name and they freeze." Sirhan Sirhan

"Then he said, he made, you know, a kind of a brief speech, saying that politics are part of his whole commitment in life..." Walter Crowe

Sirhan developed a close friendship with a non-Arab student, Walter Crowe Jr., and knew another student, Tom Goode, quite well during the short time they spent at Pasadena City College. Sirhan had known Crowe since he was 11 or 12, when they had both delivered newspapers. The three friends saw themselves as anti-establishment intellectuals who took positions on issues that were strongly left wing.

Crowe was born in Pasadena, California, on August 3, 1945, after his family moved there in 1948. He graduated from John Muir High School in 1963; Pasadena City College in 1965; and obtained a bachelor's degree in History from the University of California at Los Angeles in the spring of 1968. The friendship between Crowe and Sirhan was closest when both men were taking an Arabic language course together at Pasadena College and their relationship deepened when Sirhan assisted Walter in learning the language. Sirhan would come to Crowe's home and the two young men would practice speaking Arabic together. As a result, Walter was able to attain high grades in the subject. Although Crowe remained friends with Sirhan during the time they spent at Pasadena College, they drifted apart when Crowe transferred to the University of California at Los Angeles (UCLA) and Sirhan found employment at the racetracks.

Both Crowe and Sirhan admired the author C. Wright Mills and his book, *The Power Elite*. They were also admirers of authors Paul Goodman and Albert Camus, who argued that western society was bourgeois and corrupt. Sirhan described these books as "Terrific... it opens your mind. What a contrast to the bourgeois stuff around here."[215] Crowe also said Sirhan thought "Hitler was a hero, I mean, fine, I don't know if he was racist in terms of black people."

Crowe openly admitted he was a communist and became involved with leftist groups. He attempted to organize a chapter of the Students for a Democratic Society (SDS), and helped to form the Ad Hoc Committee for Negro Rights, although he was unsuccessful in his attempts to form an SDS chapter.[216] Crowe's parents were concerned their son had joined the Communist Party, but dismissed the matter as an attempt to express himself and gain notoriety as an intellectual. Marilynn Brunton, Crowe's older sister and a teacher in Stockton, California, met Sirhan when he visited Crowe's home and noticed how her brother's friend had made "occasional anti-Israeli statements."[217]

A friend of Walter, William Divale, said he and Crowe shared a mutual belief in the Marxist doctrine, which resulted in their friendship. A communist himself, Divale had become acquainted with Crowe in 1964 while attending Pasadena College. Divale also attended UCLA with Walter from September 1966 until July 1967, when both men shared an apartment. They participated in demonstrations, attended club meetings and engaged in philosophical debates. He recruited Crowe into the Communist Party in spring 1967 and described him as an "intellectual communist".

Divale became aware of the Sirhan family through discussions with Crowe. In 1967 Divale and Crowe had been discussing racial prejudice and Crowe had used the Sirhan family as an example of how they had experienced discrimination and had been mistakenly identified as members of the Mexican American community in Los Angeles.[218] Crowe also told Divale that the Sirhan family were "somewhat kooky" in their behavior and that "one of the brothers" had made an attempt on the life of a girlfriend who had rejected him. [219]

Crowe had misgivings about trying to recruit Sirhan as a member of the Communist Party. He believed Sirhan was left-wing on many issues, but that he was also reactionary about Jews and the state of Israel, saying that Mary Sirhan propagated these views to her son.[220] Crowe also said Sirhan's mother was a "very bitter" person and a "racist". Once, during a discussion about the Arab–Israeli conflict, he said, Mary Sirhan asked Crowe, "Have you ever smelled a Jew?"[221] By way of explaining Mary Sirhan's character, Crowe's mother said she had an "inferiority complex" and that "Sirhan was aware of this."[222] John Strathman also believed Sirhan had been heavily influenced by his mother's views.

In 1965, during conversations with Sirhan about the Middle East while both students attended a meeting of the Organization of Arab Students, Sirhan told Crowe of his admiration for President Nasser and his hope that Arabs would someday "rid Palestine of the Jews."[223] Both men had been aware that Palestinian organizations were beginning to carry out terrorist acts. Crowe told Sirhan that the Arab cause was a fight for "national liberation" and, echoing sentiments held by many left-wing radicals of the time, said the conflict in Palestine was an internal struggle by Palestinians who were oppressed by the Israelis.[224]

The terrorist organization Fatah had been founded in 1959 by five Arabs: Yasser Arafat, Khalil al-Wazir, Salah Khalaf, Farouq Qaddoumi and Khaled al-Hassan, who had met in Kuwait. Fatah (or Al-Fatah) was an acronym standing for Harakat Al-Tahrir Al-Watani Al-Filastini (Palestinian National Liberation Movement). In Arabic, HTF means death; when reversed to FTH it means victory. They saw themselves as a new generation of Arabs who were destined to become the "revenge generation". Since 1965 Fatah had been building ties to other liberation movements, including communist Cuba. They had adopted a Leninist philosophy and saw Mao and Che Guevara as heroic 'partners'.[225]

Fatah's new sponsor became the radical faction of the Ba'ath Party in Syria. The organization believed there was no room for Israelis in the new Palestine. From 1965 to 1967, Fatah pursued a policy of terrorist attacks on Israeli settlements; only a few incursions into Israel were aimed at military targets. Other Palestinian militant groups such as the Popular Front for the Liberation of Palestine, led by Christian Arab George Habash and the Popular Democratic Front for the Liberation of Palestine had mounted 113 sabotage and terrorist attacks against Israel. Fatah, meanwhile, claimed to have carried out 300 raids.

Fatah advocated a revolutionary approach to reclaiming the land, which it saw as belonging to Palestinian Arabs. "An armed Palestinian revolution is the only way to liberate our homeland," the group pronounced.

> In the initial stages at least, the revolution must be conducted by the Palestinian masses, independently of party and state. Although the active support of the Arab world is essential for the success of the operation, the

> Palestinian people shall retain its discretionary powers and primacy… Only the idea of the armed struggle can bridge ideological differences and accelerate the process of unification.[226]

Following the defeat of the Arab states in the Arab–Israeli War of 1967, Fatah was the first Palestinian group to recover. Its leaders decided that a major guerrilla war against Israel was the only viable option, and so launched a major guerrilla offensive. The organization had some 2,000 men under arms.

After 1967, Palestinians gave up seeing themselves as Syrians, Jordanians or simply Arabs, with a majority now seeing themselves as 'Palestinians'. Unlike the Palestine Liberation Organization (PLO), which was originally created by Egyptian President Gamal Abdel Nasser, Fatah was an authentic Palestinian nationalist movement. However, it was not until 1968 that Yasser Arafat took control of the PLO and he and other Fatah founders believed that Palestinians had to cease waiting for Egypt, Syria and other Arab nations to 'liberate' them. Instead, they would have to 'free' themselves. In April 1968, an historic meeting between Arafat and Nasser sealed the ties between the Arab states and the terrorist organization.[227]

In early 1968 Fatah groups of armed guerrillas were forced to withdraw from Israeli territory and operate from Jordan. In January of that year, Fatah convened a conference in Cairo with all Palestinian groups to coordinate terrorist activity. In March, a group of terrorists used a land mine to destroy a school bus in Israel's Negev Desert. Two adults were killed and twenty-eight children wounded. On March 21, the 'Battle of Karameh' was fought and would be a turning point in the Palestinian struggle against Israel. Karameh, in Jordan, was just across the border from Israel and was used as a base for Fatah fighters. Approximately 120 Palestinians were killed when Israeli Defense Forces crossed the border in an attempt to put an end to Fatah's constant incursions into Israel. The Israelis were forced to withdraw when Jordanian soldiers entered the fray, but the Fatah leadership decided they had won a victory, enhancing its stature amongst young Palestinians. Feeling victorious, the incursions continued. In April 1968 a passenger bus was stopped by Israeli police a few miles east of the Sirhan's village of Taybeh. Three young Palestinian terrorists were shot and two of the victims died.[228]

Whilst little known to the American public in general, Fatah had been promoting its interests in the United States since June 1967. Its terrorist exploits had been well-publicized amongst students on the West Coast, who received copies of Fatah statements and communiqués, according to the Christian Science Monitor's Beirut correspondent. The statements exhorted Palestinian Arabs to pursue a more violent agenda to rid the Jews from Palestinian soil.[229]

In July 1968 Fatah joined the Palestine Liberation Organization and the terrorist group became the main component. The PLO had vowed from its inception to have as its main objective the destruction of the Jewish state. It created the first terrorist training camps, invented suicide bombings and had been the chief propaganda machine in the West in its attempt to persuade Westerners that the terrorist armies were really missionaries for social justice. Relying on Western 'imperialist guilt', the PLO sought to tie the conditions of poverty, racism and oppression to the Western democracies who, they argued, were ultimately to blame for the conditions of the Palestinians in Lebanon and Jordan's refugee camps.[230]

Walter Crowe believed Fatah's terrorist acts were justified and that Palestinian terrorists had gained the respect of the Arab world. Sirhan agreed and spoke of "total commitment" to the cause. Sirhan was also for "...violence whenever, as long as it's needed," Crowe said. He came to believe that Sirhan "...could have seen himself as a fighter...a committed revolutionary willing to undertake revolutionary action."[231]

Later, when Crowe was interviewed by the Los Angeles Police, he was asked what kind of thinking influenced Sirhan to commit an act of violence. Crowe replied, "I said that the struggle inside Israel was going to be a long, long thing. And that it was akin to a liberation struggle. I said that it would not be resolved by a war. I said that... Al Fatah had given...their people... morale...and that [Sirhan]...could have very easily said, well, it's up to me to...do it here... [Sirhan] could have seen himself as a fighter." Crowe felt guilty about the part he may have played in putting ideas of terrorist acts into Sirhan's head and reinforcing his resolve to commit a violent political act.[232]

Because Crowe was a committed communist, the SUS investigated the radical student about his connections to Sirhan. They found him to be truthful when he denied he had been part of any conspiracy to kill Robert Kennedy, but the polygraph test taken by Crowe revealed he had lied when he said he did not have foreknowledge of Sirhan's crime. The LAPD concluded that Crowe's polygraph tests showed he "had some knowledge of Sirhan's intention to kill Kennedy." However, they also concluded that it was "improbable that Crowe could have influenced Sirhan, based on the conversations with Crowe."[233]

Thomas Good was a member of the Young Democrats at Pasadena City College and associated with Walter Crowe. He knew Crowe was a friend of Sirhan and had known him since Sirhan arrived in the United States. Good said Sirhan was "very anti-Israel…and a very distant individual, no matter how friendly one became with him." Good had the opinion that Sirhan was someone who "seemed to be alienated from people in general, even from other Arabs" and that Crowe appeared to be Sirhan's only friend. Even this friendship, Good said, was "not a close one." Good also believed that "of the many Arab students who attended Pasadena State College with whom he was acquainted, Sirhan had stronger ideas of Arab nationalism than any of the others."[234]

Sirhan's hero-worship of the Egyptian leader Gamal Abdel Nasser had existed since he was a young boy living in Jerusalem. In the years following the Suez Crisis of 1956, Nasser had become the greatest Arab leader since Saladin. His following was especially great with the Arab youth and he had a great impact throughout the Middle East and in Arab communities in America. Nasser believed that the State of Israel had been instituted to rid the world of Arab states. "We all know," he said after the 1956 War, "why Israel was established. Not to set up a national home, but to be one of the factors in liquidating Arab nations."[235]

Nasser believed in the 1903 *Protocols of the Elders of Zion,* which pretended to be minutes from gatherings of Jewish leaders planning to seize the world's economies and media. The Egyptian leader had been influenced by this anti-Semitic Russian forgery, which had also been used by Nazi Germany to justify its assault on German Jewry. Nasser believed in the book's thesis and quoted from it, including the paragraph which spoke of "…proof beyond all doubt that 300 Zionists, each knowing the others, controlled the fate of the European continent and elected their successors from themselves." The book inspired Nasser to exhort parents to teach their children that the Jews controlled the world's wealth and mass media. Jews had deliberately instigated the French and Russian revolutions and the First World War so that they could wipe out the Islamic Caliphate and establish the League of Nations "…in order to rule the world by their intermediary."[236] The book has been called 'The Father of the Holocaust'.[237] Sirhan would later write in his notebooks, "Long live Communism. Long live Communism. Long live Communism. Long live Nasser. Nasser. Nasser. Nasser… Nasser is the greatest man who ever lived in this world…."

Since 1964 the Israelis had known of Egypt's intentions to strike at their country. The 'Cairo Accord', as it became known, resulted from a meeting between Arab nations led by Egypt's Nasser. At its conclusion of the conference, the group of nations announced that all neighboring Arab countries had made a vow to destroy Israel. Three years later, the Israeli Defense Force had no choice but to have a pre-emptive war against Egypt Syria and Lebanon for the preservation of their country. It became known as the Six-Day War.

The 1967 pre-emptive war was begun by Egypt's decision to close the Gulf of Aqaba to Israeli shipping and to order the removal of UN troops from the Sinai Peninsula. An Israeli master spy (a Druze Arab), acquired information that the Egyptians were going to attack Israel on June 6, so the Israeli Defense Forces wiped out the assembled attack aircraft on the ground, preventing the air attack on Israel. During the tense days before the Israeli strike, the Sirhan family had been receiving reports about the situation in the Middle East from friends who lived in Jerusalem.[238]

Sirhan blamed the Jews for all the ails of the world and spoke of how 'they' controlled the United States. His anti-Semitism has been well documented, even by members of his own family; he once denounced one of his brothers for "going to work for a Jewish man".[239] Sirhan refused to see the movie *Lawrence of Arabia* as he believed it to be anti-Arab. He also disliked the movie because it had a Jewish director, Sam Spiegel. He became incensed when he saw the movie, *Exodus*. "Every time I hear that song," he said, "I shut it off. It bugs me. The memories. Those Jews.... 'The f***ing Arabs' is what they're trying to say every time they play that song." [240] Sirhan said he had learned "...from history books and reading that the main cause [of the Middle East conflict] was that the West wanted to bring in persecuted Jews from Europe and expel the indigenous Arabs to accommodate the Jews." [241] He described himself as "...not psychotic...except when it comes to the Jews."[242]

However, it was in 1967 that Sirhan's emotional stability was crucially affected. He said he "sincerely tried to find a job" and after his dismissal from college and the loss of his dream of becoming a jockey, he had:

> no identity, no hope, no goal, nothing to strive for and I simply just gave up. There was no more American Dream for me... I was a foreigner in this country... An alien. A stranger. A refugee. I wasn't an American. I was an Arab... And that's my greatest setback I've got in this country,

> especially after the Arab-Israeli War. Because everybody in America loved a winner! And the Israelis won...but I was a loser and I did not like it one bit.[243]

On 2 June 1967, after watching newscasts about the build-up to war between the Israelis and the Arabs, he wrote in his notebooks "A Declaration of war against American Humanity...when in the course of human events it has become necessary for me to equalize and seek revenge for all the inhuman treatments committed against me by the American people..."[244]

Sirhan became depressed that the territories gained by Israel during the war, which included his West Bank homeland, would never again belong to the Arabs. His anger about the war and the decision by President Johnson to aid Israel was ignited by

> ...old memories ...what we used to watch on TV during the war. They... the old city of Jerusalem... They showed...the doctor, in fact, the doctor who signed the medical certificates for us. They...showed him on TV saying that he and his...clinic were running out of supplies because... he was taking care of so many injuries and so many dead people that he didn't have medical supplies. And that...really got us, you know, not angry, not just angry, but wishing that we could help by sending some... support to him because...that he was in dire need of...medical supplies to help...the injured over there...in Arab...Jerusalem, the whole city.[245]

He said that his identification with the Arab cause influenced his self-esteem following the Arab defeat. He believed the war was his "denouement, psychologically speaking." Sirhan also became bitter towards the country that had given his family a safe haven. His intense hatred for the 'Zionists' applied equally to anybody who appeared to be aiding the cause of the 'Zionists'. He embraced the Arab proverb that "The friend of my enemy is my enemy." From June 1967 he was "very resentful towards the United States for their foreign policy...; for their one-sided support...for Israel against the Arab people."[246]

According to his brother Adel, every time Sirhan saw the television news about the Arab–Israeli conflict he would become angry. "He just walked across the room real fast" Adel said, "and got out and if he happened to see, and here I mean members of the family watching it, especially if it was about our part of the country [the West Bank], which we naturally like to see once in a while, he would say, 'How can you sit there and watch these things which are done to our people?' He did not like it at all.[247]

Sirhan was not alone in believing America was biased towards Israel. Many Arabs living in the United States found it difficult to understand why their adopted nation sided with Israel. A friend of Adel told reporters it was no secret that the Arab community in Los Angeles were upset at the American government's overt support of Israel. "We were shocked when America started helping the Israelis," she said. In 1967 and 1968 she and others joined in a demonstration with marches on Hollywood Boulevard and the Hollywood Bowl.[248]

However, Arab communities in the United States failed to grasp how the majority of Americans saw Israel as an island of democracy in a sea of dictatorships beleaguered by aggressive Arab states. Furthermore, American support for Israel had been linked to the Cold War realities of a superpower's response to the growing friendliness between Arab states, especially that of Nasser's Egypt, with the Soviet Union.

Sirhan said he 'hated' President Johnson and felt the American president was acting with duplicity when he said the president upheld the "integrity of all nations in the Middle East". Sirhan said, "...I hated his guts. At one point, he said the United States supports the territorial integrity of all nations and he stressed all nations."[249]

In fact, Sirhan wanted to assassinate Johnson and would likely have chosen him as a target had it not been for the president's stringent security arrangements. Vietnam War protests made it unfeasible for the president to give speeches anywhere but military bases. In his notebooks, Sirhan wrote:

> Sirhan...Sirhan Sirhan. Must begin work on...solving the problems and difficulties of assassinating the 36th President of the glorious United States... The so-called president of the United States must be advised of their punishments for their treasonable crimes against the state more over we believe that the glorious United States of America will eventually be felled by a blow of an assassin's bullet — bullets, bullets.

Sirhan had also developed an intense hatred for other leading American politicians, although he did express admiration for President Kennedy, who he said had been working with Arab leaders to try to bring about a peace settlement between Arabs and Jews. He said JFK "was going to put pressure on Israel...to help the refugees...he was killed and it never happened."[250] However, Sirhan also believed Robert Kennedy was antithetical to his brother because he "listened to the Jews" and saw him as having sold out to them.[251]

At the time of the Six-Day War, Sirhan was unemployed and spent a lot of his time visiting the Pasadena Public Library on Catalina Street, especially during the summer of 1967. He said he "read everything about the Arab-Israeli situation that he could lay his hands on," including publications from the Arab information center in the United States. He also read a Jewish publication, *B'nai B'rith Messenger*, because he was keeping track of "Zionist intentions." The family also received reports about the situation in the Middle East from friends who lived in Jerusalem. When the United States voiced its support for Israel in the United Nations Assembly, it enraged Sirhan. He said, "At the time I would have killed [US Ambassador to the United Nations] Arthur Goldberg if I had a gun." He wrote in his notebooks, "Ambassador Goldberg must die die die."[252]

The Sirhan family watched television reports and read Los Angeles newspaper stories about the war. Sirhan's brother Adel said his brother became angry with television reports of the Arab-Israeli conflict. "This Israeli business," Sirhan said, "it really bugged me. I couldn't believe it. I would rather have died…rather than live with it...the shock of it, the humility, and all this talk about the Jews being victorious."[253]

Sirhan also became upset at the 'bias' of magazines such as *Time, Newsweek* and *U.S. News and World Report*. His anger was fuelled by the Arab newspaper *Al Bayan*, published in Brooklyn, which promoted anti-Israeli rhetoric. Some of its articles were overtly anti-Semitic. The *Los Angeles Times* editorial of June 6, 1967, said that the US had an obligation to maintain the territorial integrity of Israel. Beginning the week of June 5, the newspaper reported television comedy shows which broadcast anti-Arab jokes that reflected the general atmosphere of joy throughout America at the Israeli victory.

Sirhan voiced his anger to strike out at American society in his notebooks. In an entry dated June 2, 1967, he wrote, "…it has become necessary for me to equalize and seek revenge for all the inhuman treatment committed against me by the American people." He intended to, "acquire $2,000 for the purchase of arms" and the "victims" would be "the President, vice, etc.—down the ladder." He then expressed his wish to be "recorded by history as the man who triggered off the last war."

Shortly after the end of the 1967 Arab-Israeli War, Sirhan visited Patricia and John Strathman. Patricia said he "came over...and that was the first I had ever really saw him burning mad about anything. He was just furious about the war... He didn't like the American policy toward the Arab nations…"[254] She said she never saw Sirhan with a temper except when he discussed the Arab–Israeli conflict. "He seemed very logical, and, you know, rational about little things. The same night he was telling [us] about mysticism...the night that we started talking about the Arab-Israeli War, and on that point he really flipped. You know, well, I never seen him that upset over anything."[255] Patricia also claimed Sirhan "admired the way [Hitler] handled people... Apparently not so much what he stood for, but the way he was able to just control…he was kind of interested in controlling people…because he didn't think they were getting their fair share and all that stuff, and he was mad about them giving support to Israel."[256]

Her husband, John, said Sirhan had been impressed by Hitler's *Mein Kampf* and the German leader's solution to the 'Jewish Question', believing Hitler had possessed hypnotic powers over the German people. John said he was "intense" and "mad" about the Six-Day War and hated the fact that the United States was aiding Israel.[257]

6

MIRROR-GAZING JANUARY 1967 – APRIL 1968

"...I have a bug. I have built in a bug in this brain of mine against the Jews and the Zionists, sir, and Israel; anything...that is involving them turns me on." Sirhan Sirhan

In January 1967, despondent that his career ambitions had faded away, Sirhan began drinking. He was introduced to Tom Collins cocktails at the Fez, where his brother Adel worked. From that date onward, Sirhan complained about headaches, became more and more irritable, brooding, and was quick to anger.

Sirhan dreamed of being something big in Jordan after his studies in the United States, but that dream had ended when he flunked out of college. Holding unrealistic expectations, he held out for a professional job, made excuses in rejecting work he felt was unfit for him, and spent the next nine months unemployed. "He didn't work for a long time," Mary Sirhan said. "He was looking for a job... He stayed at home. I used to feed him and give him books and give him even cash in his hands if he needed it. For a long time...longer than six months..."[258]

During this period of unemployment, Sirhan also became increasingly interested in mysticism, a subject he had first been attracted to in 1966, and spent long hours reading works on the power of the mind. He began to use what he had learned by writing in his notebooks and "experimenting" when he dabbled in mysticism. After one experiment of 'thought transference', Sirhan came to believe he had influenced a horse, Press Agent, to crash against the rails of the racecourse simply by concentrating his mind. He also believed he could 'kill' his former boss, Bert Altfillisch, by using the powers of his mind.[259]

After Sirhan had gone to work at the racetrack in 1965, John and Patricia Strathman had lost touch with him when the couple moved to San Marino and did not see him at all until after Sirhan's accident at the Grande Vista Ranch in September 1966. After the accident, Patricia said Sirhan was "very able to grasp everything we were talking about, and languages, and philosophies, all sorts of things."[260]

According to Patricia, Sirhan

> always would have some project going, learning something. He and John would get together and go wild over some new language that they were interested in, and then Sirhan was teaching John Arabic and all sorts of things, and John was trying to get him interested in Chinese, and then he seemed to kind of lose interest in things and just seemed to be kind of wandering around, you know, the streets [of] Pasadena. He would go to that Armenian bakery on Lake Avenue, right below Maple Street, quite often. And he seemed to have lost a lot of his enthusiasm for things, and that's when he started studying this mysticism. At least that's when he started talking about it to us.[261]

However, Patricia said that although Sirhan was still "intense, stubborn, withdrawn and helpful...he no longer talked about the racetrack or making lots of money." She thought the fall from the horse, or the "frustration of not being successful," changed his interests. "He was so intense, and he was so depressed the last few times we had seen him."[262]

Patricia said Sirhan showed her some of his experiments.

> We went over to his house one day and he showed us a couple of books he was studying. I don't remember what they were, but he was really interested in it. He was doing little minor experiments...where... transferring thought and trying to control people's actions through his mind towards theirs, and I don't know, that's about the last time...I ever really saw him.

She said Sirhan believed you could see guardian angels out "the corner of your eye...if you concentrate[d] hard enough to bring them into focus, so you really have communication with them."

Patricia remembered Sirhan saying he wanted to control a person's mind through extrasensory perception. He told her he had

> brought something out of the wall...that he had gotten this guardian angel figure [which] came out of the wall, and I vaguely remember that it had a long beard, and it was dressed in grey, and the way he described

> it, it kind of reminded you of an old Jewish rabbi or something which wouldn't appeal to him much...and then the other thing I remember talking about [is] the mysticism that he was concentrating on it, you know, controlling people's actions with this. He was studying late one night and he tried to make his mother wake up from that and go to the bathroom, so he concentrated on that for about five minutes and just when he was about ready to give up hope, she got up and heard the toilet flushing.

The Strathmans became embarrassed at Sirhan's obvious fantasies. During this period, Patricia noticed Sirhan had become "... very intense. He was always, you know you didn't see him walk around smiling or anything, but he was awful nice, really. He's the only person I really know who would truthfully go out of his way to help somebody if he found them in distress." He wanted lots of money, she said, "...and he was always studying and working... but he seemed to lose interest." The last time she saw him was the last time he ever came over to their house.

> [It was in the] early part of 1967, perhaps toward the summer, when we were on Maple Street. He was studying and he had told us [about] a fall from the horse, and he was really upset about that. I don't know how serious it was, really, but it sounds like it was a culmination of all sorts of frustration for him because he said he couldn't be a jockey anymore because of his eyes.[263]

Walter Rathke last saw Sirhan in June 1967 in Pasadena at the Sirhan family home. During the visit, Mary Sirhan told him, "I just can't talk to that boy anymore." Rathke noticed a big difference in Sirhan's personality after his injury and thought he seemed to be a "different person." Sirhan appeared very serious and did not laugh anymore, Rathke said. He "was not his jovial self."[264] Sirhan told Rathke he no longer belonged to the Rosicrucian Order. He was upset that, due to his riding accident, he did not have any money and could not keep up his dues and "they terminated him." He told him he was joining the Theosophical Society.[265]

Rathke said the Theosophical Society and Rosicrucian Order had nothing in common, describing the Rosicrucian Order as a mystic or occult type organization which directs its followers, while the Theosophical Society's only purpose was the brotherhood of man.[266]

Theosophy borrows from the philosophy of the Hindu religion without adopting the external forms of Hindu worship and was founded by Madame Blavatsky. In 1888 Blavatsky wrote *The Secret Doctrine* in which she attempted to set out the principles of God wisdom, or theosophy, that the God masters of Atlantis had imparted to her. Blavatsky claimed that they were the progenitors of the human race and that while some people retained the Atlantean purity of their ancient ancestors, others, notably the Jews, had not. Propagandists of the Third Reich were the first to latch on to her theories of racial purity. The philosophy's strain of anti-Semitism doubtlessly appealed to Sirhan.

Sirhan had read Truman Capote's *In Cold Blood,* published in 1966, in which Capote had described how Perry Smith and Richard Hickock had murdered a Kansas farmer, his wife and two teenage children in 1959. Both Sirhan and Smith had chips on their shoulders, were short of stature, embittered with the way their parents had brought them up and had both suffered unhappy childhoods. Their only sisters had died young. Both were singled out by other children as different. They each, in their own way, acted out the bitterness that had haunted them through their formative adolescent years. Both men's emotions were easily triggered by any feeling of being tricked, slighted, or labelled inferior by others. Perry Smith reacted through an orgy of violence. Sirhan responded by embracing Arab nationalism, which spoke to his feelings of inferiority and which also gave him pride and self-esteem. After his trial Sirhan told Robert Kaiser that one of the memorable parts of Capote's *In Cold Blood* was Perry Smith's confrontation with his parole officer, who let him leave prison before he was ready. Sirhan quoted Smith, "You had me and you let me go!" Then Sirhan turned to Kaiser and said "You had *me* and you let me go. And look what I did!"[267]

Capote's book also chronicled how killer Perry Smith "...foretold events, had premonitions...was most respectful of his superstitions... The compulsively superstitious person is also very often a serious believer in fate...some of his thinking [reflected] a 'magical quality', a disregard of reality...." Smith also had bouts of "shivering", "amnesia" and "trance-like states." Like Smith, Sirhan engaged in "mirror-gazing" and fell into "trances."[268]

During the following months, Sirhan's life centered around going to the racetrack and dabbling in mysticism. He frequently visited Broughton's Used Book Store near Colorado on Lake Street. Henry J. Ruthhardt, who worked at the bookstore, saw Sirhan on five or six occasions in the store and he was always alone. Sirhan invariably looked for books on metaphysics, cultism, and Eastern religious teachings, and, on one occasion, asked for books on black magic. Although Ruthhardt attempted several times to engage Sirhan in conversation by asking questions, Sirhan would answer the question briefly, then terminate the conversation. The last time Ruthhardt remembered seeing Sirhan in the store was in May 1968.[269]

During this time of unemployment, Sirhan "went to bed early, he got up early, read books and periodicals either at home or the city library and sometimes he would play music," his mother said. Between July and September 1967, she and her youngest son, Munir, said Sirhan went often to the Pasadena Library and borrowed books and often drove his mother to work. She said he "...stayed at home for over a year [*sic*] with no job [October 1966 to September 1967]." During this time, he saw the movie *Bonnie and Clyde* and was "fascinated" with it.[270]

Following the Six-Day War, Sirhan became upset that the Israelis had been receiving aid from the American government to the tune of "$370,000,000 cold cash, tax-deductible, out of the back door of the United States to give to Israel." He railed at the thought of American cities going up in flames in city riots and that Israelis were taking "money by the truck load…for another government and another country economically motivated." He was unemployed and "didn't have a damn job… I was looking for work… and here's the money getting out of the country. Why?"[271]

On July 20, 1967, Sirhan visited Pasadena City College to look at job vacancies. He saw an opening for an executive trainee for Safeway Stores on a bulletin board. The job paid $135 a week. It was the first attempt Sirhan had made to find a job since he resigned his racetrack job in December 1966. "When he handed me the application, he hadn't filled it out," job counsellor Jeanne Herrick said, "...he wouldn't put his work experience. The job he was asking for, he had no qualifications for. It said a man 5' 10" inches tall and he was 5' 2"...he wouldn't give me any further information...so I tried to tell him that we had to have further information...he was a foreign student...he [needed] a permit from Dean Lewis…." The permit was a policy of the institution which applied to foreign students.

Sirhan was incensed and went to see Lewis to complain about Herrick. When she proceeded to interview Sirhan again, with Dean of the College Dr Lewis present, Sirhan began to lie about the first interview. Herrick said, "He said I told him that he should go back to his own country, he didn't have any right here, and he ought to go back where he came from...he was extremely touchy…" After requesting and then tearing up his second application, "...[he] leaned way over the desk and shook his finger in my face, and said, 'Now, this will teach you to underestimate jockeys'...and he was serious!" Because Sirhan had been aggressive to Herrick, she did not follow up on the interview.[272]

Over the following weekend Sirhan seethed at the injustice metered out to him and returned to the college demanding to see the president. The president's secretary told Sirhan that he could see the vice-president instead, as the president was at a meeting. Placated by the attitude of the vice-president, Sirhan calmed down and filled out a new application. He was unsuccessful. He had further unemployment counselling from October 6, given vocational tests on October 20, had additional discussions on October 26 and on November 6 he said he was interested in a job in 'electronics'.

During the time Sirhan was unemployed, Adel's fiancée Myleen Kaye visited the Sirhan home several times. She met Sirhan about three times and also talked to him on the phone. She said Sirhan was very quiet and an 'odd ball' when she was around and she got the impression that he was a loner spending much of his time in his room by himself. She also said Sirhan was a "such a bum" and when she once asked him why he didn't get a job, Sirhan told her he had other things to do and that he had spent a lot of his time in the library reading. She realised she had offended him by her bluntness and subsequently never got along with him.[273]

In December 1967 Sirhan and his brother Munir bought a small pistol, a .22 calibre Iver-Johnson cadet model 55 SA with a snub-nosed 2.5-inch barrel. The serial number was H-53725. It had a dull blue steel finish with an eight-bullet chamber, double action. It was a relatively cheap weapon that sold for $31.95. Munir said that Sirhan had asked him, "See if you can see that guy to get me a gun." Munir spoke to his friend George Erhard in the parking lot of Nash's store. Erhard had mentioned to him he had a pistol for sale. "So, [Sirhan] says I want a gun," Munir said.

> He wanted a gun to go to the firing range...he didn't want it for a rifle range. That's what he kept saying. I don't know why. He said it and then as I said he's a stubborn type...he's got a book, someone's book he was reading. Well, he's always sitting down reading books and he was reading this special one. It was about guns... He used to always mention the ROTC, this and that, and he handled a lot of guns in the ROTC, and he wanted to know how they worked, this and that.[274]

The gun had originally been purchased by Albert Leslie Hertz, a resident of Alhambra, a small town south of Pasadena. He bought the gun at the Pasadena Gun Shop on August 10, 1965. Hertz was a retired civil engineer, having worked on projects in Argentina, Saudi Arabia and Korea, and had purchased the gun for protection during the 1965 Watts riots. He had never used it and kept it in its original wrapping paper and box. Hertz's wife had decided the gun was too dangerous to have around the house, so she gave it to her daughter, Dana Westlake. Westlake had been living in Pasadena when her mother gave her the gun and she hid it in the attic away from her small children. In December 1967 she decided she no longer wanted the gun around the house, so she gave it to her next-door neighbor's son, George Erhard, a gun collector.

When Munir and Sirhan purchased the gun from Erhard it was witnessed by William Price, a friend of Erhard. At this point, according to Munir, he asked Erhard to bring it around to the house since his brother was interested in buying it. When Munir brought Erhard to the family home to listen to some records, they met Sirhan, who had been sitting in the dining room. Sirhan began a discussion about his time in the California Cadet Corps. Although it was illegal for non-citizens to own a gun, Sirhan insisted they buy it. At first Erhard and the brothers haggled over the price. When the sale was agreed Munir produced $19 and the $6 balance was paid by Sirhan.

It was evident from Munir's police interview that he had aided in the purchase of the weapon. And it was also evident from a polygraph of Munir that he had been lying when he said his brother Sirhan had purchased the gun. In fact, Erhard had never been to the Sirhan home, and the purchase of the weapon was completed in a clandestine manner as they were fully aware that aliens had no right to purchase guns.[275]

According to Sirhan, he first shot the recently acquired pistol in March 1968 and practiced with it about a half dozen times, between March and May of that year.[276] Munir said Sirhan kept the gun in the glove compartment of his De Soto and, "played with it often and it made a 'click, click' sound." [277] Munir said he had been "frightened" by the look in Sirhan's eye when he handled the gun. In fact, Munir was so worried he made Sirhan swear on their dead sister Aida's life that he would not use it in a "bad way".[278]

To his mother Sirhan seemed to be a friendless young man.[279] He was borrowing money from her and moping around the house and becoming frustrated in his inability to fix his De Soto car. In September 1967, Mary tried to help her son find employment and contacted John Henry Weidner, who she knew from her church attendances. Weidner was a refugee in Holland during the war and Mary knew he was always willing to help the downtrodden like the Sirhans. Sirhan could have approached Weidner himself, but his 'Arab pride' would not allow it.

The 42-year-old Weidner owned a health food store on North Lake Street in Pasadena. The store described itself in its advertising as "Pasadena's largest natural foods center—Certified raw milk, fertile eggs, dried fruits, live food juices, fresh organically grown fruits and vegetables."

"His mother presented him to me as 'Sol'," Weidner said.

> His sister was a customer in my store, and I became friend [*sic*] with her—I became close to the mother. I am a 7th Day Adventist...so sometimes when we had a special meeting at the church I invited her, and she came several times, and she had no car, so I took her from the home to the church...sometimes in the evening, sometimes on Sunday morning...so we came quite close, and at the same time, even before I became so much close to her boy [Sirhan], Munir came to my store... I gave a job, and I think he worked for one week.... One night in car, she say, 'Can you find something for Sirhan, he's without work actually'. So, I told her he could see me, starting 17th September, he could come every Sunday... [280]

Weidner was a former captain in the Dutch Army and during the Second World War had organized resistance to Nazi occupation. Born in Holland, Weidner was like many Europeans who had come to America after the War. He cherished the rights and freedom of America, which he said was "lost in Europe." His organization received many Jews, airmen and many others who were victims of the Nazis. "It was our plan to bring the people from Holland to Paris, then to Southern France," Weidner said, "and into the mountains to Switzerland. And so, during the war, I brought these people over there... It was difficult to find people who were ready to risk their lives. If you were caught... you were deported instead of the Jewish person—deported to the concentration camp."[281]

Weidner's Dutch Reformed minister father and his sister died in concentration camps and John was tortured by the Gestapo, escaping from the Nazis five times. "I was a witness to the barbaric treatment of the Jews by the Nazis," he said. "I personally observed the crushing of the skull of a Jewish infant who was torn out of the arms of its mother. I was determined to heed the teachings and example of my father and I did everything that I could to save as many lives as possible." For his heroism he was made a member of the Order of the British Empire and held the French Croix de Guerre, the US Medal of Freedom and the Dutch Order of Orange-Nassau for saving more than 1,000 people from the Nazis.[282]

After the war a woman who had worked in his organization operated a "very nice boarding house" for "young American citizens." She introduced Weidner to a young Jacqueline Bouvier. "So, you see," Weidner said, "why I feel that the deaths of President Kennedy and Senator Kennedy meant more to me than to many people—because of this early acquaintanceship…"[283]

On November 19, Weidner hired Sirhan full time as a stocker and delivery clerk-salesman in the store. Carol Burgess met Sirhan during her employment there, which lasted from November 1967 to January 1968. He was introduced to her as 'Sol', although Sirhan lied to her, saying he had changed his first name to Sirhan so he would have two similar names. Sirhan was always by himself, Burgess said, and no one came to the store to visit him. He told her that he was close to his brother, had "nice parents", but "he never spoke of a girlfriend and at one time he said he had bad luck with girls." He did not explain the remark.

Sirhan worked in the stockroom, waited on customers and delivered orders, but he also did many different types of work including loading and unloading merchandise for delivery, building and painting shelves in the store and on one occasion he helped John Weidner's brother-in-law Henry Peters enclose an over-hanging outdoor patio area at Weidner's home in Monterey Park. However, John came to see that Sirhan was so honest he was able to trust him to handle some of the store's banking. The only problem was that he was extremely sensitive to anything that seemed like criticism. He said Sirhan "...found it hard to take my orders and he didn't like to have things explained to him. His attitude seemed to be 'I'm as good as you are'." Sirhan's Arab pride also caused difficulties. He would not wear an apron, believing it was a garment worn only by women and also felt shame that his mother had helped him find the job.[284]

Weidner believed Sirhan was "…an Arab...till the end." Sirhan told him that the Jews had stolen his country and that "They have no right to be there." It belonged to Jordan, he told Weidner, "And they have taken it." Weidner also said that Sirhan had a bitter view of how Jews in America operated. "The Jewish people were dominating," Sirhan said. "They had a lot of wealth, a lot of power…there is no freedom in America." John's wife Naomi once observed Sirhan losing his temper when he discussed "the Jews".[285]

Weidner believed Sirhan suffered from an inferiority complex. "I think he was a man of revolt," Weidner said. "He was a kind of anarchist against society, against law and order, against those who possess. Against those who have more than he has and are more successful in life." Sirhan told Weidner, "In America, freedom does not exist. I agree with the violence."[286]

Weidner, a committed Christian, tried to engage Sirhan in discussions about his faith and the virtue of forgiveness, but had little positive response from him. "I would like to be like you but I can't forgive the Jews for what they have done to the Palestinians—and they are still doing it!" Sirhan told him. Weidner suggested he should "ask God to give him the strength to forgive." Sirhan replied, "…There is no God. Look at what God has done for the Arabs! And for the Palestinians! How can we believe in God?" They also argued about the Six-Day War. When Weidner told Sirhan he had forgiven the Nazis for what they did to his family and he should look into his heart to forgive his enemies, Sirhan replied, "Don't you think Jews can also be cruel? We have to fight, there is no other way to find peace."[287]

It was Sirhan's touchiness, arrogance and feelings of inadequacy that caused friction between employer and employee. According to Weidner, "You had to be careful not to walk on [Sirhan's] feet. He wanted you to respect him intellectually. He was a man who said, 'I'm going to have my rights'." [288] Weidner said he sometimes felt that Sirhan "had turned against the whole American way of life, and that he was an anarchist in revolt against society." He thought Sirhan had the potential for being violent and described him as resenting all forms of authority. Sirhan would become very belligerent at times, Weidner said, and "seemed to be trying to prove something." He believed Sirhan's small stature might have had some bearing on his personality. However, he respected the fact that Sirhan had "beliefs and principles." "Personal honor and self-respect were important to him," Weidner said. "And second only to that he esteemed patriotism. He had strong patriotic feelings for his country [Palestine]. Yes, I would say he loved his country."[289]

Henry Peters, who was in his sixties, was related to Weidner through marriage and became an ardent supporter of the Seventh-day Adventist Church. He resided in Wisconsin but came to California during the winter months and helped at the store, sometimes working with Sirhan. During all these different types of jobs, Peters said Sirhan was always very courteous and helpful. Sirhan appeared to be very strong looking, alert and in "top physical condition. He never had difficulty in performing his daily tasks."

Following a mistake in a delivery order, Weidner blamed Sirhan for the error. Sirhan told his boss it was his poor communication skills that were to blame, and walked out of the store in a rage. However, he returned later to complete the two weeks' notice he had given. The following two weeks were fraught with conflict between the two men.

Finally, on March 7, Weidner told Sirhan he had to listen to him without complaint or leave the store immediately. Sirhan refused, sat down, and demanded Weidner give him a further two weeks' salary because he was being fired, even threatening to take his case to a labor tribunal. Weidner had no other recourse but to call the police and when they arrived, Officer R.E. Reinek questioned Sirhan about his citizenship. Sirhan exploded, insisting the police had no right to ask that question. He showed them his immigration card and said, "I am a Palestinian." Reinek told Sirhan to leave the store and no further action was taken.

Sirhan did have some support amongst the store staff. Elsie Boyko said Weidner was a domineering taskmaster, harsh and rude to his employees, particularly Sirhan. "At first, Sol would try to stand his ground—'You just don't talk to me like that. You have to treat me like a man', he'd say, then walk away in desperation and frustration." Boyko tried to mediate, but after a while, there were arguments almost every day. "Sirhan wanted Weidner to fire him so he could get some severance pay," she said, "but Weidner sensed this and would not fire him."[290]

Approximately one week after Sirhan quit his job, Weidner paid a visit to Sirhan's home to persuade him to return to work, but he refused. Weidner concluded that Sirhan had "no forgiveness in his heart."[291]

On January 9, 1968, Senator Robert Kennedy proposed the sale of 50 jets to Israel. This proposal was published in the *New York Times*. The Departments of State and Defense were opposed to the sale, worried that the arms transfer would break a policy of US neutrality Later, that same month, on January 31, Sirhan wrote in his notebooks, "RFK must die". The sentence is repeated over and over and over again on that page, and it's followed with the question and answer, "Who killed Kennedy? I don't know."[292]

On March 7, 1968, the day Sirhan quit his job, he filed a petition with the California State Division of Labor Law Enforcement in Los Angeles. He claimed that his boss was refusing to pay $156 for seventy-eight hours of work performed by him and sought $180 severance pay.

Sirhan had attended two services at the Seventh-day Adventist Church in Pasadena. The church had undertaken a series of *Bible* lessons that advertised and offered them to the general public, and John Weidner's brother -in-law, Henry Peters, encouraged Sirhan to study the *Bible* and offered to visit his home to conduct lessons. Sirhan's mother had also encouraged Sirhan to study.

Peters visited Sirhan at his house about once a week during the months of January and February1968 in the evening hours, taking *Bible* lessons to him. He made approximately four or five separate visits to the Sirhan home. The last meeting with Sirhan was held on Tuesday, March 26, 1968. Every meeting took place in the dining room of the Sirhan home during the evening hours and always on a Tuesday evening. Mary was present almost every time he met Sirhan.

During their discussions, Peters said that Sirhan told him he had won a case in court and that he had collected approximately $2,000. He also told him of his hatred for John Weidner and of how he had refused to pay him some money that had been promised to him. Sirhan said that Weidner had belittled him and that he should have paid him the money he was due as he had allegedly promised.[293]

Sirhan did not appear to enjoy his meetings with Peters and he became bored. Adel saw how Peters would become "quite impatient" with Sirhan and Munir because they chose to watch TV rather than attend the *Bible* readings. On one occasion when Peters suggested changing the meeting date from a Tuesday to a Friday evening, Sirhan stated this could not be done because he also had some other studies on Friday nights which had to do with the "study of mysticism".[294]

Peters stated that since he was leaving the state during the second weekend of April, he requested another church member to administer the lessons to Sirhan. He planned to return to his home in Milwaukee, and that prior to leaving Los Angeles he talked to Pastor Charles Mitchell of the Seventh-day Adventist Church and asked him to assign someone to continue the Bible lessons with Sirhan.[295]

The church assigned Margaret Heacock to finish up the lessons. Heacock met with him at his home and the meetings lasted for approximately one hour. The primary topic of conversation was religion, but once again Sirhan complained about his boss. She had the impression Sirhan felt 'hatred' towards him. Sirhan told her that

Weidner's "manner and attitude toward him was very rude and that Weidner was very demanding of him [and]...on many occasions customers were present when he was being insulted." Sirhan told Heacock that the customers would get so disgusted at the way Weidner treated him that they would place their merchandise, which they were preparing to buy, on the counter and leave the store without purchasing anything. Sirhan told her of one incident where he had been asked to carry jars of honey from one section of the store to another. He was trying to be careful so as not to drop or break anything. However, Weidner thought Sirhan was too slow and began to "insult and berate him in front of some people." In Sirhan's opinion, Weidner was a very poor example of a Christian. At the conclusion of their first meeting, Sirhan told Heacock that he did not wish to continue with his *Bible* lessons. Heacock attempted to win him back and continue the lessons, but Sirhan was adamant.[296]

Linda Kamakian, a Sirhan family friend, said the family were "very jealous of their privacy." She spoke to Sirhan in March 1968 on Lake Avenue. She gave him a lift, talked with him for an hour and said he had just returned from a job interview but was turned down due to lack of educational background. Sirhan looked very ill, she said, "thin and weary looking", and was very disappointed at not getting the job.[297]

From March until June 1968, Sirhan busied himself by looking after the garden at 696 East Howard, cooking and making repairs around the house and fixing small mechanical problems on his beloved De Soto car. Sirhan had paid $410 for the pink and white 1958 vehicle, raising the money through odd jobs. His mother said that Sirhan did not have his car for a long time. "It was ruined," she said. "Over a year I should say or around a year and I told him many times that I had to fix his car, pay for it, just have it done. Well, he didn't do it because, I don't know. He couldn't do it. He said, 'Mama, it cost a lot. It needs a lot of money to fix it. It isn't worth fixing'."[298]

In April 1967, Sirhan had been dropped as a member of the Rosicrucians when he failed to pay his $4 monthly dues. However, on February 5, 1968, the Rosicrucians received a money order for $16 from Sirhan. On March 26, a second money order of $20 was received. Receipt of these money orders reinstated Sirhan as an active member of the Order, which began mailing literature and magazines to him.[299]

Marilyn Hunt, a waitress at the Hi-Life Bar, 1775 East Colorado, Pasadena, had been employed there since March 1967. She recalled seeing Sirhan in the bar several times in 1967 and 1968. He always seemed to sit very quietly alone at the bar, she said, and never caused any trouble.[300] The only other Pasadena bars that Sirhan was known to frequent were Shap's Bar, on East Colorado Boulevard, the Poodle Steak Tavern and Jerry's Family Billiard Centre. Peter Selfe knew Sirhan and was also a frequent customer at Shap's. He said Sirhan had five close friends he drank with in the bar and described them as two Jordanians, one Cuban, and two Americans.[301] Selfe also said Sirhan placed his illegal horseracing bets there. Howard Rice, an employee of Jerry's Family Billiard Center saw Sirhan on infrequent occasions playing pool. At other times Sirhan would stand and talk with other patrons, Rice said.[302]

The last time Sirhan saw his old boyhood friend John O'Hanian was in April 1968. O'Hanian saw him walking south on Lake Avenue in Pasadena. To O'Hanian, Sirhan appeared to be "depressed and dejected."[303]

That same month, Sirhan became fascinated with the circumstances surrounding the assassination of Martin Luther King. He had been at the racetrack the day King was shot on April 4, and he remembered a horse, Pink Pigeon, was racing that day. He said an African American, who had been holding a portable radio approached him crying and shouting, "They shot him! They shot him!"[304] Sirhan was empathetic to the plight of African Americans and believed the only way they could attain equal rights was through violence.

Sirhan's brothers often saw a garbage collector, Alvin Clark, a man in his forties, talking to Sirhan. The trash would be collected between 10 and 11.30 am each Wednesday by the Pasadena Sanitation Department and a female neighbor of the Sirhans witnessed the meetings and became disturbed at the way Sirhan "would stare at her." The brothers thought it seemed a little pathetic on Sirhan's part as he used to rush out with cookies and juice to greet Clark when he saw the garbage truck in the area. Mary Sirhan was also concerned that her son was giving lemonade and cookies to him.

On the Wednesday after Martin Luther King's assassination, Sirhan had expressed his concern to Clark about how it would affect "Negro people and how the Negroes would vote in the coming election." When Clark told Sirhan he was going to vote for Robert Kennedy, Sirhan replied, "What do you want to vote for that son-of-a-b for? Because I'm planning on shooting him." Clark tried to explain to Sirhan that Kennedy had been a friend to African Americans and had even paid the expenses of bringing Martin Luther King's body back from Memphis to Atlanta after the Civil Rights Leader's assassination. Clark, who did not take Sirhan's remarks seriously, told him he would be killing "one of the best men in the country." Sirhan was not persuaded and told

Clark that Kennedy had made the offer to the King family merely for the publicity.*

On April 23, 1968, Weidner and Sirhan appeared before the Labor Commissioner for a hearing on his case. Weidner said he had fired Sirhan because his work was unsatisfactory. After hearing the statements of both men, the Labor Commissioner concluded that the evidence was insufficient to find in favor of Sirhan. The case was dismissed without prejudice.[305]

On April 5 Sirhan received his insurance check for $1,705 from the Argonaut Insurance Company. As he already had $200 saved, he thought he might purchase a Mustang car if he gambled some of the money at the racetrack. Within a week he had lost a few hundred dollars at Hollywood Park.[306] Thereafter his 'investments' would get worse, and he was left with only a few hundred dollars. Luck also seemed to escape Sirhan. While fixing a bent axle on his De Soto, the jack slipped and bruised his shoulder. Thinking he had mended the car correctly, he took it for a test run on the San Bernadino Freeway. But the back wheels seized up, bringing the car to a halt. Sirhan was experiencing one bit of bad luck after another: He was out of work, had lost most of his money, and had no luck with girls.[307]

To fill in time during his period of unemployment, Sirhan would often visit two elderly ladies, Anna Sylvan and Olive Blackslee, who lived down the street, and play Chinese checkers with them. His last visit was in May 1968. According to Anna and Olive, Sirhan did not discuss politics but liked to talk about spiritual ideas, philosophy and theosophy. They said Sirhan practiced yoga and mentioned "the powers of mind over matter". The women said he was "always experimenting with new religious thoughts and concepts." On his last visit Sirhan played only one game of Chinese checkers, which Anna thought was "quite unusual" as he always wanted to play "two games."[308]

The owner of the Fez, Lou Shelby, said that his only detailed conversation he had with Sirhan occurred on Easter Sunday, April 14, 1968, when Shelby and his family were traveling to the homes of family friends. He had known Sirhan's brother Adel for seven years, but it was the first opportunity to talk to his younger brother. Sirhan was interested in his opinions because Shelby had graduated from UCLA with a Political Science degree and had completed a year and a half of

* Alvin Clark's integrity has not been seriously challenged. His story did not change, nor did he try to embellish it. Additionally, a search of contemporaneous newspaper accounts of the period indicates Clark did not seek publicity following the trial, nor did he try to exploit his 'star witness' status for financial reward.

graduate work at UC, Berkeley, specializing in International Relations and Middle East politics.

Sirhan was definitely unhappy with the establishment, Shelby said, and "frustrated in his political feelings." They had "a really big argument on Middle East politics," Shelby said, and "switched back and forth between Arabic and English". Shelby realized that Sirhan's outlook was "completely Arab nationalist—the Arabs were in the right and had made no mistakes." He tried to reason with Sirhan and tried to point out that "one could be in the right but still make mistakes." Sirhan was adamant: "America was to blame for the Arabs' misfortunes because of the power of Zionism" and the "only Arab leader...was Nasser." "Sirhan thought Nasser's policies were right," Shelby said. Sirhan insisted, "The Arabs had to build themselves up and fight Israel, that was the only way. The only outside friend the Arabs had was Russia, but Russia had not proved a good enough friend during last June's fighting [the Six-Day War]."[309]

Shelby also discussed the problems of youth in America, the hippie movement and civil disobedience. Sirhan told Shelby that United States foreign policy "was not stopping a world-wide Zionist plot." Shelby discovered that he was "extremely politically oriented with his primary concern being the Israeli-Arab problem."[310]

7

THE FINAL MONTH

"...from 1967, from June of that year on... I was very resentful towards the United States for their foreign policy... in the Middle East; for their one-sided support... for Israel against the Arab people." Sirhan Sirhan

"The friend of my enemy is my enemy." Old Arab proverb quoted by Sirhan Sirhan at his trial

Sirhan began to use his mind-control techniques in setting his goal of killing Robert Kennedy. It is likely he decided to kill Kennedy in early 1968, when he made an entry in his notebook dated January 31, stating, "RFK must die."

Sirhan admitted he always became "terribly mad" every time he heard the news stories about the Middle East. As an avid reader of political periodicals, he could not have failed to notice that Robert Kennedy met with the Israeli Premier, Levi Eshkol, in January 1968 and expressed his support for Israel. In January and February that same year, Kennedy made at least three statements recommending arms aid to Israel. "[Robert Kennedy] would seem like a villain to me. Like a man who wants to kill," Sirhan said. "Like a man who wants to throw those bombs on the people and destroy...all of a sudden, he wants to send the very same things that we're going to withdraw from Vietnam to Israel. It seemed paradoxical to me...I couldn't believe it."[311] Sirhan was also angry at the way the American press was treating the defeated Arabs. "I read this magazine article on the 20th anniversary of the state of Israel," he said. "I hate the Jews. There was jubilation. I felt they were saying in the article, 'We beat the Arabs.' It burns the shit out of me. There was happiness and jubilation."[312]

Walter Crowe moved back into his parents' home in Pasadena in 1968. After having been approached by Mary Sirhan, Crowe's mother asked her son to telephone his old friend as a friendly gesture. She worked with Mary Sirhan and was concerned about her welfare. After many reminders, Crowe called Sirhan and arranged an evening out. On May 2, 1968, Sirhan came to the Crowe home and the two left together in Sirhan's vehicle, a Volkswagen sedan. They bar-hopped with two other friends, Ivan Garcia and Joseph Marcovecchio, who were students with Sirhan and Crowe at Pasadena City College. From Bob's Big Boy restaurant, they moved on to a 'topless' bar, the Hi-Life on Foothill Boulevard and later to another topless bar called the Black Cat. The group of friends concluded the evening at Ernie's Taco Restaurant on Colorado Boulevard. Crowe said that they were together for about two hours and the conversation during the evening centred around politics and career goals.

Crowe and Sirhan discussed Crowe's involvement with the US Communist Party and Sirhan talked about Al Fatah. The conversation then moved on to Sirhan's hero-worship of Hitler and of how the Nazi leader was his idol. Sirhan made no response to Crowe's enthusiasm about communism and the subject was dropped. Crowe said that because of Sirhan's actions and demeanour, and the discussion of Al Fatah at their meeting, Sirhan may have seen himself as a revolutionary who had decided to commit an act of terrorism. Crowe later told his mother that he felt Sirhan had seemed withdrawn and that it had been difficult re-building their friendship. Sirhan acted as if he resented his superior educational attainments, Crowe said. During the night out Sirhan became upset at the way the strippers demeaned themselves in front of the bar's customers and became contemptuous at the way the women dancers 'cavorted' onstage. After the group consumed four pitchers of beer, they left.[313] The last time Crowe saw Sirhan was on the Pasadena College campus on May 23.[314]

On May 18, Sirhan made a notebook entry: "My determination to eliminate Robert Francis Kennedy is becoming more of an unshakable obsession." On the same page he wrote, "RFK must die RFK must be killed Robert Francis Kennedy must be assassinated. Robert F Kennedy must be assassinated before 5 June '68." Sirhan also wrote in his notebooks, ".... Senator Kennedy must be sacrificed for the cause of the poor exploited people...the glorious United States of America will eventually be felled by a blow of an assassin's bullet..."

His notebook entries about Robert Kennedy were likely inspired by a sermonizing article entitled *Put It in Writing* by Arthur J. Fetting, which was published in a Rosicrucian magazine in May 1968. The article exhorted readers to:

> Try it. Pick a goal. Set a target date. Now, start working to make it come true…Read that goal every morning when you get up and every night before you go to sleep. Read it, believe it, and start doing things you feel you should to make it come true. This simple formula of writing it down and believing works….[315]

According to Democratic Party consultant Stuart Gerry Brown, Robert Kennedy was "tougher and more specific in communicating his support for Israel than his rivals" for the Democrat party presidential nomination.[316] On May 20, Sirhan watched a CBS documentary on television called *The Story of Robert Kennedy*. That night he brewed himself some tea and went to the living room to watch television. As he did not have any favorite program, he flipped the channels and heard Robert Kennedy's name mentioned. The narrator told of how Kennedy had visited Palestine as a war correspondent in 1948, "…. living with Israeli troops, seeing war and death at close hand for the first time... seeing the Jordan River red with blood of Jews and Arabs...he wrote his dispatches and came to his decision…" The program ended with an Israeli flag waving in the breeze: "...Bob Kennedy decided his future lay in the affairs of men and nations."

Sirhan became intensely angered when he heard the narrator proclaiming how "...Robert Kennedy was for the underdog, for the poor, the scum of society." Sirhan later said, "…And there he was…in a film from 1948 in Israel helping the Jews...celebrating…the declaration of their new nation. And the emotion with which the narrator spoke… that burned me up. Up to that point I liked Robert Kennedy. I hoped he would win the presidency. But he was doing a lot of things behind my back that I didn't know about." [317]

Sirhan said watching the TV 'burned' him up [318] and he left the room, "putting his hands on his ears, and almost weeping," according to his brother Sharif.[319] When his brother Adel was asked how Sirhan behaved when stories about the Arab–Israeli conflict appeared on television, he said his brother "(did) not like it at all."[320] Mary said Sirhan, "favored the Arab position in the Arab–Israel conflicts. When he would watch programs on television and comments would be made favorable to Israel, he would either leave the room or turn off the television."[321]

During the second fortnight of May 1968, Sirhan, according to a later comment by psychiatrist Seymour Pollack, "was disturbed that both his mother and his brothers did not see—didn't perceive—Senator Kennedy as the same destructive and malevolent and dangerous person as Sirhan perceived him to be; and I gather that he and his family, his mother and brothers, had some arguments about this." [322]

The last time Michael Haggerty saw Sirhan was on May 23 in Pasadena's Denny's Restaurant, when Sirhan entered with a group of friends. Haggerty walked over to Sirhan's table, but Sirhan ignored him and left the restaurant without speaking. This jarred with Haggerty's memory of how they were once friends around 1964 and 1965, when they had both attended Pasadena College.[323]

Joseph and Margaret Sheehan attended the Kennedy rally at the Los Angeles Sports Arena on Friday, May 24, 1968. Following Kennedy's speech, the Sheehans waited outside the arena to catch a glimpse of the presidential candidate. In the crowd was Sirhan, who looked, "completely out of character with that crowd…very quiet, intent and purposeful in a frightening way." Margaret Sheehan thought Sirhan was "intense and sinister."[324]

On May 26, Robert Kennedy told Congregation Temple Neveh Shalom in Portland, Oregon that "the United States must defend Israel against aggression from whatever source. Our obligations to Israel, unlike our obligations towards other countries, are clear and imperative… The United States should, without delay, sell Israel the 50 Phantom jets she has so long been promised." The next day Kennedy made a strong plea for the defense of Israel and his photo appeared in the *Pasadena Independent*. He repeated the message when he arrived in California.[325] The article enraged Sirhan. He wrote in his notebook, "Robert F. Kennedy must be assassinated before June 5, 1968" — the first anniversary of the Six-Day War.[326]

Sirhan attended a meeting of the Rosicrucians on Tuesday, May 28 at Pasadena's Akhnaton Lodge. The meeting was attended by twenty-four people and he was greeted by member Willamay Harrison. It was his first lodge meeting. He was asked to put on a membership apron and Verna C. Miller gave him a name tag. He was alone and hardly spoke to anyone there, but he did volunteer to undergo an experiment in testing sensory perceptions. He was blindfolded and asked to identify various objects that touched him. He left the meeting early but not before he looked at a display of occult books.[327]

On May 31 he wrote in his notebooks, "My determination to eliminate RFK is becoming more of an unshakable obsession."

Sirhan said he had fired his pistol at shooting ranges approximately six times between March and May 1968. On Saturday, June 1, Sirhan drove to the Corona Police Department Shooting Range. The roster indicated he had started firing at 12.50 pm and finished at 3 pm. On the way home he stopped at the Lock Stock 'N Barrel gun shop situated at 8972 East Huntington Drive in San Gabriel, part of the Los Angeles sprawl, to buy more mini-mags, two boxes of hollow-point ammunition, .22 calibres. On Sunday, June 2, he drove his mother to church and picked her up after the service. Later, police checked gun ranges in the Los Angeles area but could not confirm that Sirhan had practiced his shooting skills that day.[328]

That night he was seen at the Ambassador Hotel at approximately 7.30 pm. Sirhan had read an advertisement which read, "You and your friends are cordially invited to come and see and hear Robert Kennedy on Sunday, June 2, at eight pm at the Cocoanut Grove, the Ambassador." He had taken the newspaper advertisement with him. "A guy like me," Sirhan said later, "A nobody getting a personal invitation to go down to the Ambassador! Too much out of my class!" Sirhan believed if he took the newspaper cutting with him, "they couldn't throw me out of the place."

Bert Blume used to work for the Showcase Liquor Store, on Lake Street, situated near John Weidner's health food store. He had seen Sirhan on many occasions but had very little conversation with him. Blume, recently out of high school, was at the rally in the Ambassador's Palm Terrace. He observed Sirhan in the lobby area adjacent to the Palm Terrace Room and also walking past him toward the Bell Captain's desk.[329]

Sirhan elbowed his way to the front of the crowd, waiting for the senator. He stood near Paul Redding, who was attending the rally with his wife Susan and his mother. He remembered Sirhan had his hands clasped behind his back "like an umpire" for an hour awaiting Kennedy's entrance. Sirhan was positioned near the aisle Kennedy was due to walk down towards the stage.[330] Later in the evening, Sirhan caught a glimpse of Kennedy standing on the outdoor terrace of the Ambassador. His attitude was suddenly different by observing the man he wanted to 'blast'. "My whole attitude toward him changed," he said. "Before I had pictured him as a villain...But when I saw him that night, he looked like a saint to me." It was an impression that may have remained with him, had his old enmity not been resurrected by a newspaper advertisement two days later announcing a parade celebrating the first anniversary of Israel's victory in the 1967 Six-Day War.

On Monday, June 3, Kennedy departed Los Angeles airport for San Francisco at 10 am to give a speech at Fisherman's Wharf. The senator returned to the Los Angeles area at 4 pm, made a brief speech in Long Beach, and then toured the Watts and Venice area campaigning. He flew to San Diego at 8 pm for a rally at the El Cortez Hotel and Convention Center, scheduled to return to Los Angeles after midnight.

During the two weeks prior to the California primary elections, Sirhan had been going to the horse races and betting almost daily. On June 3, Sirhan asked his mother for the remaining $500 of his Workman's Compensation award, which he had turned over to her, as he planned to attend the races on Tuesday, election day, at Hollywood Park. Originally, he planned to attend a Rosicrucian meeting that same evening. Sirhan drove his mother to work at approximately 8 am that day. Around 11 am he stopped at the Richfield gas station at 2529 E. Foothill Boulevard in Pasadena and filled his car with gas. He was recognized by Jack Davies, the garage owner, who had employed Sirhan as a part-time worker from March 1964 to June 1965.

According to Mary Sirhan, her son was at home between 11 am and 4.30 pm watching television and he stayed at home all evening. However, Sirhan said he had been at home all day raking up leaves and sleeping, reading the newspapers but later drove out to Corona. He had been driving there every day "since he had his car fixed". Sirhan said he drove there or "someplace in that direction" because it was a beautiful place. He later told investigator Michael McCowan he had put 350 miles on the car's odometer. The 260-mile round-trip from Pasadena to San Diego might partly explain the extra miles Sirhan clocked. On June 3, Kennedy was due to speak at a campaign rally there. On arrival at the El Cortez Convention Center, Kennedy collapsed from exhaustion during his speech and the rally was cancelled.

When Sirhan saw the race entries in the newspaper for June 4, he concluded that he did not like the horses that were running. He said he changed his mind about going to the races and decided to go target shooting at the San Gabriel Valley Gun Club instead.[331]

Sirhan's anger became unbearable when he realised that people in Los Angeles had announced a parade to celebrate the first anniversary of the Six-Day War. "I was really curious," he said, "at how they can see themselves as celebrating...misery...the misery of the Palestinian people, and the loss of the Palestinian people. My father was there at the time, I believe. And...there was...a lot of sadness, and a lot of pain and suffering by those people. And that, humanly speaking, it bothered me..."[332]

8

THE LAST DAY – 4/5 JUNE 1968 – HOUR BY HOUR

"You know, the Arabs had emotions. [Robert Kennedy] *knew how they felt about it. But, hell, he didn't have to come out right at the fucking time when the Arab-Israeli war erupted. Oh! I couldn't take it! I couldn't take it!"* Sirhan Sirhan

Tuesday, 4 June, California primary election day

8 am Sirhan awakes and dresses in blue pants, blue shirt (Penny's), white t-shirt, blue velour sweater, blue socks and Hushpuppy-type shoes. He leaves his Pasadena home and buys a newspaper at Washington and Lake streets. He is spotted by his brother Munir. Before his return home at 9.30 am, he may have stopped off to read his paper at a diner.

Sirhan's mother sees her son leave the house at "not quite 8 o'clock" and take the car to buy a paper before returning for his first cup of tea, which is his regular routine. During the time he is gone, Mary goes to work and Munir walks to the bus stop.

Sirhan begins making decisions about which horses to bet on for the afternoon races, but abandons the idea of going to the races that day after deciding none of the horses running look like good bets. Sirhan said, "I was losing all the time and that day I did not like those horse entries… I decided to go target shooting instead of going to the races, I think…"*[333]

* In fact, Sirhan had likely been lying and had planned to go target shooting all along. After his arrest and while awaiting trial, Sirhan was asked by prosecuting psychiatrist Dr Seymour Pollack if the horses were running on election day. Sirhan did not know. Later, Sirhan asked a defense investigator to find out.

9.30 am to 11 am Sirhan's brother Adel sees Sirhan at home.

THE SHOOTING RANGE

11 am Sirhan drives to the San Gabriel Valley Gun Club in Fish Canyon, in Duarte, an LA suburb, stopping off en route to buy ammunition. He had gone to gun ranges on several prior occasions and practiced with the gun because he "liked to" and "was interested...in ..target practicing perfection." He first developed an interest in guns as a member of his high school Cadet Corps.

11.30 am Sirhan is one of the first to arrive at San Gabriel Valley Gun Club. He registers using his real name and correct address then proceeds to rapid-fire his gun using a small screwdriver to remove the shells to empty the gun's chambers. After Sirhan had fired awhile on the shooting range, he buys several more boxes of bullets from Buckner. Buckner later observes Sirhan rapid fire shooting. Together with the ammunition he has brought to the range, Sirhan expended between 300 and 400 bullets.[334]

Michael Soccoman, a member of the club, talks to Sirhan and handles his pistol. He observes Sirhan shooting and concludes he is a good shot. When Sirhan fires his gun at Soccoman's target, his are the two best shots. Sirhan tells Soccoman he is going hunting and when Soccoman questions the legality of the bullets he is using, Sirhan says he does not know about the legality and accuracy of the weapon. Sirhan replies, "Well, I don't know about that. It could kill a dog." Sirhan is observed firing his gun by more gun range visitors, David Montellano and Henry Carreon, who said Sirhan shot very fast rapid fire and used mini-mags with hollow points. Sirhan tells them the mini-mags, "spread a lot more on impact."[335]

Shortly after he starts shooting, Everett Buckner observes Sirhan with a young attractive blonde woman. The woman is Claudia Williams, who is at the range with her husband. After her husband leaves her to use the rifle range, she turns to Sirhan to ask his advice about how to fire her newly acquired gun, as it was the first gun she had owned. Sirhan tells her the gun is firing to the left and she has to stand properly then squeeze the trigger slowly with even pressure. Sirhan stays with her for about twenty minutes until the range master shouts cease fire as the range has to close at 5 pm. He had been at the range all day.[336]

PASADENA

6.10 pm After leaving the shooting range, Sirhan drives to Pasadena City College campus and calls in at Bob's Big Boy restaurant, where he catches sight of an Indian student he knew, Gaymoard Meherji Mistri.

Mistri has been sitting at the counter drinking coffee. Sirhan sits at the counter next to Mistri and they talk about the horse races and horses in general. Mistri has bought a *Herald Examiner* newspaper (later found in Sirhan's car) from a newspaper rack on the college campus, but only for the classified advertisements.

Mistri hands the reading sections to Sirhan, who sees it includes a story about the Jordan-Israel conflict and that gunfire had again broken out. Sirhan becomes angry, hitting the newspaper with the back of his hand and telling Mistri how bad the situation in the Middle East is. "This is bad, this is terrible," Sirhan says.

Sirhan also notices an advertisement for a parade celebrating the first anniversary of the 1967 Arab-Israeli Six-Day War: 'Join in the Miracle Mile March, for Israel'. The advert says the parade will be "tonight" and Sirhan takes this to mean the evening of June 4. However, he is mistaken. The parade has been organized for the evening of Wednesday, June 5. Sirhan eats a hamburger and drinks his coffee. Sirhan pays for the coffee.[337]

6.40 pm The two men walk to the nearby Pasadena City College cafeteria and meet three Arab students: Marof Badran, Anwar Sayegh and Abdo J. Malki. Sirhan knows two of the men, Marouf Badren and Anwan Sayegh who were members of the Organization of Arab Students. As the students are due to attend 7 pm classes, the two friends leave after some small talk.

7.05 pm – 7.15pm Mistri and Sirhan walk back Bob's Big Boy restaurant, talking on the way about hunting and shooting.

7.15 – 7.30 pm Sirhan and Mistri stay at the restaurant for ten minutes and part company after Mistri turns down Sirhan's offer to play pool. Sirhan says he has time to kill before his Rosicrucian meeting, which is scheduled to begin at 8 pm. Sirhan shows Mistri a bullet and Mistri is puzzled. Mistri leaves in his car.*

7.30 pm After he leaves the restaurant, Sirhan looks at Mistri's newspaper again and sees an advertisement announcing, 'Join in the

* It is likely Sirhan had been showing Mistri one of either the two spent bullets found on the front seat of Sirhan's car the day following the assassination containing wood fragments, the spent bullet removed from the glove compartment of Sirhan's car, or the expended bullet removed from Sirhan's pocket at Rampart Division hours after the shooting.

Miracle Mile March for Israel' and it "boils him up" again. "A fire started burning in me," he said. "I thought the Zionists or Jews or whoever it was were trying to rub it in that they had beat hell out of the Arabs."

Seeing the sign brings Sirhan back

> ... to the six days in June of the previous year... I was completely pissed off at American justice at the time... I had the same emotionalism, the same feelings, the fire started burning inside me...at seeing how these Zionists, these Jews, these Israelis...were trying to rub in the fact that they had beaten the hell out of the Arabs the year before...when I saw that ad, I was off to go down and see what these sons-of-bitches were up to.

Sirhan drives to the 'Jew' parade, as he calls it, to "see what those goddamned sons of bitches were up to. I was driving like a maniac." According to him, he gets lost.[338]

Finding no signs of any victory celebrations on Wilshire Boulevard or Miracle Mile, Sirhan notices a storefront campaign party for Republican primary election candidate for Senator Thomas Kuchel. He steps inside and overhears someone say there were several large parties at the Ambassador Hotel, a short distance away. Sirhan decides to go to Republican Max Rafferty's primary election night party at the Ambassador. It will allow him the opportunity, he believes, to see Rafferty's daughter, Kathleen, who he knows from college.

Sirhan illegally parks his pink and white De Soto Firelite a couple of blocks from the Ambassador. The following day it is found by an FBI agent parked on New Hampshire Avenue, license plate number JWS 093. Inside the car, agents find two spent .22 cartridges on the front seat and a book in the back by Manley Palmer Hall entitled, *Healing: The Divine Art*. He leaves his wallet and gun in the glove compartment.

THE AMBASSADOR HOTEL

The head of hotel security, William Gardner has arranged for six additional guards, from Ace Guard Service, to work at the hotel. The total security force consists of eighteen uniformed guards. Six Los Angeles Fire Department inspectors are assigned to the hotel for the evening to enforce fire and occupancy regulations. Los Angeles Police Rampart Division deploys an additional eight officers, in four radio cars, in anticipation of the large crowds planning to attend festivities at the hotel. The radio cars are to be deployed normally and not specifically at the hotel. These arrangements are the total security arrangements which were made for the election night proceedings at the hotel.

6 pm Many people are crowding into the hotel where parties are beginning for Senator Kennedy, Democrat Alan Cranston and Republican Max Rafferty. Other guests are in the hotel for business conventions. In total, 514 guests are registered.

6.05 pm Ace Security Guard Thane Eugene Cesar had received a call from the Ace Guard Service manager at 4.45 pm, saying they needed an extra man for that night to be at the Ambassador. Cesar arrives there and reports to Fred Murphy, the Ace Commander, and William Gardner, the hotel's security chief. Gardner's eleven security guards are dressed in brown uniform and are unarmed. Cesar is in the full uniform of the Ace Guard Service, which requires .38 calibre guns in holsters. He is checked out by his superiors and determined to be carrying the regulation handgun. Cesar was not there to be a bodyguard for Kennedy. The guards were hired for 'crowd control'.[339] Murphy tells Cesar he is working crowd control at the Kennedy campaign party. He is told to patrol the large Embassy Ballroom on the lobby level of the hotel.

8 pm The polls close and the public bars open in the hotel. About 500 people are waiting for Kennedy's speech.

RAFFERTY PARTY, AMBASSADOR HOTEL

8 pm (approx.)

Upon entering the lobby of the hotel, Sirhan observes a sign at the entrance to the Rafferty Headquarters, which is located in the Venetian Room. Sirhan joins the Rafferty celebration, where he stays for an hour. Sirhan's main purpose is to see Rafferty's daughter, but he never sees her that evening. At the Rafferty party he orders two Tom Collins drinks.

After an hour Sirhan returns to his car and because he is not covered by insurance, which he cannot afford, he decides to return to the party allegedly to sober up with coffee. He later claims he could not remember picking up the gun from the car seat before returning to the hotel for coffee, but that he "must have".[340]

At the Rafferty party, Sirhan drinks several Tom Collins drinks. He drinks them like 'lemonade' because he "...didn't know anything about beers or liquors. I was a square. The Tom Collinses tasted just like lemonade." Sirhan wants to be "...a part of the social set... the social, environment." He sees "everybody...celebrating and enjoying the evening." He thinks he would have been out of place if he didn't "...drink...a Tom Collins or something..." According to Sirhan, he stays at the party for about an hour.

After his stay at the party, Sirhan returns to his car. "I was surprised I made it to my car", he said. He is too drowsy to drive so decides to go back to the Ambassador to get some coffee. Before returning, he places his .22 Iver Johnson pistol in his pocket. The gun is concealed by his blue velour shirt. Later, Sirhan claims he took the gun with him because he was afraid it would be, "stolen by Jews." He leaves all his identification in his car.

8.45 pm – 9 pm Sirhan is observed standing in the Electricians Booth adjacent to the Venetian Room, where the Rafferty party is being held. Having the gun with him is an "impulsive thing". He knows he should not have the gun. His behavior, he knows, is reckless because he had "consumed liquor". "I was tired" Sirhan said. "It was late. I was an early-to-rise, early-to-bed person. I was out of my element."[341] He "had never been drunk that many times in [my] life...I had to be nursed... I had to be taken care of by my brother when I got drunk that time before."

Hans Peter Bidstrup, an electrician, sees Sirhan enter the booth and sit down. Sirhan begins a conversation. He is holding a glass containing a "milky-looking liquid", according to Bidstrup. It is a Tom Collins drink. "Are you a Democrat?" Sirhan asks him. When Bidstrup nods, Sirhan extends his hand and says, "Shake hands with another Democrat." Sirhan asks Bidstrup which floor RFK is on and if the senator had bodyguards. Sirhan and Bidstrup are conversing for several minutes when Sirhan asks him if he had ever seen Kennedy. Bidstrup's first impression of Sirhan is that he is half-drunk because he is so talkative, but is unsure. Bidstrup sees Sirhan jump up and speak to Michael Wherton, a fireman who was standing near the electricians' booth. Sirhan asks Wherton about his job.[342]

Gonzalo Carillo-Cretina, a waiter, sees Sirhan with a drink.[343]

9 pm. Enrique Rabago, an unemployed auto-mechanic, and his friend Humphrey Cordeo, had gone to the Ambassador to join in Kennedy's victory celebration. They had come to the hotel together but had become separated. Rabago is standing at the entrance to the Palm Court Room.

Rabago sees Sirhan drinking from a glass. When they speak to each other Rabago thinks Sirhan is "educated and arrogant."

Rabago begins talking to Sirhan in Spanish but, realizing the short swarthy young man is not Hispanic, begins speaking in English. Rabago, worried that Senator Eugene McCarthy may have been ahead in the vote, asks Sirhan, "Are we going to win?" Sirhan answers they were, but then turns "arrogant...acting like a big shot." They have a short conversation and are soon joined by Cordero.

When one of them suggests Kennedy might help the poor, Sirhan angrily responds, "Kennedy! He should never be president. You think that he really wants to help the poor? Kennedy helps himself. He's just using the poor. Can't you see that?" Rabago asks if 'we', meaning RFK supporters, are winning. Sirhan expresses disdain for Kennedy. "Don't worry about him if he doesn't win," he says. "That son of a bitch. He's a millionaire and he doesn't need to win. He just wants to go to the White House, but even if he wins, he's not going to do anything for you or for any of the poor people." Sirhan predicts Kennedy is going to "buy the presidency".

When Cordero suggests they go back into the hotel to the Kennedy party, Rabago hesitates because they both are wearing casual clothes. Cordero asks Sirhan what he thinks of Rabago's apprehensions. Sirhan says, "Why shouldn't we go in there? We are voters; we're putting them in office." Cordero notices how Sirhan appears very aggravated by the way rich people act toward him, as Sirhan complains to Cordoro and Rabago that he has just come from the Rafferty Campaign Room, where the hostess had "looked down at him" because of his attire. Sirhan tells Cordero that he paid for a drink there with a $20 bill and left the change. He describes them as "…all smiles then; it's not what you look like, it's what you have got."

Both Rabago and Cordero last see Sirhan at 9.30 pm and both leave the hotel at 10.15 pm.[344]

9.30 pm – 10 pm Sirhan moves to the Colonial Room, situated between the ballroom and the serving pantry that leads through a passage right into the ballroom. It is an almost empty room, a small private dining area of the hotel. It has been designated as the next call for RFK following his expected victory speech in the Embassy Room. It is fitted up as a small, extra writing press room, and there are about a half dozen female telegraph operators and a dozen or so people hanging around. It holds three teletype machines, situated against the long north wall of the room.

The reporters watch RFK's speech from a television monitor in the north-west corner of the room. The main exit and entrance on the south wall open onto the lobby. There is no security posted on the swinging entrance door to the Colonial Room. Western Union operator Mary Grohs, who is stationed there, is startled to see Sirhan staring over her shoulder at her teletype machine. He looks very intense and his attention is concentrated on the material being sent. She tells him that the Kennedy teletype machine was further down the line. He walks away without saying anything.*[345]

9.30 pm Fire Inspector Cecil Lynch decides the Embassy Room has reached its capacity and admits people on a "one in, one out" basis. Supporters in the lobby complain as the doors are shut. Disappointed at not being able to secure a place in the Embassy Room to watch Kennedy give his speech, some decide to gain access by surreptitiously going through the kitchen pantry.

At the same time, Murphy reassigns Cesar to the Embassy Room kitchen pantry and tells him to position himself at the east door next to the Colonial Room, where a press conference is planned for Kennedy after his speech in the Embassy Room. His assignment inside the kitchen is to keep unauthorized people out of the area which leads to the rear of the stage in the Embassy Room.

10 pm Sirhan is observed leaning against the bar in the Embassy Room by Lonny L. Worthey and Serous A. Mashayekhi. Worthey accidentally bumps into Sirhan. Sirhan is "not in the same spirit as others in the room, not smiling."[346]

Gerry Costigan, a soundman, removes Sirhan from the Embassy stage sometime during the evening.[347]

10 pm – 10.15 pm Waiter Gonzalo Carillo-Cretina sees Sirhan standing outside the restroom adjacent to the Venetian Room. Cretina is working

---

* Sirhan frequently became fascinated by things around him, which prompted him to stare at people or objects. Sirhan later told his police interrogators, "Everything…life itself is a challenge… When you watch a barber, Sir, I just stand and watch that barber for hours…from the time I'm watching him I want to be nothing but a barber. You know, if I'm watching a dentist, boy, he fascinates me, and I want to be him. I was talking to [LAPD officer] Frank (Foster) here a while ago. The way he talked; you know…I was very fascinated and, you know, I was sort of superimposing myself in his position for temporarily." RFK LAPD Microfilm, Volume 98 (Transcripts of Recorded Interviews)

Current Section: Taped Conversations Relating to Sirhan B. Sirhan, 5 June 1968 https://www.maryferrell.org/showDoc.html?docId=99841#relPageId=311

at the Palm Court in the hotel when he is approached by Sirhan. "It's sure crowded in here," Sirhan says, and asks Cretina if he can take a folding chair and hold his drink while he puts it up. Cretina obliges Sirhan, but they do not converse.[348]

10.15 pm – 11 p.m. Sirhan is seen standing in the pantry area of the kitchen by Judy Royer. She is working on the Kennedy staff and arrived at the hotel at approximately 4 pm During the evening, she checks the pantry and kitchen area to clear it of persons who do not belong. Royer had been told that Kennedy would be going to the Colonial Room after his speech in the Embassy Room. She checks the kitchen area about twice an hour for three hours prior to midnight.

An hour or two prior to Kennedy's speech, Judy Royer observes Sirhan in the anteroom behind the Embassy Ballroom stage. She approaches him and asks if he has a pass. Because Sirhan is not wearing a press or staff badge, she asks him to leave. He turns and walks toward the doors leading out to the Embassy Ballroom. She asks Sirhan once more to leave the pantry area during the evening.

Sirhan is seen at the Embassy Room bar by Teresa Christian. She thinks he looks "nervous" and chastises him for pushing his way to the front of the crowd.[349]

10.30 pm Sirhan is seen in the pantry area by Dr Marcus McBroom. Sirhan has been leaning against a steam table. Believing he is a hotel worker, McBroom notices he is not wearing a white uniform. According to McBroom, Sirhan looks "out of place".[350]

11 pm Robert Klase is standing in the kitchen area after attempting to get into the Embassy Room through the main entrance. He has been refused admittance by a guard and is attempting to enter through the kitchen. As he stands in the anteroom, near some television equipment, a man who is monitoring a television set asks him to watch a nearby door. Minutes later, as Klase is watching the door, Sirhan attempts to enter the anteroom. Klase taps Sirhan on the shoulder and tells him no one is allowed in the area other than members of the staff. Sirhan turns around and goes back into the Embassy Room.

11.15 pm Cesar's assignment inside the kitchen is to keep unauthorized persons out of the area which leads to the rear of the stage in the Embassy Room. At approximately 11.15 pm Murphy talks to Cesar and tells him to go to the door at the west end of the kitchen area to perform the same security functions. He tells him Kennedy will be coming through the pantry on his way to the Colonial Room after his speech. Murphy tells Cesar to move from the east pantry door to the west double swinging doors, next to the backstage area. While he is waiting, Cesar talks to several of the Kennedy retinue including comedian Milton Berle, Rafer Johnson and Rosey Grier.[351]

Two guards are assigned to escort RFK through the pantry: Stanley Kawalee and Thane Eugene Cesar.

There are two Ace security guards with guns in the Embassy Room: Albert Stowers and Jack Merritt.

11.45 pm – 12 pm

Sirhan remains in the pantry area, close to Jesus Perez at the corner of a serving table. Several times Sirhan asks Perez and kitchen worker Martin Petrusky, "Is Mr Kennedy coning this way?" Perez tells him that he does not know. He also asks the other kitchen help the same question.[352] Sirhan appears to Perez to be "just standing around as everyone else was" and appears to have "some type of papers in his hands", twisting them in such a way that it gives Perez the impression he is nervous. However, Sirhan is by now well under the influence of the calming effect of alcohol, greatly reducing his inhibitions.[353]

The kitchen staff have an idea that RFK might go to the Embassy stage through the pantry as the passageways there had been lined with trellis-covered green and white wooden barriers and some of the counters have been covered with white tablecloths. Other signs which arouse their curiosity are a three-man television crew, who had set their equipment up in the ante-room just beyond the pantry. Both Jesus Perez and waiter Martin Patrusky see Kennedy when he passes through the pantry on his way to give his victory speech. They both observe Sirhan still in the pantry area.[354]

11.59 pm Kennedy steps off the freight elevator in the kitchen and walks past Cesar through the west pantry doors, out of an anteroom between the pantry and a backstage area and on to the Embassy Room stage where about 500 people await his speech.

Shortly before Kennedy's arrival in the pantry, Henrietta Sterlitz and her friend Evelyn Planavsky see "…two teenage boys and one teenage girl…pop balloons and…exclaim 'Kennedy's Dead!'"[355]

Wednesday, June 5

12.05 am – 12.10 am Martin Patrusky is with a girl who is a Kennedy campaigner and two waiter friends and Perez. He sees Sirhan standing on tray rack in the pantry looking towards the stage area. By now Sirhan has consumed at least four Tom Collins drinks by his own estimate.[356]

12.10 am – 12.15 am Barbara Rubin and Gonzalo Carillo-Cretina see Sirhan standing next to the ice machine in the pantry. Vincent DiPierro sees Sirhan in a crouched position next to the ice machine.

The original plan is for Kennedy to go downstairs to give another victory speech to the overflow of 1,500 people who are unable to get into the Embassy Room. However, because it is late, this plan is cancelled. Instead, it is decided that he should meet with the "paper press" in the Colonial Room and afterwards go to a victory party at The Factory, a downtown nightclub, partly owned by Kennedy aide Pierre Salinger and the candidate's brother-in-law, Hollywood actor Peter Lawford. Some hotel staff, unaware of the change in plans, think RFK is going to go to the downstairs ballroom. However, Kennedy aides Fred Dutton and Bill Barry are only concerned with how the candidate is going to get through to the Colonial Room and they plan the route. An Ace guard suggests they move through the crowd in the Embassy Ballroom. However, Kennedy has asked to go the 'back way'.

Thane Cesar has been waiting in the hall passageway separating the pantry from the Embassy Room with Jess Unruh and Milton Berle preceding the entrance of Senator Kennedy into the Embassy Ballroom. Klase and Judy Royer watch the Kennedy victory speech on a television in the Colonial Room. He and Judy Royer pass through the kitchen on their way there but they do not see Sirhan.

Before Kennedy nears the end of his victory speech, aides Fred Dutton and Bill Barry check the shortcut to the Colonial Room. Walking across the pantry, which was less crowded than any other passageway, they both agree this will be the safest route. Barry and Dutton return to the stage from the Colonial Room through the swinging pantry doors to the anteroom and up the inclined hallway at the back of the stage. They step through the stage drapes to the senator's retinue, which surrounds the senator as he finishes his victory speech.

At the conclusion of Kennedy's victory speech, Civil Rights veteran and campaign aide John Lewis hears ex-FBI agent Bill Barry, Kennedy's personal bodyguard, say, "Bobby, we're supposed to go this way." 'This way' means through the crowd in front of the stage. The senator answers "No" and heads toward the rear of the stage.[357] Kennedy has asked ex-FBI agent Bill Barry to protect his wife Ethel as they are both unable to catch up with the senator.*

---

* Writer Jules Witcover, who was following Kennedy after he left the stage, wrote: "The original plan had been for Kennedy to go out through the crowd to another reception on a lower level of the hotel. But there was closed-circuit television down there and that group had just seen and heard the candidate. When Bill Barry came up to Dutton in

12.14 am Kennedy leaves the stage through the drapes and steps down into the anteroom where Cesar is stationed. Cesar takes Kennedy's right arm with his left hand to assist him through the crowd. They walk east through the pantry toward the Colonial Room.[358]

Cesar and Kennedy walk through the swinging pantry doors. The security guard begins pushing people away from Kennedy as the senator is having difficulty moving forward. Kennedy and Cesar reach the ice machine shortly before the mâitre d', Karl Uecker, takes Kennedy's right hand, leading him through the pantry. Cesar moves behind Kennedy and takes Kennedy's right arm at the elbow as Uecker keeps hold of Kennedy's right hand. Cesar lets Sirhan approach from the area of the tray rack and ice machine. In front of Kennedy are about twenty people, and Kennedy is in the midst of a group of about fifty people. Perez and Patrusky both see a 'smirk' on Sirhan's face as he darts out. As the crowd enters the pantry, Kennedy pulls away. Cesar was the closest person to him. Cesar sees Kennedy turn completely sideways so that the side of his neck is facing almost perpendicular to the gunshots. Cesar is inches away when Sirhan fires his shots and thinks the would-be assassin is firing at him. Cesar ducks then stumbles and falls. When he retrieves his composure, he stands up and pulls his gun out, holding it at a 45-degree angle. After thirty seconds he puts his gun back in his holster.[359]

12.15 am Lisa Lynn Urso sees Sirhan draw his gun from his waistband and fire. Boris Yaro sees Kennedy backing away with arms up raised towards his head as Sirhan, with his gun held extended and high, "charges" towards Kennedy. Martin Patrusky sees Sirhan standing on the tray rack, pushing towards Kennedy,

---

the crush and told him the functionaries below wanted Kennedy, Dutton demurred. It would just be a repeat performance. Besides, it was already past midnight; the waiting newsmen as usual were pushing for a press conference, and the shortest route to the press room was the way Kennedy had come in, through the kitchen corridor and pantry area... Barry and Dutton discussed the matter another moment and then, as Kennedy concluded and started out, Barry moved up and told him: 'No, it's been changed. We're going this way.' 'Okay,' Kennedy said, still swamped by admirers. Dutton and Barry, expecting Kennedy to leave by way of the ballroom stage side steps that led onto the ballroom floor and then directly out into the kitchen corridor through the swinging doors to the left, moved in that direction to clear a path for him to the press conference. But Kennedy, with Ethel slightly behind, was boxed in by reaching, screaming well-wishers chanting, 'We want Bobby! We want Bobby!' Instead of following his two aides, he started off the platform, led by the assistant maître d'hôtel, Karl Uecker, through a back exit way into the dark corridor. Barry looked back, saw the new route, and raced over". Witcover, *85 Days*, 264-265

reaching around Karl Uecker and firing shots. As Perez withdraws his hand from Kennedy's, he hears shots and sees people next to Kennedy struggling with Sirhan.

Freddy Plimpton, part of the Kennedy entourage, sees Kennedy give "a slight stoop and his hands go up to the side of his face in a motion as if to push something away." She "sees an arm go up right next to Kennedy's head."

Busboy Juan Romero, a young 18-year-old whose stepfather, a waiter, had gotten him the job at the Ambassador, sees Kennedy moving through the kitchen pantry following the speech in the Embassy Room. He gets close enough to stick out his hand for him to shake. As Kennedy grabs it, Juan hears a bang and feels a flash of heat against his face. He sees "...the guy put out his hand to the Senator's head...then I see the guy put a bullet in the senator's head."

Kennedy's ex-FBI bodyguard, Bill Barry, was abreast of the Senator about 4 feet away from him. Barry sees Sirhan holding the gun in his right hand, his arm is extended and the gun is "about 12 inches from the Senator's head."[360]

Vincent DiPierro sees Sirhan's "...stupid smile he [has] on his face... kind of like an envious smile, like, you know, villainous." He sees the gun come from the right side of his eye and, as Sirhan's arm is outstretched and the assailant is "shorter than Kennedy," the gun is "going in an upward trajectory." Sirhan lunges forward, bringing the muzzle of his Ivor-Johnson revolver within several inches of Kennedy's head at "point-blank" range. He sees Kennedy's arms go up to his head. There is "nobody between" DiPierro, Kennedy and Sirhan. DiPierro watches as Sirhan shoots at Kennedy and is sprayed in the face with Kennedy's blood. He sees a bullet hit Kennedy's head and another bullet hit the top of Kennedy's jacket. A bullet tears through DiPierro's shirt, but he is uninjured. DiPierro only sees seven shots come out of the gun, but he hears "eight shots." He sees the gun, "pitched slightly *upward,* and as Sirhan is considerably shorter than Kennedy, this accounts for the upward trajectory of the bullets in Kennedy's body."[361]

The muzzle of Sirhan's gun is held at a distance of 1 to 6 inches from the senator's coat at the time he is shot. Freddy Plimpton sees "His eyes...narrow, the lines on his face...heavy and set...completely concentrated on what he [is] doing."[362]

Kennedy friend and campaign worker Frank Burns, who is standing very close to Kennedy as the senator was shaking the waiters' hands, sees him throw up his hands toward his head, "as if he was about to grab it at the line of his ears." Burns realizes the gun is close to Senator

Kennedy as he feels a burning sensation on his left cheek, just before he sees the senator falling. Kennedy's arms are near his head as he is, "twisting to his left and falling back." The gunman is almost "directly in front" of him. He is still holding the gun and coming closer to the senator. "He was aiming the gun down at the Senator as he was falling. He was *stepping forward following the fallen body* [emphasis added]."[363]

Richard G. Lubic sees Sirhan lean against a steam table and extend his hand with the revolver towards Kennedy. The first two shots are deliberate with a slight pause between, followed by wild rapid firing. As Sirhan aims his gun, Lubic hears Sirhan shout, "Kennedy, you son of a bitch!"[364]

Edward Minasian, a hotel employee, is standing "within five feet of Kennedy" when the senator is shot. Kennedy's right shoulder is very near to his left shoulder. He sees Sirhan's revolver extended, reaching around between the steam table and Karl Uecker. He sees Kennedy raise his arms in front of his face.

Valerie Schultz sees Kennedy turn "something more than 90-degree angle facing roughly... west of north where there were people standing," which places the rear of Kennedy's head towards Sirhan. The gun is "pushing...toward the Senator and the gun was to the side or back of Kennedy's head when Sirhan began firing."

Boris Yaro sees Sirhan "lunging at the senator." He also sees Kennedy "backing up" against the kitchen freezers as Sirhan fires at him at "point blank range." Yaro and DiPierro see Sirhan's firing position clearly. Although Sirhan is seen by witnesses as being in front of the senator, his outstretched arm has reached around Karl Uecker and is directed towards Kennedy's head, which has turned to the left exposing the right rear of his head.*

With an outstretched arm and gun in hand, Sirhan points his gun and 'stabs' it at Kennedy, as the senator turns his head to the left in a defensive stance. Kennedy's arms rise and his body bends in a downwards motion. The arc of the gun follows Kennedy's head as the senator stoops to avoid his assailant. A millisecond later a bullet enters the right rear of Kennedy's head.

Uecker attempts to grab the weapon from Sirhan, as Kennedy falls to the floor of the pantry. Cesar does not draw his gun until both he and Kennedy have fallen to the floor (Cesar has dropped to the floor to avoid being hit by bullets). Cesar's gun is only out of his holster for

---

* Many of the twelve eyewitnesses who were close to Kennedy when he was shot stated that Sirhan was anywhere from 3 to 12 feet away from his victim. However, the majority of the witnesses gave estimates of muzzle distance based only on the first shot and did not see Sirhan 'lunging' at the senator.

about thirty seconds and is not drawn until he begins to stand up. Cesar is in shock. He also has powder burns in his eyes. He immediately runs out of the pantry when he sees Sirhan struggling with Kennedy's aides and returns immediately with other Ace guards, Jack Merritt and Albert Stowers, who were in the Embassy Room when the shots were fired. Merrit enters the pantry with his gun drawn.[365]

The pantry erupts in chaos as Kennedy's retinue fall over each other to avoid the gunshots. They are knocking over trays, cutlery and balloons are bursting. People are shouting and screaming.

After Kennedy has fallen to the floor, former FBI agent Barry sees Sirhan holding a gun and hits him twice in the face. A group composed of maître d'hotel Karl Uecker, Edward Minasian, writer George Plimpton, Olympic gold medal decathlete Rafer Johnson and professional football player Rosey Grier, force Sirhan against the steam table as he continues firing his gun in random directions. Five members of the crowd are wounded by the random gunfire. At one point, Sirhan is able to wrestle free and grab the revolver again. He attempts to shoot it, but all his bullets are expended.

Most of the seventy-seven pantry witnesses have heard the gunshots and later describe them as "a number of shots", "a series of firecrackers", "several shots" or "a number of shots in rapid succession". In the chaos that follows the first shot, most of the earwitnesses cannot remember the exact number of shots fired. The vast majority, however, put the number at eight or less. Only a handful hear more than eight shots. Some witnesses are *certain* they hear eight shots, including Kristi Witker, Warren Rogers, Vincent DiPierro and Barbara Rubin, who were all close to Kennedy. One of the shooting victims, Ira Goldstein, says he later re-enacted the "sound and rhythm of the shots and concluded he heard seven shots." [366] As nationally acclaimed ballistics expert Larry Sturdivan told this author:

> If anybody . . . tells me he can reconstruct the location and posture of each person in that room at the time of each shot, I would conclude that he was delusional. If I were there, I would guarantee that my location and posture would change continuously between shots and there would be no way I could remember exact locations or postures at any given moment. Photographs help, but one cannot pinpoint the time of the photograph to the millisecond and that's what one would need to do to re- construct a trajectory from gun to entry point.[367]

Jack Merritt enters the pantry after the shooting. Merritt is in the hall outside the Embassy Room when informed of the shooting. He sees a group of men are holding Sirhan on a metal table and Senator Kennedy is lying on the floor.

Kennedy has been hit three times, twice in the back and once behind the right ear. A fourth bullet has gone through his jacket without touching him.

- Wound 1 is the fatal wound to the head. The bullet entered the brain and fragmented into two large and many tiny pieces. Fragments of the mastoid bone were scattered in the brain. Two wound tracks were visible in the X-rays, a result of the bullet splitting. According to coroner Thomas Noguchi, powder burns on the right ear area indicated Kennedy had been shot from a distance of 1 to 1½ inches.
- Wound 2 is the bullet that entered from the back of Kennedy's armpit, through soft tissue, and traveled upwards at an angle of 59 degrees to the vertical moving back to front.
- Wound 3 is the bullet that also entered from the back of Kennedy's armpit at an angle of 67-70 degrees to the vertical in a nearly parallel path to the bullet that caused Wound 2. The bullet did not exit the skin and lodged near the sixth vertebrae, where the neck meets the back, 2 cm from the spine. According to Dr Noguchi, who performed the autopsy, both wounds in the area of Kennedy's armpit and right side were the results of shots fired at very close range.

All three bullets traveled back to front, right to left and upwards. A fourth bullet passed through his jacket without causing injury; it traveled the same path as the bullets that caused wounds 2 and 3.

Of the three bullets that hit Kennedy (excluding the jacket pad bullet), one was lost in the ceiling, the head bullet fragmented and the third bullet removed from Kennedy's neck was matched to Sirhan's gun.

Later, Dr Noguchi said it was impossible to determine which bullet hit Kennedy first. There were five holes in Kennedy's coat—an exit hole at the right front of the shoulder—no nitrate; an exit hole three-quarters of an inch to the rear of the right shoulder seam—nitrate particles present; an entrance hole two inches below the shoulder seam in the right sleeve—nitrate deposits; and two holes in the rear right sleeve seven inches below the shoulder seam—nitrate deposits. Noguchi later stated that despite his efforts, there was really no way to accurately trace the flight pattern of so many bullets.*

---

* Noguchi found that four shots had been fired at Kennedy from 3 inches away at most. Three shots appeared to be in contact with Kennedy's back and shoulder, based on

Noguchi placed the Sirhan weapon 1 or 2 inches from the skin behind the right ear when the first shot was fired. Kennedy, according to eyewitnesses, was turning his head and upper part of his body to shake hands with the kitchen help, Juan Perez and Jesus Romero. Additionally, Noguchi and Wolfer both estimated that Kennedy's arm had been raised, thus lifting the padding up off his shoulder and accounting for the line of a bullet fired through the shoulder coat which did not graze the skin of the senator but could have continued on into Paul Schrade's head.

When the shooting ends, Kennedy is lying on the floor and whispers to busboy Juan Romero, "Is everybody OK?" He looks around and recognizes his wife, who is kneeling beside him. He calls her name several times. Los Angeles doctor Stanley R. Abo attends to him and attempts to keep the head wound bleeding to prevent a clot forming.

A struggle ensues as those present attempt to immobilize and disarm Sirhan, who witnesses say has great strength. This comes as no surprise to several of Sirhan's friends, who describe him as having great strength. Although short and slight of build, he is very strong.

A hotel employee grabs Sirhan around the wrist of the hand holding the gun, but Sirhan, who is still able to move that hand, continues shooting. Irwin Stroll, William Weisel, Elizabeth Evans and Ira Goldstein are injured by the resulting gunfire. The assassin manages to fire off all eight of his shots before Kennedy's retinue, which includes Rosey Grier, Rafer Johnson and George Plimpton, and together with Karl Uecker finally subdue him. Sirhan feels "a choking" in his throat as he was being restrained. Some were "holding me and beating me and twisting my left knee and pounding my head on the table. They hurt my left eye..."

Immediately following the shooting, Dr Marcus McBroom, a Los Angeles psychiatrist, hears Sirhan say, "'I did it for the country, I love my country' or something to that effect...He was shouting like he'd done the right thing or was attempting to do the right thing...he was trying to do something for the good of the country...I heard him say."[368] Jesse Unruh sees Sirhan being restrained on the kitchen table. "I can [or] I will explain," Sirhan pleads.[369]

---

powder burns to his jacket, Noguchi said, with one shot passing through the jacket's shoulder pad and not touching Kennedy. All three were fired sharply upward. The fourth shot was fired into the back of Kennedy's head from 3 inches away, Noguchi concluded, by test-firing a similar gun to determine how much gunpowder sprayed at various distances.

Kneeling next to Robert Kennedy is busboy Juan Romero. Romero is an admirer of Kennedy and persuaded a friend earlier in the evening to let him answer Kennedy's request for room service. When a Kennedy aide had answered the door to the room Romero pushed the food cart in and found himself standing next to Kennedy, who shook his hand.

He sees Kennedy sprawled on the floor, "looking up at the ceiling, and I thought he'd banged his head." Romero asks Kennedy if he is OK and if he wants to get up. Romero sees his "left eye…twitching" and "one leg…shaking." He lifts Kennedy's head and feels warm blood spilling through his fingers.

Ethel Kennedy pushes Romero out of the way, but moments later allows him to press some rosary beads into her husband's hands.

When asked "Why did you do it?" Sirhan once more insists this time to police officers, "I can explain." Two policemen take Sirhan to Ramparts police station.

12.18 am Geraldine Agnes McCarthy, a Kennedy supporter, is with members of her family outside the Ambassador Ballroom taking a breath of fresh air and going through a doorway opening onto the Wilshire Street parking lot of the hotel. There is a fire escape leading down from the floor above. The party consists of Geraldine McCarthy, Margaret McCarthy, Winnie Marshall, Mary Towley, Eileen Anderson, Phil Litroh, Chris Marshall and Paul Benedict. Several people come down the stairway from above and a girl in an orange dress shouts, "Kennedy has been shot!" Shortly after that, a girl in a "beige dress with black dots" comes down the outside fire escape and exclaims, "Oh my God, Kennedy's been shot!"[370] This later leads to erroneous accounts of alleged co-conspirators exclaiming responsibility for the assassination.[371]

Albert Victor Ellis, a roommate of John Shamel, the hotel's convention manager, hears a "female voice" say, "We shot him." He assumes she means "we the American people" shot Kennedy. He leaves the Embassy Room and walks to the lobby and hears "several other people…state something to the effect 'We shot him'."[372]

Laurie Gail Porter hears her friend Robin Casden shout, "We shot him" and also hears "several people" shout "We shot him." [373] *London Daily Express* photographer Harry Benson goes outside the Embassy Room and hears a man "with a United States flag in his mouth… a real nutty guy, say, 'Thank God, he's been shot'."[374]

Robert Kennedy is taken to a hospital where he undergoes surgery. He subsequently dies the next day, June 6, 1968. The cause of death is a gunshot wound that has penetrated the brain.

In the police car en route to Rampart Station, Unruh hears Sirhan say, "I did it for my country." Unruh asks Sirhan, "Why him?" Sirhan replies, "It's too late."*[375] Sirhan later tells author Robert Kaiser, "They told me...I was on television!"[376]

Later that night, Rafer Johnson turns the weapon over to the LAPD after the police track him down at Central Receiving Hospital, and it is booked into the property division at Ramparts police station.

Officer Guadalupe Dela Garza hears Sirhan voicing his dislike of the trouser waist of his jail clothing as being too large. Sirhan is quite concerned with his appearance. Garza also watches the slow, deliberate and thorough manner in which Sirhan showers. Officer Frank Foster, a jailer, converses with Sirhan, who talks about children, horses, the Boston Strangler and Foster's duty at the jail.[377]

LAPD Officer William Jordan thinks Sirhan is less upset than "individuals arrested for a traffic violation." Sirhan's mind seems "keen" to Jordan, who thinks he fancies himself "somewhat of an intellectual."[378]

---

* Sirhan did indeed shout out the motive for the crime (words to the effect, 'I did it for my country') according to two contemporaneous witness accounts: Dr Marcus McBroom and Jesse Unruh. Unruh's account may be challenged as he expressed some confusion about what he actually said, but not so McBroom.

9

JAIL

"The abuse of the insanity defense has led to what may be called the alibi of abnormality. Instability is not insanity, maladjustment not psychosis...It seems that every abuse has its apologists... A defendant in a murder case in whom nobody ever saw any signs of abnormality before his arrest, may be declared insane, spend some time in an institution, and then be [released]*...he has acquired a psychiatric hunting licence to kill."*

Dr Frederic Werthan, author of *A Sign For Cain: An Exploration Of Human Violence*

"If you look at the map today you will not find Palestine. It has been wiped from the face of the earth... What is our guilt that we should have our homeland stolen from us? Was our only guilt that of being a defenseless people who wished to live in peace with our simple customs... My son Sirhan and Senator Robert Kennedy were both victims of Zionism... Not only was Sirhan's country taken from him but he was robbed of his childhood." Mary Sirhan after hearing the news of Robert Kennedy's assassination

Around the time Kennedy was taken to the hospital, the police arrived at the hotel and took custody of Sirhan. He was removed through a hostile crowd and placed in their police vehicle. California politician Jesse Unruh got into a car with Sirhan and they were taken to the police station. En route the officers advised Sirhan of his constitutional rights. During the trip, Unruh asked Sirhan "Why did you shoot him?" Sirhan replied, "You think I am crazy? You think I will tell you so you can use it as evidence against me?" Unruh also heard Sirhan say "I did it for my country" and believed he was not intoxicated. Police officers who were with Sirhan at the time of his arrest or shortly thereafter reached the same conclusion. The police found various items on Sirhan's person, including a newspaper article, which in part noted that in a recent speech, Senator Kennedy, "favored aid to Israel 'with arms if necessary' to meet the threat of the Soviets."

Sirhan was considered by the interviewing LAPD Officer Jordan to be "rational and alert." He intelligently discussed any other topic, Jordan said, but steadfastly refused to discuss the assassination. When asked by a police sergeant if he was ashamed of what he did, he replied, "Hell, no!" In fact, he was so proud of his act that the morning after the shooting, he asked jail guards for a newspaper so he could see what had been written about him. When no news stories of the assassination appeared due to press deadlines, he became upset.[379] The doctor at the county jail who examined Sirhan immediately following his arrest also testified to his subject's alertness, saying the suspect was "...self-satisfied, smug and unremorseful."[380]

During the police station interviews, Sirhan never once asked why he had been arrested. If he had indeed been in a 'disassociated state', the first question Sirhan would have asked was, "Why have I been arrested?" Sirhan was also fully alert when he was given a police caution that he need not say anything until he sought legal assistance. He refused to give police officers any details about himself, including his name and address, but he did reveal his disillusionment with America in conversations with his interrogators. Frank Foster asked Sirhan what he wanted to get out of life, and Sirhan replied, "Nothing... They won't give me it! They won't give me it."[381]

Sirhan had brushed up on his knowledge of psychology to ready himself for his trial and perhaps wanted advice on how to cover up. He asked a deputy Sheriff to order him a book, *Psychology You Can Use*. Sirhan requested two books after his confinement in the County Jail: *The Secret Doctrine* by Helena P. Blavatsky and *Talks on the Path of Occultism, Volume I - At the Feet of the Master* by Annie Desant and C. W. Leadbeater. The books dealt with theosophy, a doctrine which gave its adherents the knowledge to "master nature and guide their destiny." Sirhan said, "The Rosicrucians taught me everything."[382]

Sirhan had known how diminished capacity can be used to excuse acts of murder. His brother Munir revealed that they used to go to trials together. Sirhan at first denied it and then admitted he had been learning about the "legal process... [I] was always interested in going down to the courtroom."[383] Following his arrest, Sirhan had asked Officer Foster about the Boston Strangler case and of how Albert DeSalvo had committed the crimes because he had suffered a deprived childhood. Sirhan responded, "...but, correct me if I'm mistaken, is it

Following the assassination, Bishara Salameh Ghattas Sirhan, Sirhan's father said, "I can say that I do not regret his death as Kennedy the American politician who attempted to gain the presidential election by his aggressive propaganda against the Arab people of Palestine... Kennedy was promising the Zionists to supply them with arms and aircraft...and thus provoked the sensitive feelings of Sirhan who had suffered so much from the Jews... It is not fair to accuse my son without a full examination of Zionist atrocities against the Arabs—those atrocities which received the support and blessings of Robert Kennedy." *California State Archives*

Sirhan's close friend Walter Crowe said Mary Sirhan propagated extreme anti-Semitism to her son. He said she was a "very bitter" person and a "racist". Once, he said, during a discussion about the Arab/Israeli conflict, Mary asked Crowe, "Have you ever smelled a Jew?" Two other close friends of Sirhan, John and Patricia Strathman, also believed Sirhan had been heavily influenced by his mother's views. *San Francisco State University Archives*

Sirhan's younger brother, Munir Sirhan, insisted the Sirhans were a "normal, happy, God-fearing family". In reality, the Sirhans were a troubled family with a doting and bigoted mother and a distant, rigid and punitive father. *San Francisco State University Archives*

Bishara Sirhan was originally from Taybeh, a village with a Greek Orthodox and Roman Catholic population. The village is built on several hills about 30 miles from Ramallah, north of Jerusalem. It is now a West Bank village and controlled by Israel. *Wiki Fair Use*

At the time of Sirhan Sirhan's birth on March 19, 1944, the family lived in a comfortable five-roomed apartment in the Musrara quarter, just outside Jerusalem's Old City walls. The apartment house on St Paul's Street had an internal courtyard and was a stone's throw from the Damascus Gate, the main entrance to the Old City. *Mel Ayton*

The Damascus Gate, Jerusalem. On December 29, 1947, the Sirhans were caught up in one of the most serious pre-war incidents of the 1948 Arab-Israeli War when Sirhan and his father witnessed dynamite being thrown from a speeding car by the Irgun, a militant Zionist force. The father and son had been about to go through the Damascus Gate when the bomb exploded. Two British constables and eleven Arabs were killed, with another thirty-two Arabs wounded. *Mel Ayton*

Robert Kennedy campaigning in Los Angeles, 1968. *Los Angeles County Sheriff's Department Records, California State Archives, Office of the Secretary of State, Sacramento, California*

During the early evening of June 4, 1968, California Primary Election Day, many people crowded into the Ambassador Hotel where parties were beginning for Senator Kennedy, Democrat Alan Cranston and Republican Max Rafferty. Other guests were in the hotel for business conventions. A total of 514 guests were registered. *California State Archives*

The Ambassador Hotel on Los Angeles' Wilshire Boulevard, with its red-tiled roofs, graceful gardens, and 23.5 acres of velvet lawns, was one of the world's most famous hotels. It was the meeting place for the rich and famous. *Wiki Commons*

Kennedy addressing supporters in the Embassy Ballroom of the Ambassador Hotel after his victory in the California Democrat presidential primary election. *Sven Walnum, The Sven Walnum Photograph Collection, John F. Kennedy Presidential Library and Museum, Boston*

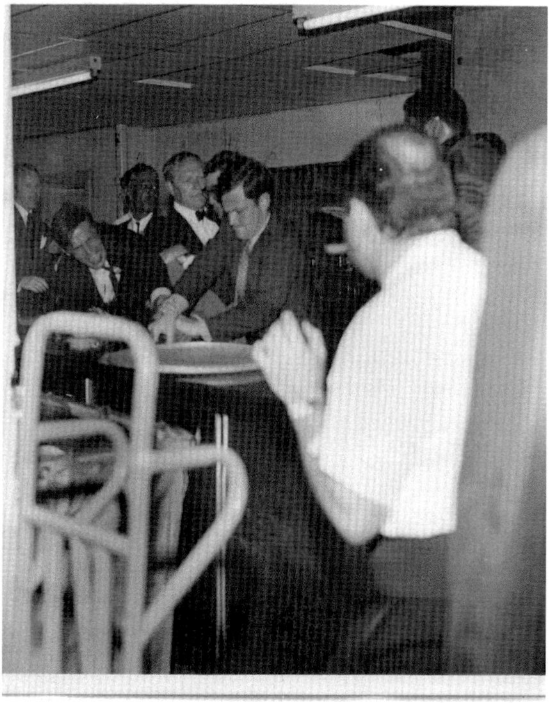

The Ambassador Hotel pantry, situated behind the Embassy Ballroom stage. A hotel employee grabbed Sirhan around the wrist of the hand holding the gun. Dr Marcus McBroom, a Los Angeles psychiatrist, heard Sirhan say, "I did it for the country, I love my country…" *California State Archives*

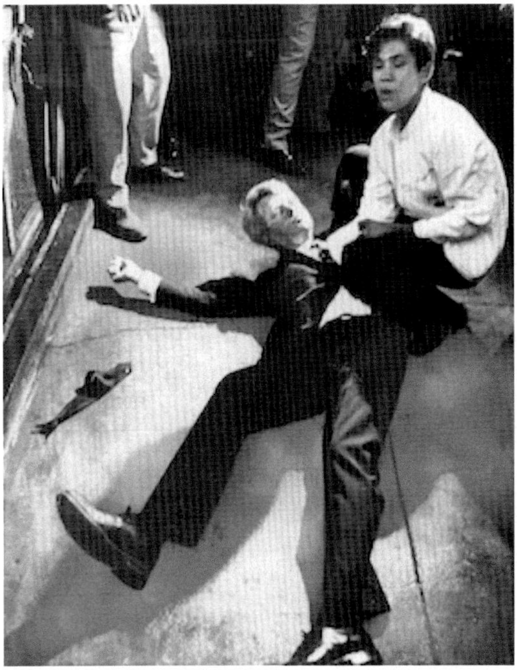

Kneeling next to Robert Kennedy is Juan Romero, a young 18-year-old busboy. He was an admirer of Kennedy and persuaded a friend earlier in the evening to let him answer Kennedy's request for room service. *Gatehouse Media, Boris Yaro*

The Ambassador Hotel kitchen pantry. The X marks the spot where Kennedy fell backwards after being shot. *California State Archives*

Sirhan at Los Angeles' Ramparts Police Station. When American Civil Liberties Union lawyer A.L. Wirin visited him, the accused assassin confessed, "I shot him". Sirhan pulled an imaginary trigger then repeated, "I shot him". *California State Archives*

The Iver Johnson eight-shot pistol Sirhan Sirhan used to murder Robert Kennedy. *California State Archives*

Sirhan surrounded by Los Angeles Deputy Sheriffs. *Sheriff's Relief Association*

A poster of Sirhan used by terrorists. The translation from Arabic reads: *A fighter not a murderer, Sirhan Bishara Sirhan. On the 5th of Haziran* [June] *1968, a year after the Zionist colonialist assault on Palestine and Arab countries, a Palestinian youth named Sirhan Bishara Sirhan shot the American senator Robert Kennedy to death. "I did this for my country." This is what Sirhan said after his arrest. Today, Zionists circles in the US attempt to distort the motives of this fida'i* [guerrilla fighter] *and extinguish the voice of the truth, fired from his gun.* https://www.palestineposterproject.org/original-copy-location/portfolio-1301-1400, http://liberationgraphics.com

The grave of Robert F. Kennedy, Arlington National Cemetery, Washington D.C. *Mel Ayton*

when…the man is self-admitting? He admits that he's, wasn't trying, but they won't believe him? Is this related to it?"[384]

Robert Blair Kaiser, who came to know Sirhan better than any of the defense lawyers, believed Sirhan knew that the Boston Strangler committed his crimes in a "disassociated state."[385] Later, when ACLU lawyer A.L. Wirin met with Sirhan, the accused assassin wasted no time in telling him, "I shot him." Sirhan pulled an imaginary trigger then repeated, "I shot him."[386] He told Robert Blair Kaiser, "For the loss of human life, I think I should be dead. But for stopping Robert Kennedy, a fucking politician, who would have been a killer if he had been elected… I don't think I should be convicted at all."[387]

When John Weidner heard the news of Sirhan's arrest he told NBC news:

> When I first heard about it my first reaction was to think about what Kennedy said about Israel a few days ago and that made me believe that it was not impossible that a hot-tempered man like Sirhan, with his fantasies, that he was able to do something like that. I tried to discuss with him about how good it was in America but he didn't want to believe it. He believed that Russia and China were maybe better… he was resentful against authority, against those who possess, and he told me America was a country where there was no freedom…. On that subject [Israel] he was fairly unstable.[388]

During the police investigation that followed the assassination, police officers interviewed Sirhan's friend Walter Crowe. Crowe said that to the best of his knowledge, Sirhan made no mention of assassinating, shooting or killing anyone. However, he was not sure whether Kennedy's name might not have been mentioned in some other context. Crowe then said that Sirhan may have said something about Kennedy, "...something like, 'Well, Walt, you know, Walter, if somebody should shoot that bastard'." Crowe became fearful police officers may have thought he had been responsible for instilling in Sirhan ideas which led him to kill Kennedy and was afraid investigators might ask him to what degree he had influenced Sirhan. However, LAPD officers thought Crowe had been "overly impressed" with the possibility he had any impact on Sirhan's state of mind. It appeared "improbable" to investigators.[389] After a polygraph was administered to Crowe, the police concluded:

Based on the available polygrams, the only sound conclusion that can be reached is that Sirhan made some statement to Crowe regarding his intent to kill Senator Kennedy. Whether or not this was a casual statement or a detailed discussion cannot be ascertained from the test... but that it was possible that Kennedy could have been mentioned…but definitely there was no mention by Sirhan about shooting Kennedy. He told Sirhan that the struggle inside Israel was going to be a long, long thing; that it was akin to a liberation struggle and would have to be resolved by war.[390]

In the pre-trial period Sirhan continued to insist he had acted on behalf of his fellow Palestinians, whilst at the same time insisting that he could not remember shooting Kennedy. He even felt that in killing the presidential candidate (which he said he "must have done"), he had "given a favor" to many people, including President Nixon. Robert Kaiser, a journalist who was given access to Sirhan in the pre-trial months, asked Sirhan what he thought of the presidential election and Nixon's triumph. "Nixon!" Sirhan said, "he's worse than Kennedy. To get the Jewish vote, he said he'd help the Israelis. But what good did it do him? Hell, he only got four percent of the Jewish vote.... hell, I gave it to him!"

During an interview with one of his lawyers, Sirhan repeated the claim he had "done Nixon a favor" and had "given the presidency to Nixon". To Sirhan that meant Nixon should therefore arrange his freedom, a passport to Jordan and $1m. He had the demands written out ready for his lawyer to use.[391] Sirhan also railed against the Democratic Party nominee Hubert Humphrey. The week before the Democratic Convention in Chicago, Sirhan told Robert Kaiser, "Hubert Humphrey, that chicken-faced son-of-a-bitch?" Sirhan had been upset with Humphrey because "...even after the assassination [of RFK] Humphrey said he would send bombers to Israel just to spite me! He said that just to spite me! Humphrey, you better have a million guards around you, because you're gonna get it, you goddamn bastard."[392]

Sirhan came to believe he was an important revolutionary—he was in the "vanguard of the Third World," as he expressed it. He said, "They [the Palestinians] want action. They want results. Hey! I produced action for them. I'm a big hero over there!" He told Robert Kaiser he believed Kennedy would be "like his brother and help the Arabs but... he fucked up. That's all he did.... He asked for it. He should have been smarter than that. You know, the Arabs had emotions. He knew how they felt about it. But, hell, he didn't have to come out right at the fucking time when the Arab-Israeli war erupted. Oh! I couldn't take it! I couldn't take it."[393]

Defense psychiatrist Seymour Pollack believed Sirhan expected to receive a sentence of a couple of years in prison for the murder. "It is the same kind of thinking that a black nationalist has who doesn't think he should get too much time for killing somebody in a racially justified situation," Pollack said. "He thought it was good to kill Senator Kennedy. He believed he was right...and that is not necessarily a delusion...He thought he would be looked up to and would be considered a hero...He believed he was doing what was not only right but should be done, a good thing."[394]

In the aftermath of the assassination, the US Justice Department reported that Arab American businessmen in Los Angeles were spreading a story that Sirhan was "a secret agent paid by the Zionists to blacken the name of the Arab world". It also reported that the Arab Higher Committee for Palestine in Beirut had instructed its New York office to offer "all possible assistance" to Sirhan. The committee's spokesman, former Grand Mufti of Jerusalem, Haj Amin el-Husseini, who visited Berlin during the Second World War and collaborated with Hitler, said it had instructed its New York representatives to legally defend Sirhan as far as United States law would permit. The committee was known in New York as the Palestine Arab Delegation.[395]

Henry Awad, the editor and publisher of the *Star News and Pictorial*, the largest Arab newspaper in America, said, "The Arab community wants this trial. We think it's the only way the US will hear about the Arab cause... Every single Arab in America regrets the killing, but the trial will bring us a chance for publicity." [396] The *New York Times* interviewed John Jabara, a celebrated spokesman for the Arab American community in the United States, who believed the trial of Sirhan would bring an "understanding of the Arab cause."[397] On June 10, *Al Anwar*, an Arab newspaper in Beirut, commented, "Regardless of everything, Sirhan's blood-stained bullets have carried Palestine into every American home. The act may be illegal, the price high and the assassination unethical. But American deafness to the cause of the Palestine people is also illegal, unethical and carries a high price."[398] A Beirut weekly magazine opened a defense fund for Sirhan and contributions flowed from every corner of the Arab world. Numerous newspaper reports in the Middle East spoke of Palestinian joy at the news of the shooting.[399]

Palestinian leaders glorified Sirhan. In April 1969 the Palestine Liberation Organization distributed several hundred thousand posters in Arab countries depicting Sirhan as a heroic Arab commando. A sample poster was front-page in a Beirut newspaper and carried a large picture of Sirhan, with a drawing of a Palestinian guerrilla with a rifle in front of him. Above the picture were the words, 'Sirhan Bishara Sirhan: A Commando, not an assassin'. [400]

TIME magazine was typical in how the American press portrayed the crime as the mindless act of a deranged individual, symptomatic of American society in general and a result of weak gun control laws.[401] *Newsweek* editorialized:

> ...but whether Sirhan is executed or locked away the trial itself has notably failed to explain, in any profound way, whatever meaning there may be behind the Kennedy assassination. Perhaps, as Albert Camus has pointed out, the only way to understand such maniacally absurd events is to see the absurd itself as all the answer there is.[402]

There were few media outlets in the United States that recognized the true nature of Sirhan's act. Those who pointed to Sirhan's pro-Palestine and anti-Israel motive were generally ignored by the mainstream media. There were exceptions. *The Jewish Observer* recognized that Robert Kennedy's assassination would leave a "deep scar on America's relations with the Arab world" and noted how the State Department played down Sirhan's Arab origins in order not to offend Arab states. They also observed that members of Congress were avoiding all reference to the Arab-Israeli conflict. Taking their cue from the State Department, politicians in Congress avoided fanning the flames and downplayed the Arab–Israeli connection to the crime. In fact, US Secretary of State William Rogers was anxious to avoid a trial which he believed would affect US relations with the Arab world. The press followed suit.[403]

According to academic Pamela Pennock, most leading Arab American organizations in the US sought to disassociate themselves from Sirhan, but "...a few activists seized on the opportunity to explain Sirhan's political passion to the public at the risk of alienating Americans even further from the Palestinian cause."[404]

Without any lead from the American government, US commentators speculated that there were psychoanalytic answers to the murder, or tried to link it with the suspicions surrounding the JFK assassination.

Pamela Pennock has written that most Arab Americans in the United States at the time of the assassination responded to Sirhan with silence, and quoted Arab American activists in Detroit as "never hearing anyone sympathising with Sirhan."[405] That was not the case, however, with Arab American residents in the Los Angeles area. Anti-Semitic feelings amongst the Arab community were prevalent in the years after the 1967 Arab–Israeli War.

Lou Shelby said that the clientele at his restaurant was composed of 70 percent non-Arabian individuals and 30 percent of individuals of 'Arabian descent'. The club and restaurant consisted of two rooms that were used by the patrons. According to Shelby, numerous fights that centred on political and religious affairs occurred in the upstairs room of the restaurant. Both Fez restaurant owners, Louis and Fred Shelby, were aware of a significant number of Arab patrons who celebrated the fact that an American politician had been gunned down.

Many customers at the Fez embraced anti-American as well as anti-Israeli sentiments. When two men, purportedly FBI agents investigating the Robert Kennedy assassination, visited the upstairs room of the restaurant in August 1968, patrons began to chant "FBI, FBI get out of here." The customers became so unruly that it was necessary for the owners to close the room for the rest of the evening.[406]

Phyliss Young began working as a cocktail waitress and part-time dancer at the Fez Club in August 1965 when Adel was working there as a musician. Adel often used to take Phyliss home for breakfast and they saw each other for social outings. She thought of Adel as a "kind and generous" man. A year after meeting Adel she was introduced to his brother Sirhan, who she remembered seeing in the club "two or three times", the last time being in April 1968.

Young said she was working at the Fez the night of the Robert Kennedy assassination. Mike Siam, the manager, and Sam, a bartender, were on duty that night and when they heard about the assassination, they "danced and sang". According to Phyllis, one of them said, "It's a great thing that Kennedy has been shot." She also said, "several of the individuals" were glad the "Jewish lover" had been shot. Many of the patrons were "Anti-American", Phyliss declared.

Phyliss Young was Jewish and in the two and a half years she had worked at the restaurant, there had always been a certain amount of friction between herself and the restaurant's Arab employees. She thought it was partly because she was Jewish and partly because she did not speak Arabic. She said she left the Fez after becoming tired of the comments and insults from some of the Arab patrons. The day after the Kennedy assassination, Young resigned her position because she was "... in fear of my life after what happened the night of the assassination."[407]

Elsa Marie Butler corroborated Young's story. Butler worked as a belly dancer at the Fez and said that many of the employees and customers had been "vociferous in their animosity towards Israel." Butler said on the night of June 4 she came to work at 8 pm and at around 1 am, customers entering the restaurant mentioned the shooting at the Ambassador Hotel and that Kennedy had been the victim. As the restaurant did not have a TV or radio, all the information about the shooting was provided by customers. When Butler finished her shift, she saw Siam was "... very elated about the news." Butler said he was clapping his hands and encouraging singing in Arabic. She could not understand the meaning but noted that the song ended with the Arabic word 'Yehudi', which means 'Jewish'. Siam spoke in English of how he was glad that the shooting had occurred and blamed the "Jewish people".

Butler realised Lou Shelby had not agreed with the sentiments of his customers and told her that Siam would not be returning as his manager. She did not return to work as she felt the "intense nationalism expressed by the customers and employees" made the atmosphere "most conducive to fights." [408]

Another employee confirmed Young's opinion the Fez patrons were "very nationalistic". She said the upper floor of the restaurant was a "very pro-nationalist environment" and several customers who were at the restaurant indicated they were "glad that the Jewish-Lover" [Robert Kennedy] was dead." She also said she sensed that amongst the many Arabs at the restaurant there was "the strong feeling of anti-Americanism."[409]

Joyce Cecelia Stone had become acquainted with the Sirhan family at the Fez. When Adel left the restaurant, he was replaced by Arab immigrant George Elias, who had previously worked at the Baghdad Café in San Francisco. According to Stone, the person who played the oud in the band was also the Master of Ceremonies as he controlled the microphone. During Adel's time at the Fez, Stone observed very little trouble amongst the patrons but by the fall of 1967, when Elias took over, the college students who frequented the Fez began to sing songs of an "Arabic political nature" and "fights broke out". Elias, she said, had problems in "handling the trouble". On one occasion Sirhan spoke to Stone and told her of his anger at the United States for assisting Israel in the 1967 war. Sirhan also told her that the

United States provided radio cover from United States ships for the benefit of Israel. It was the only comment Sirhan ever made to her of a political nature.[410]

The stories told by Young, Butler and Stone were corroborated by a source who did not want to be named, but his statement was recorded by the LAPD on June 6. In police memos he was referred to as 'C'. 'C' said he and his wife had gone to the Fez "some time ago" (before the assassination) to see "belly dancers". However, on arriving he discovered that "most of the night" was given over to the singing of "Arab nationalist" songs and of how the United States "should be punished and how the president, LBJ, should be punished." The informant said that even before a picture of Robert Kennedy's assassin had been released, he "knew he was an Arab".[411]

Zare Boujigian, a part-time waiter at the Fez and assistant to Lou Shelby, said he had numerous conversations with Sharif Sirhan prior to and after the assassination. He had been introduced to Sirhan through Adel. Sharif had talked about his frustration with Robert Kennedy and his policies, Boujigian said. On one occasion, Boujigian asked Sharif why Sirhan had shot Kennedy, and Sharif said that in his opinion his brother had become so agitated by Kennedy's pro-Israeli tendencies that he "took it upon himself to kill him". The assistant manager said Sharif had been "spending money freely" after the assassination. Boujigian also believed that because of Sharif's "free spending" ways at the Fez, the notion that the family were "in need of money" was not true. He said that a fund-raising dinner for the Sirhan family was held in Baces Hall, 1528 N. Vermont, Pasadena on Sunday, August 18 and that "All the money from this fund raising went to Mary Sirhan."[412]

At Sirhan's 1985 parole hearing, he stated, "… if you were to talk to any Arab who was in Los Angeles at the time in 1968 and 1967 during that Arab-Israeli War…he couldn't have felt any differently than I had...with the treatment of the Palestinian and Arab situation in this country."[413] Three of Sirhan's friends testified to Sirhan's claim that Arabs in Los Angeles reflected his strong views about Israel. Sirhan would occassionally meet Ali Ahmed Kalla, Jesse Karadsheh and Maroun Mansour at the racetrack. Kalla had at one time co-owned, with Jesse Karadsheh, Shakers Oasis Bar on Hollywood Boulevard, Los Angeles where Adel had once worked as a musician. Sirhan would occasionally accompany Adel, Kalla and Karadsheh for breakfast after Adel had finished work. Kalla told the FBI the men did not discuss politics as, "there was no point" as they all "thought much the same way" about the Middle East. Kalla said they all agreed that, "a great injustice had been done the Arabs by the formation of the State of Israel and all were bitter about the expropriation of their land and property....".*[414, 415]

After news of the assassination reached the West Bank, which was then controlled by Israel, 52-year-old Bishara Sirhan was living alone in a modest stone house in his Israeli-occupied village on a 'very small' retirement pension. He also earned income as a part-time agricultural worker. He had last seen his Sirhan in 1965 during his previous visit to the United States. "I am a religious man, I have been all my life," he said. "I am shocked beyond words. I had the news last night from the village mukhtar [elder] Faiz Ba'Ajis Muaddi. If my son did it, he deserves his fate… This is the blackest day of my life."[416] Bishara told a *LIFE* reporter that his son was a "religious boy, quiet and intelligent" whom he taught "true Christianity" and "raised...to love. Now I am against him." His aunt Nurrah, who also lived in Taybeh, said, "May Palestine cut off his hand."[417]

However, Bishara also told reporters that his son's trial would establish the fact that Palestinian Arabs had a legitimate cause: "A nation of our own, not Israeli, not Jordanian but Palestinian…he was a very good boy, a very studious boy. If he did this…it was because he was doing something for his country. We know he is a hero."[418]

---

* 31-year-old Merla Stephens and her sister 38-year-old Velda Hoffmeister told the LAPD they saw Kalla and Sirhan together in 1964 at the Terrace Gardens Bar in Pacoima, California, around seven or eight times in 1964 and early 1965. Both sisters told LAPD police officers Kalla had "trained" Sirhan to be an assassin and "hypnotised" him. Stephens said she came to that conclusion because of the way both men interacted and not because of anything they said. However, Stephens insisted Kalla had said, "I am training him right". She also said Kalla talked about assassinating leading US politicians.

Velda Hoffmeister was interviewed again by the LAPD on the 2nd August 1968. The LAPD officers said Velda described her memories of the Sirhan brothers as "vague" and she did not hear any conversations about "guns" or "assassinations". She could also not explain to officers her statement that Kalla was Sirhan's "trainer". Officer S. Bowles believed the sisters came forward to "bask in publicity". The sisters also make a number of other allegations which harm their credibility. Sirhan had apparently told Merla Stephens he, "was married and his wife lived in the Middle East".

Accordingly, the likely interpretation of the sisters' story, if true, is that Sirhan and Kalla were engaged in an effort to impress the young women by acting out a "hypnotised assassin" scenario. It was around this time that Sirhan had become enamoured with the subject. Additionally, it is unlikely a team of conspirators would announce, four years before the fact, their plans to commit an assassination, risking exposure by two strangers. However, this did not absolve the LAPD or the FBI who should have followed up on their interviews with Kalla.

At her home in Pasadena, Mary Sirhan said her son had killed Robert Kennedy because of his Arab nationalism. She said, "What he did, he did for his country."[419]

Over the following weeks Bishara would expand on his response to Robert Kennedy's assassination:

> I can say that I do not regret his death as Kennedy the American politician who attempted to gain the presidential election by his aggressive propaganda against the Arab people of Palestine... Kennedy was promising the Zionists to supply them with arms and aircraft...and thus provoked the sensitive feelings of Sirhan who had suffered so much from the Jews.... It is not fair to accuse my son without a full examination of Zionist atrocities against the Arabs – those atrocities which received the support and blessings of Robert Kennedy.[420]

Bishara Sirhan requested the Jordanian Bar Association for assistance in his son's trial and it chose four lawyers: Fouad Atallah, Ahmed Al Khahil, Mohamed Barada' h and Hassan Hawwa. However, the lawyers were discouraged in their efforts by the Jordanian government, who felt that they would cause a strain on the United States and Jordanian relationships.

The week after the assassination, Bishara visited Amman, Jordan, to draw funds from his bank account for his projected trip to Los Angeles to see his son; a trip that was later aborted. On arrival at the Hotel Continental, he held a press conference in which he appealed to Pope Paul VI and "the conscience of the world" to secure a fair trial for his son. He told newsmen that he regretted the death of "Kennedy the human being" but that the senator's "unbalanced" support of Israel in his presidential campaign statements "provoked the sensitive feelings of Sirhan who had suffered much from the Jews."[421]

Bishara told journalist Salah Abd as-Samad for an *Ad-Diffa* (Arab newspaper) article:

> The murder of Senator Kennedy saddened me because he was from the Kennedy family, but the picture [of him] has a second face...the political face. For the Senator was also an American politician, so on this I have a view to express... I believe that the imbalance in Senator Kennedy's speeches while electioneering for the Presidency was the primary cause of what happened. He was promising certain parties to supply them with arms and aircraft with full awareness of the consequences of that promise. Its consequences would be more displacement of children, more orphans and more widows. This, in addition to the degradation of and contempt for the Arabs in his speeches, a thing that made my son Sirhan

> feel insulted in that society where Senator Kennedy was speaking…this is what pushed my son to act as he did… [If Kennedy] merely called for peace in the Middle East, nothing would have happened.

Bishara said his son was a "fervent Arab in every drop of his blood" and went on to tell the journalist:

> I believe there are in the world people of free conscience. I believe world public opinion will be on my son's side because Sirhan was a model boy and did not commit his action except to prevent further tragedy and further displacement of children from their homes. Sirhan imagined that Senator Kennedy would add to those tragedies… For all that, I hope that people of conscience in the whole world will stand by my son... I only wish the Los Angeles Court, and the American people and members of the Kennedy family would imitate me.

When he was asked how members of the Kennedy family could "imitate him," Bishara replied, "In my toleration. My son Munir was killed in Jerusalem in 1945 after a car ran over him. But I pardoned the culprit and gave away...compensation, 300 diners...to mosques and churches..."[422]

Bishara dwelt at length on what he claimed were his son's "painful memories" of the 1948 Palestine war—memories, perhaps, of a cruel father who "once beat one of his sons until the boy was unconscious and chased away neighbors who sought to intervene."[423]

In a volte face of his original statements to the American media, Bishara said he still believed in his son's innocence, "despite the accusations", and said Sirhan's motives should be scrutinised to find out what "led him to such an act". To Bishara, his son's motives were "His love for his homeland and religion [which] must have overcome everything else and incited him to act." He said he did not support violence or political assassination, "But Kennedy was rash in his statements… The late Senator Kennedy was the man who lit the fuse on the mine inside my son Sirhan."[424]

Sirhan was considered a high-profile inmate and was housed at the Central Jail while security measures were being implemented at the Hall of Justice Jail, where he was held during the time of the trial. He spent four and a half months there. His secured cell area on the thirteenth floor of the Hall of Justice was self-contained. During his stay, Sirhan read books and newspapers, ate candy bars, and smoked cigars and Winston and Viceroy cigarettes. The Sheriff's Department deputy sheriffs were given a unique opportunity to observe the accused assassin, and they recorded his every movement and every conversation he had with them. His trial was held in the same building in a permanent courtroom on the eighth floor of the Hall of Justice.

When Sirhan's attorneys visited him each morning to discuss what was to take place in court that day, a deputy would sit outside the cell and the attorneys would sit in the cell with him. The deputy was close enough to hear everything that was discussed. Each day, his attorneys advised Sirhan on what to say during his appearances in court especially things not to mention and how to present himself.

Sirhan constantly asked the deputies many questions about how the press was reporting him including:

"What are the papers saying about me?"

"Is the press playing this thing up big?"

"Is the press still hot on my case?"

"What's in the headlines this morning?"

"I got my picture in the paper. What do you think of it?"

He also wanted to know if there were any TV cameras in the courtroom. One deputy wrote, "[Sirhan] appeared extremely anxious to know if he was still the subject of conversation amongst the public" and was "anxious about Middle East reaction to the assassination." [425]

To the sheriff's deputies, Sirhan was more forthcoming about the assassination than he was to the jury. The deputies recorded that he told Dr Bernard L. Diamond that he did not receive any help from anyone in shooting Robert Kennedy; that nobody told, suggested or paid him to kill Kennedy; that he did not meet a girl at the Ambassador Hotel (who would later figure in conspiracy stories as 'The Girl In The Polka Dot Dress' – *see Appendix*); and that he did not know her name or was assisted in any way to shoot Kennedy. Crucially, the Sheriff's logs clearly reveal Sirhan was more stridently committed to the Palestinian cause than he ever revealed to his lawyers or the court.[426]

During one visit, Mary told her son, "It's very difficult…for all of us. Everyone is very upset...you didn't think of me, before you did this, if you had you wouldn't have done it." She also told him to "face up" to what he had done.[427] It was revealed in the logs that during one of her earlier visits, on July 12, Sirhan had told her he had "acted alone." Following the visit, Mary made this known to FBI agents.[428] She also repeated what Sirhan had told her to one of her neighbors, Betty Wansink: "What [Sirhan] did he did alone".[429]

Particularly pertinent in the jail logs is the recorded admission by Sirhan that he was not sorry he had killed Kennedy[430] and a confession to Deputy I.B. Mills that, "I sure got myself into a hell of a fix."[431]

Deputy Paul Harman was the security deputy who was sitting right outside of Sirhan's cell when Sirhan's defense attorneys scheduled a psychiatrist, Dr Bernard Diamond, to examine the inmate in his cell. As this was taking place the psychiatrist pricked Sirhan's hands with needles, Harman wrote, and also led him through the assassination by hypnotising him.

During the hypnosis, the psychiatrist told Sirhan, "You're entering the Ambassador Hotel; what are you doing?" Sirhan said, "I'm looking for a place to hide where I can surprise Kennedy." The psychiatrist then asked, "Where did you go?" Sirhan: "I went in the kitchen."

"What are you doing in the kitchen?"

"I'm waiting."

"Kennedy's coming through the door; what are you doing now?" Sirhan: "I'm looking at him."

According to the logs, when Sirhan was told Kennedy was "coming at you" he brought his hand up as though he was drawing a gun from his waistband and pointing his arm as though he was firing it. Then he began rapidly pulling his finger back as though he was pulling the trigger over and over again. He continued to fire the make-believe gun even after it would have run out of ammo. Deputy Harman wrote that he was "stunned" at what he had just witnessed.[432]

Another Sirhan confession was recorded by Deputy B.E. Mitchell. Though Sirhan had willingly participated in a re-enaction of the assassination, he did not "believe in psychology or any of that bullshit. I make these people believe what I want them to believe."[433]

Bernard L. Diamond, a professor of law and psychiatry at the University of California was hired by Sirhan's lawyers to examine him. During his meetings with Diamond, Sirhan said that when he was mad, he did not "give a damn what happens." [434] During the same meeting with the psychiatrist, he said, "[Robert Kennedy] would have been a killer if he had been elected, he would have sent those fuckin' jets. I don't think I should be convicted at all." He told prosecution psychiatrist Dr Pollack that he felt he had committed an act that was criminal, but did not really feel it was criminal; he should be punished because he took the law into his own hands, but he should be punished for only a few years and then released. [435]

The day Sirhan was indicted he received a letter from an anti-Israel activist from New York City named John M. Lawrence. Lawrence wrote of how he believed Sirhan's motives were clear: "Our pro-Arab political organization extends our friendship to you in your time of trouble. We are proud of you personally for that part of the showing you made establishing you have great heart for the suffering Arab peoples in and about Palestine. We, of course, regret that in your political naivety, you foolishly used the method of assassination."[436] He referred to Sirhan alternately as a "Palestinian freedom fighter", a "moderate Christian Socialist" and an "anarchist".[437] Lawrence also compared Sirhan to the nineteenth-century anti-slavery activist John Browne.[438] There were no tears for Robert Kennedy amongst Arabs, he said, a man who he described as "the advocate of sending American jet bombers to Israel so Jews may kill more Arabs."[439]

Lawrence offered Sirhan assistance in promoting the cause of Palestinian nationalism. "We want you to know that in us...you will have loyal friends. We want to be in touch with you to be of all the help we can in your hard days ahead. To us you are a soldier in the cause of justice for the Arab people who in good faith made a bad judgment... Day by day the militancy of the Palestinian freedom fighters grows."[440] A subsequent letter included a money order for an unspecified amount.[441] The newsletters Lawrence sent to Sirhan included the phrases, "Remember Deir Yassin! Remember that Jewishism [*sic*] is Nazi barbarism!"[442]

Four days later, a friend of Lawrence's, Dr M.T. Mehdi, the 'Secretary-General' of the Action Committee on American-Arab Relations, issued a press release where he, like Lawrence, directly connected the killing of Robert Kennedy to US Middle East policy. The press release stated:

> Sirhan Sirhan is a Christian Palestinian refugee whose people have been either killed or expelled or subjugated by the Zionist Jews. It was morally wrong on the part of Senator Kennedy to submit to the pressure of the Zionist and promise sending fifty jet fighters to Israel so that more Israeli Jews might kill more of Sirhan's people and occupy more of Sirhan's home... Senator Kennedy is in a very real sense an indirect victim of Zionism.[443]

Sirhan replied to Lawrence with a telegram in which he wrote, "Respected Sirs: Grateful for $ [*sic*], enjoyed 'Insight.' Please send more issues. Anxious about Mideast reaction." The deputy in charge that day was asked by Sirhan, "Can the contents of this telegram be kept from the press?" The deputy assured him they would.[444]

Deputy T.I. Greene recorded a conversation he had with Sirhan in which the accused assassin asked him to "read something." It was an article about how Malcolm X was hailed as a great leader and mentioned how the Black Muslim leader had not experienced any discrimination during his trips to Arab countries. After reading the article, Greene said nothing. When Sirhan asked him what he thought of the Black Movement he told him, "I'm for it."

When Sirhan asked Greene what he thought about Malcolm X, Greene said he was a "great leader". "You damn right he was," Sirhan said. Greene said Sirhan appeared to be "even more pleased than before." Sirhan then handed Greene another article for him to read. "This one was about the Blacks in New York wearing the African costumes, etc. and mentioned identification," Greene wrote.

> I read it and sat it down on the bunk. He wanted to discuss the articles but I just smiled. He smiled also and said, 'I understand'. However, within a very short moment he asked, 'What do you think about Stokely Carmichael?' I told him that I knew Stokely. (I really don't). He lit up like a X-mas tree and asked several times, 'Personally, personally? [*sic*] To this I smiled and lowered my head. [445]

During discussions with his jailers about "life, death, hell and heaven," Sirhan asked Deputy Dyson, "Do you think I'll go to hell when I die? Wouldn't it be something if that son-of-a-bitch [RFK] were waiting for me?"[446]

Sirhan would frequently launch into 'monologues' about horse racing, horses, and jockeys and the racetracks he used to visit, and books he read which were "mostly Theosophy." One deputy reported that Sirhan "often [whistled] for periods up to half an hour." Sirhan told one deputy that all the deputies who guarded him were "going to be famous one day" and frequently engaged them in conversations about how the newspapers were going to report him that day.

Sirhan was also interested to know if there were "any female nurses on the same floor" of the Hall of Justice building. He told Deputy Mills he could not "... wait until tomorrow. There's this good-looking woman in the jury; boy, if she could talk like she looks—wow—you know... Yeah, and a special [smile] for that good-looking bitch...what I need, I sure as shit can't get it in here. Boy, oh boy what I couldn't do to that good-looking bitch." On January 16 he said he "heard her speak... and everything was fine until she indicated that her husband was a mortician. I could just see her getting f***** by her old man after he had been messing around with dead bodies," Sirhan said. Sirhan jokingly asked Deputy Mills if he should "...get [his lawyer] Cooper to ask the judge if I could have a girl—I sure could use one." [447]

Sirhan also joked about the trial, at one point saying that he was thinking about changing the venue to Tel Aviv and also changing his name to 'Sirhanstein.' He pointed to a map of Israel and said, "This we will take back."[448]

On January 25, 1969, Sirhan asked Deputy C.M. Foster who he had voted for in the presidential election. Foster replied that he was a "conservative-type." "You didn't like Kennedy...?" Sirhan asked. "Would you have voted [for] him if he had lived?" When Foster said "No," Sirhan replied, "I made a few people happy, then."

During the time he spent at the Hall of Justice, Sirhan met with writer Robert Blair Kaiser who had been hired as a defense investigator to allow him access to the assassin. Kaiser had many conversations with Sirhan, who knew he would be writing a book about the case. When Sirhan discovered the author had been talking about him on television and radio shows, he wrote to his lawyer, Grant Cooper:

> Hey Punk. Tell your friend Robert Kaiser to keep mouthing off about me like he has been doing on radio and television. If he gets his brains splattered, he will have asked for it like Bobby Kennedy did. Kennedy didn't scare me; don't think that you or Kaiser will: neither of you is beyond my reach. (A)nd if you don't believe me—just tell your ex-monk to show up on the news media again—I dare him. R.B.K.* must shut his trap or die.

As author Dan Moldea observed, "Sirhan's own words in this document appear to contradict the theory promoted by Sirhan's apologists that he was programmed to kill by persons unknown and then programmed to forget about it."[449]

Sirhan's trial had begun on January 5, 1969. Emile Zola Berman, a Jew, became one of Sirhan's lawyers and was praised for defending a Palestinian. However, he may well have been used by the defense team to remove the political aspects of the crime from being addressed. It was Berman who advocated Sirhan's defense be built around the plea of diminished capacity to prove that he had been mentally ill, but Sirhan protested this line of defense. Before the trial he told his

* Robert Blair Kaiser was acting as a defense investigator.

lawyers, "Have you ever heard the Arab side of the story?.... I mean on the TV, the radio, in the mass media? That's what bugs me! There's no Arab voice in America, and goddamn it, I'm gonna show 'em in that courtroom. I'm gonna really give 'em hell about it."[450]

The remaining members of Sirhan's defense team were comprised of three notable attorneys: Grant Cooper, Russell E. Parsons and Emil Zola Berman. Later, Russell Parsons brought pro-Palestinian activist and lawyer Abdeen Jabara on to the defense team. Issa Nakhleh, chief of the Palestinian Arab delegation to the United Nations, acted as a defense consultant. The prosecution consisted of lawyer David N. Fitts, Lynn D. Compton, and John Howard from the District Attorney's office.

It was undisputed that Sirhan fired the shot that killed Senator Kennedy. The evidence also established conclusively that he shot the other victims. Sirhan's lawyers decided that the best defense for their client was to prove he had been acting spontaneously and that it was the act of a deranged mind. Specifically, it was argued that because of one of any combination of the following abnormalities (intoxication, hypnotism schizophrenia-paranoid type, paranoia) were present when Sirhan shot Kennedy, he was unable to maturely and meaningfully pre-meditate and deliberate. Since premeditation and deliberation are one of the essential elements necessary to prove first-degree murder under California law, evidence of intent or state of mind in this regard was crucial.

Bernard L. Diamond stated that Sirhan was probably suffering from a condition known as 'diminished capacity' and believed he inadvertently exhibited this condition in court when he became violently upset at the mere mention of his childhood. During the trial Sirhan repeatedly voiced his political motives, but his lawyers went ahead with their trial strategy after the judge rejected a second-degree murder plea that would have saved Sirhan from the gas chamber.[451]

Sirhan strongly disagreed with his lawyers' decision to argue that he had been mentally ill when he shot Robert Kennedy, which accounts for why Sirhan became angry when his lawyers promoted it in court. Sirhan reacted this way because in Arab culture there is a great stigma attached to mental illness. In most Arab countries it is better to be a criminal than to admit insanity.

Twice during the course of the trial, Sirhan had to be restrained in the courtroom. His outbursts helped the defense in their plea of diminished capacity, but overall, it was damaging. Sirhan's first out - burst came as a result of the prosecution introducing his notebooks, which made reference to his "determination" to kill Senator Kennedy, into the court as evidence. Sirhan also disrupted the court twice saying that he would change his plea to guilty if the notebooks were introduced. He was so outraged at the possibility the world would witness his maniacal ramblings that he interrupted the court on February 27 to demand he be allowed to change his plea to guilty and to request his own execution. He said, "I want to withdraw my plea of not guilty and plead guilty to all counts as charged... I want to disassociate myself from my counsel... I killed Robert F. Kennedy wilfully and premeditatively and with twenty years malice aforethought..."[452] The judge denied the request, saying that this had to be proved in a court of law.

Sirhan's last outbreak in court came during the testimony of the prosecution's witness, Dr Seymour Pollack. Pollack said he believed Sirhan was lying when he took the stand and that he had lied during his psychiatric investigations. Pollack could not accept that Sirhan was unable to remember his notebooks or of shooting Kennedy. Sirhan leaped to his feet during Pollack's testimony and said he was not "going to let him call me a liar."[453]

When Sirhan was returned to his cell, he told his jailer, I.B. Mills, "It's not very many people my age who is considered a martyr by his people. You know, I am. What's more, with such strong feelings, I don't think I'll receive the death penalty...just think, I'll go down in history as a martyr and will always be remembered, at least by my countrymen."[454]

On April 17, the jury returned a guilty verdict. Some jurors later confessed they were confused about the psychiatric evidence, with one, Benjamin Glick, saying, "Not even the experts could get together among themselves." Another juror, Alberto Frederico, said, "All these psychiatrists! They really had us all stirred up. It was confusing."[455] At one point during the trial, jurors even administered the Rorschach Ink Blot Test that the defense experts used, with some finding they had responses similar to Sirhan's "paranoid reactions."[456]

After Sirhan was found guilty, his attorneys arranged a press conference where he said he was sorry for what he had done and that he felt sorry for the Kennedy family. When he returned to his cell, he told Deputy Harman, "I hope that's what the bastards wanted. I don't feel sorry for what I did; if I had it do over again I would do it exactly the way I did."[457]

During the penalty phase, Prosecutor John Howard demanded death for Sirhan. "In resolving the question of this defendant's guilt," he told the jury, "you have found him lacking in honesty, in integrity, and even in the courage of his own convictions. You could not have failed to see the smirk…when he declared 'I don't know who killed Senator Kennedy'."

On April 23, the jury passed sentence on the penalty that Sirhan should receive. He was condemned to the gas chamber after eleven hours and forty-five minutes of deliberations. Three years later, the sentence was converted to life imprisonment when the state of California banned the death penalty.

On May 23, 1969, Inspector Welch, Captain Carpenter and Senior Deputy Torcaso took Sirhan from his cell to Grand Street heliport, where he was put on board a helicopter and flown to Van Nuys and then escorted to San Quentin prison.

Following the assassination of Robert Kennedy, Saidallah continued to display his weak character and took every opportunity to cash in on the family connection. In fact, the whole family expected to benefit financially from the assassination, believing they would receive $100,000 from a deal which involved selling Sirhan's story to a major media outlet. Robert Kaiser asked Adel Sirhan why the Sirhan family would expect to make money just because Sirhan killed Senator Kennedy. Adel replied, "Look, as long as there is money to be made…"[458]

On July 3, 1968, in the early hours of the morning, Saidallah had reported to the Pasadena Police Department that he had been shot at while driving on the Pasadena Freeway. He gave an account of how he had been returning from Los Angeles when two vehicles had moved into position alongside him and that a man in one of the vehicles had fired two shots at his vehicle. During the follow-up investigation, several inconsistencies appeared in his account, including the reasons for his being in Los Angeles at that hour of the morning. A polygraph examination determined that Saidallah had been lying and it was proven by physical evidence. The shooting incident had been fabricated.[459]

The trial brought further problems for the family. On November 1, 1968, Saidallah visited his mother to ask for money. He said he knew she had received some funds from several Arab Church groups to help with Sirhan's defense. Mary Sirhan denied she had, but this did not prevent Saidallah from refusing to leave the house, even threatening to hit her if he did not receive his share of the alleged sums of money. When police officers were called, Mary refused to press charges of disturbing the peace and Saidallah left without further incident.[460]

During Sirhan's trial, Sharif, who had not spoken to his brother Sirhan in five years, had threatened Sirhan's lawyer Russell Parsons and defense investigator Michael McCowan. McCowan knocked Sharif unconscious after believing he had been tampering with his car. Sharif was angry because he believed the family had 'isolated' him.[461] Sharif had also caused trouble for the family by telling Sirhan's lawyers that, a few days before the assassination, Sirhan had told his brother Adel that he (Sirhan) would soon become famous. Adel denied this.[462]

Zareh Bouigian, assistant manager at the Fez club, said he had numerous conversations with Sharif prior to and after the assassination. During these conversations, Sharif had talked about his frustration with Robert Kennedy and his policies. On one occasion, Boujigian asked Sharif why Sirhan shot Kennedy, and Sharif answered that, in his opinion, "Sirhan had become so agitated by Kennedy's pro-Israeli tendencies that he took it upon himself to kill him."[463]

In 1973, Sharif was convicted in a federal court of writing a letter threatening Israeli Prime Minister Golda Meir.

10

SEEKING FREEDOM – SAN QUENTIN AND SOLEDAD

"I was young, Sir. I was young. I…I was, I was impetuous, maybe. I was a youthful offender. That's, that's what really comes in within that realm, my behavior and my attitudes, and all of that."
Sirhan Sirhan to Parole Presiding Commissioner Garcia

For the following fifty years of his life, Sirhan adopted a two-track approach in his quest for freedom. The first involved insisting that the crime he had committed was justified and that he had been acting as a hero to his fellow Palestinians. However, he knew that in seeking his freedom through the California parole system, he would have to show culpability and remorse. To those ends, he would claim he could not remember shooting Kennedy but accept the evidence that he "must have" done so. He also knew he would have to profess remorse for his act and claim he had sympathy for the Kennedy family.

The second track approach to his freedom included relying on his conspiracist defenders, including his lawyers, to promote the idea he was a 'hypnotised patsy' who had been controlled by others and thus bore no responsibility for Robert Kennedy's death. In other words, he was not guilty at all.

Sirhan's claim that he had no recollection of the assassination began shortly after his arrest. He admitted he did go to a shooting range earlier in the day of the assassination, and admitted he "must have shot Kennedy," even though he had no recollection of the event. However, during his trial, he had accepted culpability for the murder and it was only at a later date that he began to claim his admission of guilt was part of his defense lawyer's strategy to spare him from the death penalty rather than argue his innocence.

When his death sentence was commuted to life in prison in 1972 after the California Supreme Court invalidated all pending death sentences imposed in the state prior to that year, Sirhan began his life sentence. Since that time, Sirhan has had multiple parole hearings. California parole hearings are held every five years, although extra hearings may be held. Each hearing takes into account various factors, such as Sirhan's behavior in prison, his understanding of the crime, his rehabilitation efforts, and the opinion of the victim's family, among others.

However, Sirhan's claims he had undergone strenuous efforts to change his behavior had little effect with the parole boards. They repeatedly rejected his claims of remorse, concluding he had none and was devoid of any insight into the crime he had committed. Additionally, as the decades passed, Sirhan would change his position continually on the questions of actual guilt, moral guilt and whether or not he actually committed the murder.

During his decades-long parole hearings, Sirhan had support from Palestinians and Arab exiles living in the United States. M.T. Mehdi, then secretary-general of the Action Committee on American-Arab Relations and one of the earliest pro-Palestinian activists in the United States, believed that Sirhan had acted in justifiable self-defense, declaring, "Sirhan was defending himself against those 50 Phantom jets Kennedy was sending to Israel." He also wrote a 100-page book on the subject entitled *Kennedy and Sirhan: Why?* It was this relationship with Mehdi and Sirhan's insistence he acted as an avenger of Palestinians that would persuade nearly every parole board to conclude that Sirhan had not changed and was unsuitable for parole.

When Sirhan was found guilty and sentenced to death, he dismissed his attorneys and appointed Abdeen Jabara, a Long Beach attorney, and another appellate lawyer to handle his appeal. Jabara spent a career fighting for the civil rights of Arabs and Arab Americans.

Years later, in 2018, Jabara would say:

> My concern was to what extent Sirhan's and his family's experience in Palestine played a role in what happened. And if it played a role, it should be exposed; it shouldn't be swept under the rug for political expediency. So I went there to monitor the situation and to ascertain if Sirhan's defense was tailored in the best way to secure justice for him.

Jabara also said Sirhan was experiencing a severe mental condition at the time of the shooting, which was linked to the trauma he had experienced as a young boy in Jerusalem "and the tragedy that befell the entire Palestinian people." In 2018 Jabara said he could not be certain there was not some sort of conspiracy, but he had "little doubt Sirhan shot Kennedy. Sirhan never said there was somebody else," he said. [464]

Following his 1969 trial Sirhan was transferred to the Adjustment Centre at San Quentin State Prison to await appeals and his pending execution. Before he was transferred from his Hall of Justice cell Sirhan's attitude to the Sheriff's deputies changed considerably. For his remaining few months there before his transfer to San Quentin Prison he adopted a "belligerent tone" with his guardians and was, as one deputy wrote, "to say the least, difficult". Deputy Torcaso wrote, "he has quite often become boisterous in his use of profanities, with complete disrespect for the deputies assigned to this detail. He never addresses us in the proper way, often calling out our last names and sometimes by first names...everything has been done to appease this inmate...we have at all times been fair and courteous to him..." [465] Sirhan's time at San Quentin was also not without early behavioral problems. In 1970 he became upset and threatened a staff member.

In the coming months and years Sirhan would continue to show very little remorse for his crime. He became fixated on promoting the Palestinian cause and seeking his freedom through the parole system. He was also hopeful that his defenders in the media and his many lawyers would persuade the American public that he was an innocent 'patsy'.

Many people around the world identified Sirhan as a Palestinian terrorist. In 1970, when the Popular Front for the Liberation of Palestine (PFLP) hijacked three aeroplanes and landed them at Dawson's Field airstrip near Zarqa, it was believed that part of their demands for the release of the passengers included the release of Sirhan. After Sirhan's mother made arrangements to fly to Jordan to negotiate with the terrorists, she was denied permission to leave America by the US State Department to fly to Jordan. When Sirhan found out that his mother had been denied permission to leave, he became extremely upset. He "went wild and teargas was used to subdue him" according to San Quentin prison officials. Sirhan was eventually locked up in solitary confinement. An overwrought Mary Sirhan said, "I am a mother and I feel like any other mother... But...I believe in America. America is great and there is lot of justice in it. My son will be out with the justice of America!"[466] (It was later discovered that Sirhan's release was not part of the hijackers' demands.)

In 1972 Sirhan again threatened a staff member and on one occasion even threatened a hunger strike. He also became angry over security measures and sometimes came into conflict with other inmates. He said his problems were the product of his having been placed in an environment which "he could not at the time cope with." "The changeover of the inmates" he said, "there's always people—there are always people coming in and going out, so that really, it's like a revolving door for these people. And I have to adjust to different personalities, to different behavioral patterns with all the prisoners that come in and leave."[467] When Sirhan met the Parole Board psychologist who was responsible for evaluating him, he said he "really didn't want to commit homicide" when he shot Senator Kennedy, but merely wanted to "attract attention to the plight of his fellow countrymen."[468]

In March 1973, the characterization of Sirhan as a 'terrorist' was once again bolstered when Black September terrorists took ten hostages, including the US ambassador to the Sudan, Cleo A. Noel; the Deputy Chief of Mission, George Curtis Moore; the Saudi ambassador, Shaykh Abdullah al-Malhouk, along with his wife and children; and the Belgian and Jordanian charges d'affairs to Sudan.

At first, the militants demanded the release of some members of West Germany's Bader-Meinhoff extreme left terrorist gang as part of a prisoner exchange, which included Sirhan. Then they asked for the release of ninety Arabs being held by the Jordanian government, including Abu Daoud, who was said to have planned the 1972 Munich attacks. When President Nixon refused to negotiate, PLO leader Yasser Arafat ordered the gunmen to torture and kill their three Western hostages before they were captured by Sudanese authorities. Arafat took credit for these murders during a private dinner with Romanian president Nicolai Ceausescu two months later. The US government kept this attempt to free Sirhan and the subsequent murders of the three diplomats a secret for fear of creating an obstacle to any future diplomatic settlement of the Arab-Israeli conflict.[469]

This incident did little to help Sirhan with his legal efforts and his pleas for a new trial. As Stephen Flatlow observed:

> At least 144 American citizens have been murdered by Palestinian Arabs since the 1960s. Robert F. Kennedy was the first. Successive U.S. administrations have refused to demand that the Palestinian Authority hand over the killers for prosecution, and major news media outlets have consistently refused to treat it as a serious issue or even ask Palestinian

> spokesmen about it. That's because keeping Sirhan Sirhan and other Palestinian killers of Americans out of the spotlight is also a way to keep promoting the Palestinian cause.[470]

In 1974 Sirhan's attempts at freedom were further damaged when Bill Ayers and Bernardine Dohrn dedicated their communist manifesto *Prairie Fire: The Politics of Revolutionary Anti-Imperialism* to Sirhan (along with 200 others), hailing him as a courageous political prisoner.[471]

In April 1975 Sirhan once again threatened a San Quentin prison official with whom he was displeased. He wrote a letter to him which stated, "When I panic at the loss of my teeth, I want you to rest assured that I am going to kill every one of you sons of bitches. You are responsible for my continued torture and physical disadvantage. You are not all the gods you seem to think you are. You believe just like the lowliest convict under your tyranny."[472]

In another incident that year, Sirhan told his San Quentin guards that he was going to hurt them and could injure their brains. He afterwards said his remarks were purely an act of self-defense in which he was "verbally protecting himself." That same year, he was admitted to the prison hospital for twenty-one days for depression, which he said was his way of escaping "the other inmates." [473]

In May 1975 Sirhan was transferred to the State Correctional Training Facility at Soledad in Monterey County, California, a prison 120 miles south of San Francisco. Sirhan lived in Maximum B Protective Housing Unit No. 1, a two-story concrete building he shared with 124 other men. Sirhan did not have a job at Soledad, but he participated in Alcoholics Anonymous and served as the chairman of the program. From 1979 through 1984 he was involved in 'Project Soledad', which was run by Hartnell College. He took courses in art; life career planning; self-hypnosis; stress reduction; biofeedback; Tai-Chi and individual counselling sessions. He was held in Soledad from 1975 through 1992, when he was transferred to Corcoran State Prison.

Much of his time was passed in his 7 by 10-foot cell on the second floor. It had a bunk, a toilet and a washstand. There were no bars on the window, but it was covered with wire mesh. The door was solid and also had a wire mesh window. At fixed hours he went downstairs for meals in the dining hall or visited the exercise yard. At others, his cell door was open and he could mingle with other prisoners on the second floor. He used body building exercises to stay in shape and took extension courses gaining junior college credits in English and Math, although this ended around 1979, when he exhausted the prison's school offerings.

A British journalist, Paul Callan, visited Sirhan in 1978. During the interview in Sirhan's Soledad prison cell, the assassin once again admitted shooting Kennedy. Sirhan "...coiled his fingers around an imaginary .22 calibre revolver—and aimed it at my head," Callan wrote. "It was terrifying... I have never doubted that he was the man who took the senator's life." Callan also remembered that as they parted, Sirhan showed no real contrition and in apparent mitigation for his crime, he quoted Nietzsche: "One should guard against being spiritually disturbed after committing a great act." "A great act?" Callan thought, "The brutal murder of Robert Kennedy?"

Callan had also heard, in Sirhan's own words, the political motive for killing the senator. "I have a hazy memory of that day" Sirhan told him.

> ...I am deeply remorseful at having killed another human being. I have a deep hatred, in principle, of killing anyone...[but] I was not regretful about killing a man who was threatening me, my life, my country, my Palestine, my beloved homeland...What I did was a political act. I was the instrument...Some of that time was hazy. But I remember I was greatly agitated and in a highly nervous condition... Then I read in the *Los Angeles Times* that a Zionist organisation [he spat out the word 'Zionist,' Callan said] was planning to hold a victory march in the vicinity of the hotel where Kennedy was speaking. It was that march that compelled me to go down—my lovely Palestine was emotionally in my heart. Like most Arabs, I do not drink alcohol, so my body was not used to it. I remember returning unsteadily to my car to rest. I had to get my mind straight. I also had to go and get the gun because I was afraid the Jews would steal it.[474]

At his 1979 parole hearing, Sirhan told the board that he was drunk at the time of his crimes, saying, "I don't feel myself to be responsible beyond the first shot."[475] However, Sirhan's statement was refuted by Carmen Falzone, an inmate friend of Sirhan's at Soledad. Calzone said Sirhan had re-enacted the shooting to him and that he had:

> ...actually raised his hand and everything. He had a perfect memory, absolutely perfect at the time he was in the kitchen, at the time of the shooting, during the shooting. He told me that hypnosis or that mind blank thing that he claimed was just a game and that he was never hypnotized... Sirhan is saner than you or me. He told me he made up all that trance and hypnosis stuff... He told me the love for the Kennedys was declining, so now he wanted to make himself look more sympathetic in the media... I found out Sirhan was highly intelligent, one-directional,

> emotionless, and suspicious, the perfect terrorist… I asked Sirhan, 'If you were angry because the U.S. supported Israel, why didn't you kill the president, kill LBJ?' He started to tremble, those dark eyes popping, and he said, 'Don't you understand, I did kill the president. Kennedy would have been president. And if he was that pro-Israel when he wasn't president, imagine how he would be as president. So, I decided to change history.'[476]

In an interview Sirhan gave to M.T. Mehdi in September 1980, the assassin insisted he did indeed shoot Kennedy, who, he said, had "provoked" him. He said his anger over the anniversary of the 1967 Arab-Israeli War had triggered his actions the night he assassinated Kennedy. "You must remember the circumstances of that night, June 5," he said. "That was when I was provoked... That is when I initially went to observe the Jewish Zionist parade in celebration of the June 5, 1967, victory over the Arabs. That was the catalyst that triggered me on that night." Sirhan then added, "In addition, there was the consumption of the liquor, and I want the public to understand that…" In his book, *Kennedy and Sirhan,* Mehdi had contended that both Sirhan and Kennedy had been victims of 'Zionism' and in the interview Sirhan agreed. "We are, we are," he said. "He more than I as it turned out, unfortunately. I have nothing but respect and admiration for all the Kennedys, but except for that single moment when he said that he was going to send instruments of death and destruction against my people. I am not going to accept that, and never will I accept or acquiesce to it." [477]

Sirhan was visited every couple of months or so by his mother and his brothers, Adel and Munir, and all spoke with him regularly on the telephone. In 1982, on a visit by Adel and his mother, Mary Sirhan said, "It is a double tragedy for me. I'm a mother, I feel for people and I want people to feel with me. My son has had a tough life in there [prison]. I hope God will change our hearts to love one another." Adel and his mother often spoke to their son in Arabic during their visits. When speaking to the press about Sirhan, she became emotional at the alleged injustice metered out to her son, begging that people try to understand him as she did—as a sensitive boy who was scarred by war in their homeland.[478]

The same year Sirhan gave another prison interview to his friend M.T. Mehdi, who had remained a frequent prison visitor. Mehdi published articles in a publication entitled *Action Magazine.* He said Sirhan had received offers of refuge from Libya, Syria and Jordan and he chose Jordan to live in if he succeeded in gaining parole. It was "where his father lived," he said. Sirhan told Mehdi that he was "... really obsessed with the matter of the Palestinian people's rights. I don't think I'll ever settle, rest, have my inner feelings of peace as long as my own countrymen are being deprived." During the interview, Sirhan did not show any remorse for killing Robert Kennedy.[479]

In the published article of the interview Mehdi wrote: "I've previously made this statement to Sirhan in a question-and-answer session—'Sirhan Sirhan is legally guilty and Robert F. Kennedy is morally guilty'. Sirhan is legally responsible for the death of one person directly. Robert Kennedy is responsible indirectly for the death of thousands of Palestinians, Lebanese, Syrians." Sirhan "wholeheartedly agreed" with Mehdi.[480] Mehdi also told his readers that Sirhan may have been prepared to die in 1972, "but now he wants out. He's just tired of the whole thing." Commenting on the article, the UPI reported that Sirhan was still "absorbed in Mideast politics" and he "measured world leaders in relation to them... He has said he is sorry for Kennedy's widow and children. He has always stopped short of apology for the assassination."[481]

Sirhan's seventh parole hearing was held on February 10, 1982. Once again, he repeated his belief that if "Robert Kennedy were alive today," he would not "countenance singling me out for this kind of treatment." Sirhan added, "I think he would be among the first to say that, however horrible the deed I committed 14 years ago...it should not be the cause for denying me equal treatment under the laws of this country." His parole was denied and the board cited the severity of the crime and concerns about his potential for future violence as reasons for the denial.[482] Sirhan's eighth parole hearing was on March 21, 1984. Again, his parole was denied due to the gravity of the crime and concerns regarding public safety.

In 1975 the California state legislature had moved to introduce fixed sentences and give those on indeterminate life sentences 'a date certain' for their release. Although Sirhan had earlier been given a parole date of February 23, 1986, in 1982 the District Attorney, John Van de Kamp, petitioned the Board of Prison Terms to consider rescinding it. The request was granted. Van de Kamp said, "The message must be sent out in clear and unmistakable terms that political assassination will not be tolerated in this society—and those who engage in it must pay the price."[483]

At his 1985 parole hearing, Sirhan admitted to writing the incriminating entries in his journals that had been found by police in his bedroom after his arrest. Since his trial, he had always stated he had no memory of the entries. But Sirhan had already confessed at the time of his trial that he could remember them. When asked by prosecutor Lynn Compton if he was "charged up, you were mad, and you were writing something down about eliminating or killing him, right?" Sirhan answered, "At the time, yes."[484]

At the same 1985 parole hearing, Sirhan stated that "liquor [was] the main culprit" for his crime. Sirhan also introduced his belief that a Jewish cabal in the United States was preventing his release. He told the parole board:

> ...this is what it is...I want to look out for Sirhan now rather than look out for others... I'm not interested in being a trouble-maker anymore... I feel that punishment was due in this case. But not to the degree that it has been meted out so far. That was my impression from what I've read in some of the (Board's) decisions. That you're holding my political opinions against me...as grounds to deny me parole or some grounds to agitate against me...there is a tremendous Jewish interest in this country and I don't know how influential they are...in persuading you to work against me. And a I feel it was political... Robert Kennedy was a political martyr and all his, you know, supporters are agitating against me, too.

When Sirhan was asked if he considered himself to be a political prisoner, he replied, "In the sense that you are holding my political opinions as a point...to retain me in prison, I would say that."

During the hearing, he finally confessed he had written about killing US Ambassador Goldberg in his diary. It was yet another contradiction of his long-held excuse that he could not remember the writings in his notebooks, in which he ranted about killing Robert Kennedy, as well as others he had a grievance against. Presiding Board Member Castro told Sirhan the threat was "...found in your diary" and asked him, "Do you know how it got in your diary?" Sirhan replied, "Well, I wish I had never written it. In all honesty."

Sirhan continued to insist he had suffered 'diminished capacity' when he committed his crime, even though he had originally raged against his lawyers' defense that he was suffering from a mental illness during his trial. He compared himself to another assassin, Dan White, who murdered San Francisco Mayor George Moscone and Supervisor Harvey Milk. White had been released after five years' imprisonment and Sirhan suggested he be given the same leniency. His state of mind was "...not up to par to the standards required for a first-degree murder," he pleaded. As deliberation, premeditation and malice aforethought had to be established, he argued, he did not have the mental wherewithal to legal requirements to really be convicted of first-degree murder. Sirhan repeated he had the thoughts which were chronicled in his notebooks, "but I just cannot in all sincerity remember [them]. I don't really remember that far back—my emotional feelings and I don't exactly recall them at the moment." Perhaps disingenuously, Sirhan claimed there was a 'filmstrip' showing that he was "not responsible for more than one shot." No such filmstrip exists.

After arguing his innocence Sirhan decided he would provide the parole board with yet another reason why he had killed Kennedy but, on this occasion, he was met with the same disbelief amongst parole board members he had been faced with during previous hearings. Sirhan's weak excuse this time was, "I had nothing else to do, you know, to occupy my mind at the time to, you know...to do anything, you know, constructive—and—it just happened."

At the close of the hearing, Commissioner Rudolph Castro called the 1968 assassination "an attack on the democratic system of government [which] with three shots disenfranchised millions of people. Sirhan still does not accept the enormity of his crime..." and his appeal was dismissed.[485]

During his time at Soledad, Sirhan had positive remarks made about him by prison staff concerning his relationships with staff and other inmates. The staff also recorded that Sirhan had participated in education programs, as well as 'Project Soledad'. However, a remark he made to the 1986 parole board clearly showed he had a lack of self-awareness. His very telling response to a question put to him by a board member revealed his narcissistic personality. He said he truly wished that his murder of Robert Kennedy "hadn't happened... Not so much for Kennedy's sake, but for my own." The board concluded, "It seems to me that there has never been any change in Sirhan's attitude towards these offences."[486]

During the time he spent at San Quentin and Soledad, Sirhan had been reported for a number of "infringements of rules," including a threatened hunger strike; anger over security measures; disrespect; and threatening comments. These "problem areas of the past" had diminished by 1984, but he was told that "when subjected to stress in the institution, emotionally it would get to you, and you have had some outbursts wherein staff was threatened one or two occasions maybe an inmate. These threats have never been carried out. There's never been any violence." The closest Sirhan ever got to violence was when he grabbed a prison officer's nameplate so he could turn it over and read his name. Nevertheless, it was acknowledged by the board that the incident was only "remotely related to violence."[487]

In 1985, in a series of interviews he held with the *Los Angeles Times'* Bill Farr, Sirhan once again lied about not knowing Robert Kennedy would be at the Ambassador Hotel on the night of the assassination. He took responsibility for the assassination and said there was no conspiracy but insisted that he did not even know that Kennedy was going to be at the Ambassador. "They claim I was lying in wait. How could that be? I did not know what way he was coming out. In fact, only a last-minute decision by a Secret Service man prompted Kennedy to leave through the kitchen." Sirhan's preposterous claim is, however, contradicted by trial witnesses Enrique Rabago, Humphrey Cordeo, Jesus Perez and Martin Patrusky.[488]

By 1986 Sirhan had only two disciplinary reports: the 1972 incident, when he had "become upset and threatened a staff member" and a second incident when Sirhan complained of being "depressed" with "an element of suicidal ideation" and prison staff had attempted to take a sharpened mirror away from him, which he finally handed over.

During Sirhan's 1986 parole hearing, he repeatedly indicated his intense dislike for the parole board and for all American jurisprudence and the criminal justice system. He believed he had been treated unfairly throughout the entire process: at the trial, in his sentence, in his parole granting, and, of course, in its denial of parole. The parole board said Sirhan showed a lack of appreciation for the enormity of his offense and that his claim of amnesia was "preposterous." The State Board of Parole Hearings spokesman, Tip Kindel, said Sirhan was, "...very hostile He hates Americans... He continues to pose a risk to public safety."[489]

At his 1987 parole hearing, Sirhan admitted he had shot Senator Kennedy, but denied shooting the other victims. He said that he committed the crimes in retaliation for Senator Kennedy's statements of support for the United States' military aid to Israel. Throughout his parole hearings, Sirhan could not provide a credible show of remorse as he claimed not to remember shooting Kennedy. During the hearing he equated his memory problem with President Reagan's. "You know, President Reagan has a problem with his memory," he said. "...Just remember some things that he hadn't done three or four months [before], never mind having to put for something that he [made] some decision or some action that he made nineteen or twenty years ago." He told the board that he suspected he had blocked the shooting from his memory for his self-preservation.[490]

These actions did nothing to advance Sirhan's relationships with future parole board members, while his interview to a foreign journalist in November1988 and his previous complaints about the parole boards did not go unnoticed during his next hearing in 1989. The board brought up the issue of terrorism, citing an investigation about an interview he had given to Nadeem Nasser, who was a personal acquaintance of Sirhan and his family. Sirhan had made known his desire to be forcibly removed from prison by "foreign terrorists" and had expanded on that idea in his interview. He said that terrorism could create political pressure on his behalf and gave examples of how this would occur, including help from Arab countries, "who were going to have to remedy the injustice" of his continued imprisonment. Sirhan was quoted as saying that he was very much disillusioned by the American justice system because he was not being treated in the same manner as someone else who may have committed first-degree murder. He said he was "being treated this way because of his Palestinian heritage and would seek…action on his behalf." Sirhan also said that would include "any terrorist group which would aid in his release from prison and help him get out of the United States."

During the Nasser interview, Sirhan said he had been forced to resort to "other means" as his only resource in seeking his freedom. According to a staff member who monitored the interview, Sirhan expressed his lack of faith in the American system of justice and said he would seek others to take action on his behalf, including any terrorist group which would aid in his release and help him escape from prison. In mitigation, Sirhan said he had been "pushed to the breaking point by the [Parole] Board's actions," meaning the board had not previously sanctioned his release.

The California state investigation of the interview also disclosed that on at least two occasions Sirhan had expressed his desire to receive aid to gain his freedom. Additionally, during an interview with his Correctional Counsellor at the time, Sirhan indicated that he "was ready to resort to other means to gain his release and clarified the statement by explaining that terrorists in Arab countries could play a role by applying political pressure on his behalf."[491]

During the 1989 parole hearing, Sirhan, knowing he would have to give the parole board members some kind of credible answer as to why he assassinated Senator Kennedy, struggled with his responses. He claimed he was "drunk" on the night he assassinated Robert Kennedy.

> I don't know what my capacity is, but…how much I can drink and…I get high and then start drinking, again…when a party, whenever. But I don't really know how much I can drink, but I know now, that I drank too much and should never have gone that night… two or three times before that I drank was…when I went to pick up my

> brother, who works in a nightclub at the time and then I just sat there waiting for him and then I kept sipping that stuff. That's how I got introduced to Tom Collinses. And that's easy because it doesn't have all that...foul taste and smell of cutty sark-type liquors, because I remember smelling the Cutty Sark and I don't like it. And that's why he recommended the Tom Collins, because it was easy to drink; it was like lemonade.

As usual, Sirhan attempted to show some remorse:

> I already said I'm very sorry, I'm very remorseful. Life was taken...after 21 years I have come to think about it, in terms of my own problems and my family's problems concerning their support of me while I'm in prison. And more than this...[I] became quite convinced that my act, was very wrong, morally and...towards Robert Kennedy and express remorse for his family... I realize the mistake of it and I wish from the bottom of my heart...that this crime is [a] horrible offense...

But he then launched into his mea culpa, saying:

> You know, a lot of people seem to ignore or not be knowledgeable that Robert Kennedy was my hero...and he was my choice for president in '68 and his support for Israel at the time, money sent them, 50 Phantom jet bombers, to drop arms and rain death and destruction on my countrymen. That was nightmarish to me too. In fact, those 50 war planes were nuclear capable that Israel received and the same ones that Bobby Kennedy was talking about. And it made me wonder, makes me still wonder, what did Israel need planes designed to carry and to deliver and drop nuclear bombs in 1968? After Israel had vanquished and annihilated five Arab Armies and Air Forces, you know, that's what really bothered me. I'm a human [being].[492]

When challenged by the board about the statements he made in 1988 regarding his willing acceptance of aid in securing his freedom, including from terrorist groups, Sirhan said it was because he was "angry and frustrated and, really, I tell you, I felt tremendous feelings of rejection by the Parole Board... I mean any other lifer...because you, I sense that, you know, you're nit-picking at, you know, rehashing this whole pot of stew, you know, all over again, every time I come up here. You know, when is this case going to be put to rest? And I, pray that it does..." Sirhan added that he would "never identify any of fellow Palestinians as terrorists... I would never call them as terrorists...even though their deeds might be violent... I would view them more as nationalists, trying to liberate and regain and to return to their homeland, just like I would want to do."[493]

Board Commissioner Maureen O'Connell responded to his remarks by asking him if he would refuse to call any Arab a terrorist. "That's what you, in the west would call those people," Sirhan said, "and maybe rightly so, but as an Arab, I don't think that I would...call them, would label them, as terrorists... I would call them my Palestinian countrymen, but I would also, at the same time, condemn their violent acts."[494]

The same year, 1989, in a television interview he gave to David Frost, Sirhan repeated his claim of acting in defense of his 'people' when he murdered Robert Kennedy, who, he said, was a consistent supporter of Israel. Sirhan said it "infuriated" him. "My only connection with Robert Kennedy was his sole support of Israel and his deliberate attempt to send those fifty bombers to Israel to obviously do harm to the Palestinians."[495]

During his 1989 hearing, Sirhan was asked about the remarks his fellow inmate Carmen Falzone had made about him in 1979. "You remember that?" the chair of the 1989 Parole Board asked. Sirhan replied, "You know, that this inmate was a paid, I believe, informant for the LAPD and District Attorney's Office."

In 1985 Sirhan had mentioned the case of Armenian terrorists who were shown leniency. During the 1989 hearings he again sought to link the case with his own. He spoke of how he had been unfairly treated in comparison with other terrorists and once again cited the case of Armenian terrorists who committed murder. Sirhan was referring to the case of Gourgen M. Yanikian, who had killed two Turkish consul officials, Mehmet Baydar, the Turkish Consul and another official, Bahadir Demir, in Santa Barbara in 1973. Yanikian served ten and a half years. Sirhan said that Yanikian:

> ...served only some 10 years of his sentence and was paroled after that and in given his social, unstable social history and background and the horrors and strife of his youth and witnessing killings and massacre of Armenians in Armenia and Turkey, you people have seemed to have neglected or overlooked his, you know, ugly young life. And yet you would highlight mine as a factor of aggravation and negativity, huh? And then right is wrong.

During the hearing he frequently clashed with board members. When he was accused by one member of acting as a 'loner' in the prison system, Sirhan said he did not want to associate with other inmates "too much" because,

> ...the living style is the living process and in prison just sort of forces the idea of [being a loner]. If you don't want to mix with child molesters or rapists or, you know, defilers or whatever... that's my choice to, to do that. What would be better, [Presiding Board Chairwoman] Ms O'Connell, for me to spend a couple hours in my cell listening to classical music or to... one of my favorite reading programs, or to be out on the tier slamming dominos on a table, making noise and hollering about the score that I'm making or playing cards, which I don't even know how to do. Because I don't see any benefit to me from doing that.

Once again, the board rejected his parole pleas, citing his refusal to accept full responsibility for his acts. One of the ways Sirhan did this, the parole board concluded, was by denial. They cited his frequent claims of, "I didn't know what I was doing. I don't remember what I was doing." The board chairman also cited Sirhan's interview with David Frost about the "fighting in the Middle East" and of how he likened his crime to killing Hitler. "Of course, it's an absurd illusion," the chairman said.

> Sirhan is an angry man, he's angry obviously with this board. He is angry with the American system of justice. He is angry with the situation that he finds himself in. Then on November 3rd, 1988, we hear reference of the interview by the British journalist Nadeem Nasser, where he speaks of being disillusioned with the American System of Justice, purports or reports that he's not being treated like other first-degree murderers, he's being discriminated against because he's a Palestinian. And [he] states that if he is denied parole this time, he would seek others to take action on his behalf, including any terrorist group, which would aid in his release from prison and help get him out of prison.[496]

The following year Sirhan again repeatedly claimed he had been kept in prison because the parole board had treated him differently from others. Sirhan once again mentioned the Armenian terrorist case and added that he was treated differently from other murderers, again referring to Dan White. On this occasion Sirhan described his purported amnesia after he shot Robert Kennedy as a "...fugue state." "There was some liquor," he said, "but [I'm] not trying to mitigate or excuse my action, I take full responsibility for it, but I can't honestly say...that I had full composure of my mental abilities at the time. If I did, I assure you, we wouldn't be sitting here right now."

In 1990 parole board members were informed that Sirhan had been given support for his release from the mayors of Bethlehem and Nazareth and "about 80 percent" of the "respected leaders" in

Jerusalem and the West Bank. The board members also heard how Sirhan had worked as a tier tender in Death Row and other institutions, had served food, mopped floors and cleaned toilets. "I've done sone of the lowliest jobs and I've got excellent reports on them," he said. "... Some of these assignments are menial, let me tell you." He told the board he wanted to "bury a bad memory [of his crime] and go on with life. To relive it is to open up old wounds and it's not really wholesome or healthy." He said he avoided confrontation because he had "all the fire" burned out of him.[497]

The 1990 board concluded that Sirhan continued to see himself as a political prisoner. Members rejected his excuse on national television that he acted as a Jewish person would act if given the opportunity to assassinate Hitler. The board also concluded his proclaimed 'protector of all Arab people' was the basis for their refusal to release him. Additionally, the board said that Sirhan had "periodic explosive outbursts when he is frustrated or feels threatened" and that although he was "very self-defacing, an element of narcissism" kept arising. "A continued degree of obsessive-compulsive thinking is noted," the board concluded.[498]

Sirhan had spent nearly twenty years in Soledad prison before being moved to the California State Prison in Corcoran, near Fresno. It was at Corcoran, where his prison mates included notorious killer Charles Manson and serial murderers Patrick Kearney and Juan Valejo Corona, that Sirhan's quest for freedom saw a new approach. He would now enjoin with his conspiracy-minded defenders to argue that it was someone else who had fired the fatal shot that killed Robert Kennedy, and that he was not guilty at all.

11

SEEKING FREEDOM – CORCORAN AND RICHARD J. DONOVAN PRISONS

"I would not want to take the blame for this crime as long as there is exculpatory evidence that I didn't do the crime." Sirhan Sirhan's admission to investigative journalist Dan Moldea in 1993

"This case may be the final chapter in an American tragedy." Beverly Reid O' Connell, District Judge, May 1, 2015

From 1992 through 2009, Sirhan was confined at the California State Prison in Corcoran, in the San Joaquin Valley, near Fresno, California. On arriving at the prison, Sirhan was immediately provided with work. In June 1992 he was assigned as a clerk typist. In January the following year he joined the yard crew and then in March was the 'third watch porter'. In July 1994, Sirhan joined the 'food tram' and the 'food cart', but decided he did not like the work. "I just couldn't—couldn't tolerate the work," he said. "There was too much…too violent. Typing Incident Reports, stabbings, woundings, cell extractions. And…every time I go to my cell after my work assignment, I never felt good about it. Because there was nothing positive…that I can think of, having done that day because of the negative reports that were involved…in my job."[499]

In 1992 a prison counsellor report stated, "If Sirhan does not like the rules of society in which he resides, voluntarily or otherwise, then he will live by his own rules." The counsellor described Sirhan's "difficulty in accepting authority and following directions" that he considered "foolish and unnecessary."[500]

From 1994 through 2005 Sirhan was represented by attorney Lawrence Teeter. Since 1994 he had been attempting to persuade state and federal courts to overturn Sirhan's conviction, arguing his client was hypnotized and framed like the assassin in the fictional film *The Manchurian Candidate*. The assassination was the result of a government conspiracy, Teeter argued. Sirhan was in the wrong position and too far away to have fired the bullets that killed Kennedy and that, although Sirhan did fire a gun that night, he did so in a hypnotic trance, induced either by the CIA or 'the military industrial complex'. Teeter also argued that Sirhan's lawyer, Grant Cooper, was compromised by a conflict of interest and was, consequently, grossly negligent in defense of his client. Teeter's team of defense lawyers moved for a new trial amid claims of setups, police bungles, hypnotism, brainwashing, blackmail and government conspiracies. All of Teeter's claims were rejected by the California courts. He died in 2005, and Sirhan declined other counsel to replace him.

Dan Moldea, who had spent years investigating the assassination, interviewed Sirhan three times for his book about the murder. *The Killing of Robert Kennedy – Means, Motive and Opportunity*, was published in 1995 to the acclaim of the *New York Times* and *Newsweek* magazine, as well as a host of other critics who praised his book. During his interviews Moldea asked Sirhan if he had been a participant in a conspiracy. Sirhan replied, "Do you think I would conceal anything about someone else's involvement and face the gas chamber in the most literal sense? I have no knowledge of a conspiracy." Sirhan admitted to Moldea that his "defense attorneys developed the idea of the 'Manchurian Candidate' theory."[501]

Moldea said that until Teeter was hired as Sirhan's defense attorney, Sirhan never mentioned CIA brainwashing schemes and "just claimed he was drunk and couldn't remember that night... Now he's saying he didn't do it, but he was heavily influenced by Teeter, who believed that the CIA was responsible for anything that went wrong in society and was a real conspiracy buff." The connection between Sirhan and the CIA "was complete bullshit," Moldea said. Sirhan had:

> Acted on his own accord out of a desire for fame and anger over Kennedy's support for Israel against Palestine... Sirhan was a kid, an average guy who was 24 and the same age as Lee Harvey Oswald. He was checking out girls that day at Pasadena City College, and before that was even practicing firing his weapon at a firing range. He went to the Ambassador because there were three different election-night parties there, had several Tom Collinses when he got there, and it was hot and he got drunk.

Moldea added, "Sirhan Sirhan shot Bobby Kennedy and he acted alone. When a civilian investigator is looking for a conspiracy in a highly publicized case like this, he's probably gonna find it, but you have to run through the gauntlet of re-examining the evidence and in this case, all of the large questions that would indicate a second gunman at the crime scene go by the wayside."[502]

At Sirhan's tenth parole hearing on June 18, 1997, Sirhan insisted he had not committed the crimes and was innocent. The parole board head called Sirhan's denials of guilt "preposterous", and he was denied parole for the tenth time. The commissioner afterwards said:

> You can imagine my surprise when I picked up the psychological evaluation for this particular hearing and also the departmental evaluation prepared by the correctional counsellors in which Mr Sirhan told the psychiatrist or the psychologist and to the correctional counsellor that he considers himself innocent of these offenses. If I was surprised by reading those words in these reports, I was shocked today when I heard the words that this is nothing more than an out-and-out frame-up by the district attorney's office. Mr Sirhan has never come to grips with the enormity of this offense. He has never come to grips with his own responsibility for this offense. He has never unequivocally acknowledged responsibility and accepted responsibility, and he has never in a really heartfelt manner expressed remorse for these particular offenses. It is shocking to me that he can stand here after all these years, or sit in here after all these years, and deny that he's guilty of these offenses in the face of what I consider to be overwhelming evidence.[503]

A psychiatric report, dated January 31, 2001, was looked upon as unfavorable to Sirhan's chances for parole release because the examining doctors Julie Olson and Greg Hirokawa indicated he had a personality disorder with paranoid and narcissistic features, "based on his demonstration of withdrawn behavior due to his mistrust of others, a lack of intimate contact with others, a lack of empathy for his commitment offense [and] grandiose sense of self-importance, shallow affect..."[504]

In 2001, during a parole 'forensic evaluation', Sirhan said he felt distant from responsibility and guilt and that he doubted he had committed the crimes. At the hearing, Lawrence Teeter said, "Mr Sirhan is quoted as saying that he had an anti-Israeli and a pro-Palestinian motive for this go back to a time when, well, in order to understand those references, we have to remember that, under hypnosis, Sirhan was told by the prosecution psychiatrist, it's because of the Jews, isn't it? In other words, that motive was put in there through hypnotic implantation." That statement is in direct contradiction to the numerous friends, relatives and acquittances who testified to Sirhan's virulent anti-Semitism.[505]

After 9/11 Sirhan was bizarrely accused of some connection to the suicide bombers because he had suddenly shaved his head and wore a towel around it around the time of the attacks. Sirhan had also obtained a TV, having shown no interest in television previously. Sirhan's brother Munir said the towel was solely to keep him warm, while the TV was an entirely coincidental gift from a departing prisoner.[506] Sirhan did not appear at his 2003 parole hearing.

At his 2006 hearing a prison counsellor's report dated March 13 was introduced. The report quoted Sirhan as saying, "I don't want to live in this country. I want to go; I want out of this country. I want to be deported to Palestine of any Arab country that will take me." [507]

Sirhan said he felt traumatized by the assassination every time he thought about it. "But I cannot remember the...shooting," he said. "I have said many times before that I do not remember any details of the actual shooting of Mr Kennedy, may he rest in peace. All I can say now about the shooting is that my part in it cannot be undone. So, I'm stuck with this." Contradicting himself, he also said he did indeed remember the shooting, but it was

> Vague, vaguely right now, but you know...so much time has elapsed that I...just don't think about that anymore. No politics. I'm not interested in all that. Just as, just as an aside, I have a brother who is nearly blind, my surviving brother. I'm so concerned about his welfare and his, and his ability to live, you know, uh, safely. That, uh, that is all what occupies my consciousness right now. I want to go home and be a helper to him...and I'm very sorry that it took place.

Sirhan then claimed he was only "partly" responsible for the shooting.[508]

In October 2009, ostensibly for his safety, Sirhan was transferred to Pleasant Valley State Prison in Coalinga, California, 200 miles northwest of downtown Los Angeles. He was housed in a cell by himself before being subsequently returned to Corcoran. The following year, continuing on his 'two-track' approach to securing his freedom, Sirhan told Dr Carrera that he was responsible for shooting two bullets, but as he had been grappled by the maître d', who deflected his shooting towards Kennedy, it precluded him firing the fatal shot at Kennedy himself.[509]

Following Lawrence Teeter's death in 2005, Sirhan did not have an attorney for some time. However, in 2011 he appointed a new defense team of William Pepper and Laurie Dusek and they represented him at his March 2011 parole hearing. When Parole Commissioner Mike Prizmich questioned him about his reading of the *Koran,* he said he used it to 'keep up' his Arabic but claimed he had been a practicing Christian all his life. It was a lie that ignored the overwhelming evidence, presented in this book, that at the time of the assassination he was a committed atheist. Sirhan continued to repeat his decades-long mea culpa that he could not remember shooting Kennedy. He said he continued to have no memory of the assassination nor of any details of the shooting which he gave at his 1969 trial, nor did he acknowledge his confession at the trial.

William Pepper repeatedly tried to claim that Sirhan had been a 'hypno-programmed' patsy in the Robert Kennedy shooting and his memory of being programmed was 'wiped' by unknown conspirators who were purportedly behind the assassination. He told the commissioners he hired Dr Daniel Brown of Harvard Medical School to spend more than sixty hours with Sirhan to recover his memory of both the shooting by placing him in a hypnotic state. Brown's attempts, Pepper said, were without apparent success. However, during the hearing Sirhan accepted that he did commit the crime because of his "state of mind at the time". He said he had "consumed some four glasses of Tom Collins. And I'm not a drinker. So, the Tom Collins to me was pretty much like a Kool-Aid or lemonade, because it was easy to guzzle it." He also dismissed the seriousness of the suffering of his other Ambassador Hotel pantry victims by describing their injuries as 'flesh wounds'.[510]

At the hearing a doctor's report was introduced in which Sirhan talked about his crime. The doctor said that Sirhan had expressed remorse and regret for his role in the assassination of Senator Kennedy and took responsibility. The doctor's examination, however, concluded that Sirhan took "... more of a victim's stance on several issues including the court process" and he claimed he had been a "victim, much like the senator." Sirhan was denied parole on the grounds that he still did not understand the full ramifications of his crime. He was also denied parole due to the nature of the offense, the impact on society, and the risk he might pose if released.[511]

The 2011 Presiding Board Commissioner Mike Prizmich told Sirhan that he failed to meet the state's criteria for suitability for parole by blaming others for his problems, behaving immaturely and not seeking enough self-help programs. "At this hearing," Prizmich said, "you're interrupting me time and time again, demonstrating a lack of control and impulsivity." Prizmich noted the impact on the Kennedy family which "had endured another tragedy five years before with the killing of President John F. Kennedy." Sirhan interjected. "That's not my responsibility," he said. Primich told him, "In this way, interrupting me indicates a lack of control of yourself." He added he was not impressed with Sirhan blaming others for all of his problems. "You have made statements that someone set you up, the CIA set you up, the DA set you up... Everything that occurred in a negative way to you, you say it was someone else's fault. We believe you minimize your conduct."[512]

In April 2011 Sirhan's claim that he suffered from amnesia was brought into question by a document released to the press by Michael McCowan, one of Sirhan's trial defense investigators. McCowan was a private detective who assisted Sirhan lawyers. He had worked for the LAPD for ten years while attending law school. In 1995 Dan Moldea had reported that Sirhan told McCowan of the moment when his eyes met Kennedy's just before he shot him. In the pre-trial period, McCowan had been talking to Sirhan about the shooting and had been startled to hear how Sirhan's eyes had met Kennedy's in the moment just before he shot him and before Kennedy had fully turned to his left at the time the senator was shaking hands with the kitchen staff. McCowan asked Sirhan, "Then why, Sirhan, didn't you shoot him between the eyes?" Without hesitating, Sirhan replied, "Because that son-of-a-bitch turned his head at the last second."[513] When Dan Moldea published the story in his book *The Killing of Robert Kennedy*, in 1995, he was attacked by Lawrence Teeter, who claimed McCowan had been lying.[514]

However, in 2011 McCowan produced a manuscript of notes he had made with Sirhan present. This new evidence in the case effectively destroyed the amnesia defense Sirhan continually used at his parole hearings. The historically important manuscript shows, clearly and vividly, in Sirhan's own hand, that he did in fact remember the events of 4/5 June 1968, directly refuting his defense that he suffered from amnesia or was hypnotized and then programmed to forget. The behavior described in the manuscript was controlled and intentional, the *Los Angeles Times* stated.[515]

McCowan's story is also supported by another telling incident reported in Robert Kaiser's book, *RFK Must Die*. During Sirhan's trial, hotel workers Jesus Perez and Martin Patrusky both said Sirhan had approached them to ask if Robert Kennedy was coming through the pantry following his speech. Sirhan had contended he did not remember anything after he had collected his gun from his car. Yet, following the testimonies of the hotel workers, Sirhan had told Michael McCowan, who was seated next to him, that he had not approached either witness. When McCowan reminded Sirhan that he supposedly remembered nothing of this period before the crime, Sirhan "nodded and gulped."[516]

Additional evidence showing that Sirhan had lied about his memory loss includes a conversation with Robert Blair Kaiser in which Sirhan told him he thought Lee Harvey Oswald and James Earl Ray had acted as cowards in shooting their victims from behind. Kaiser asked Sirhan if his act was less cowardly. Sirhan responded, "Hey, when you shoot a man in the back? There you go! At least Kennedy saw me." Sirhan quickly and disingenuously added, "I think, I don't know."[517]

On November 26, 2011, William Pepper and Laurie Dusek filed court papers for a new trial, alleging that "expert analysis of recently uncovered evidence shows two guns were fired in the assassination and that Sirhan's revolver was not the gun that shot Kennedy." Pepper argued that Sirhan should be freed from prison or granted a new trial based on "formidable evidence". Pepper said his client was innocent and suffered "horrendous violations" of his rights.

In December 2011, California Attorney General Kamala Harris, through her Deputy Jamie Fuster, requested assistance from this author and Dan Moldea in her preparation of a brief challenging Sirhan's claim that he was innocent of the murder of Senator Kennedy.[518] This author and Jamie Fuster worked with Moldea in reviewing the evidence presented by Sirhan's lawyers, and the government's legal briefs cited the investigative work of both authors.[519]

On January 5, 2015, the results of Sirhan's efforts to secure a new trial based on his innocence and the bizarre notions of his purported hypnotic state, his alleged amnesia, the contorted theories about the ballistics evidence and a flawed examination of the acoustics evidence which purportedly showed fourteen shots had been fired in the pantry of the Ambassador Hotel were handed down by the California courts. Sirhan was denied freedom by US District Judge Beverly Reid O'Connell. O'Connell accepted the "Report and Recommendations of Magistrate Judge Andrew J. Wistrich," and concluded that Sirhan "failed to meet the showing required for actual innocence." Sirhan's case was not strong enough, she said, and "Petitioner does not show that it is more likely than not that no juror, acting reasonably, would have found him guilty."[520]

On November 22, 2013, Sirhan was transferred from Corcoran to the Richard J. Donovan Correctional Facility in San Diego County. Donovan prison is on Otay Mesa, close to the US-Mexico border and houses more than 3,500 inmates. The transfer occurred on the fiftieth anniversary of the assassination of President John F. Kennedy. A spokesman for the California Department of Corrections and Rehabilitation said that the transfer was "a routine matter of housing allotments" and its timing was "simply an unfortunate coincidence."

Sirhan was adamant he did not want to attend his fifteenth parole hearing in 2016 as he was upset at the way he had been treated at his 2011 hearing. However, Sirhan lawyer Laurie Dusek and his brother Munir persuaded him it was in his own interest to attend. During the hearing, Sirhan claimed he was not "legally guilty" of "anything" and did not have a "proper defense" at his 1969 trial because his trial attorney did not conduct a crime scene investigation. Sirhan also claimed his 1969 lawyer "never really examined any of the witnesses [and] conceded everything before even examining the bullets...there was hardly anything that he did other than concede my guilt." Sirhan was represented by William Pepper, who attempted to re-litigate the crime before the parole board. He was given short shrift and was told that his conspiracy theories were not the place or forum to discuss them.

During the hearing Sirhan said he did not remember the details of the crimes, but believed he was innocent based on what he had read about the case in his attorney's briefs. He told the board that "legally speaking, I'm not guilty of anything."[521] Sirhan and the deputy commissioner clashed:

> *Deputy Commissioner Stanton:* Okay. You told Commissioner Roberts that you do have remorse. And you said that was for what—when he asked you what it was for what you were legally responsible for. Is that correct?
>
> *Sirhan:* Yes.
>
> *Deputy Commissioner Stanton:* All right. But right before that didn't you tell him that you were not legally responsible for anything?
>
> *Sirhan:* Okay. Are you saying that I'm contradicting myself?
>
> *Deputy Commissioner Stanton*: No. I'm just saying that the two are inconsistent. You just said to Commissioner Roberts before making that statement, legally I'm not responsible for anything. Then when he asked about your remorse...he said what are you remorseful for? And you said for anything that I'm legally responsible for. But you just said previously I'm not legally responsible for anything.

When Stanton asked Sirhan to explain his memory loss, Sirhan said:

> It's a horrendous experience that for me to keep dwelling on it is harmful to me, to my survival even in prison. And that's why I tried to not avoid it, not to forget it, not to dismiss the responsibility for whatever the extent of my guilt is. But for my own mental health I try to avoid it, thinking about it and recall and, you know, do all this self-analysis about it, you know, from 50 years ago.

However, the parole board members dismissed Sirhan's pleas and concluded he had been lying about his memory loss.

One of Sirhan's shooting victims from the night of the assassination, 91-year-old Paul Schrade, testified in support of Sirhan. He said it was his belief a second shooter killed Kennedy and that Sirhan was intended to be a distraction from the real gunman. Sirhan repeated his claim to have no memory of the shooting, saying: "It's all vague now… I can't deny it or confirm it. I just wish this whole thing had never taken place... It's the loss when the news came to me that three members of my family died within six months when I was locked up... at Corcoran, the remorse, I mean the sadness and the sense of loss, I mean I experienced human death." The commissioners noted how Sirhan had repeatedly thought only of himself. His parole was denied on the grounds that he had not expressed adequate remorse for his crime or acknowledged its severity.[522]

On August 30, 2019, the 75-year-old Sirhan was stabbed multiple times and his throat was slashed by another prisoner. Officers responded quickly and found him with stab wound injuries. The California Department of Corrections and Rehabilitation said, "The suspect in the attack has been identified, and has [been] placed in the prison's Administrative Segregation Unit, pending an investigation." Sirhan survived the attack and was transported to an outside hospital for medical care before being returned to prison two days later. The prison authorities refused to give any information as to his assailant.[523]

Prior to his upcoming 2021 parole board hearing, Sirhan had been examined by a prison psychologist. He said that he was innocent of the crimes and "was in the wrong spot at the wrong time," thus portraying himself as the victim. The psychologist said he "denied planning the crime and denied remembering committing any illegal act on the night in question." The psychologist noted, "despite multiple attempts, Mr Sirhan would not report his understanding of the facts of the crime, as he instead referenced others' reports" Sirhan had been citing conspiracy theories concocted by his lawyers and others who promoted the notion that he was the victim of the CIA or other dark forces who used him as a 'patsy'.

The psychologist observed that "Mr Sirhan reported significant memory impairments" that were only present "when [he was] discussing his history of engaging in antisocial and violent actions." While the psychologist found that Sirhan's "current cognitive abilities appear grossly intact," his answers were "evasive" and Sirhan "appeared to be engaging in significant impression management," and "overall, he was not believed to be a reliable source of information."[524]

In 2020 Sirhan began working with several prisoners who were trained to help other inmates with conflict resolution and concepts, such as empathy and remorse. The group worked with Jen Abreu, a facilitator for the 'Alternatives to Violence Project'. In August 2021 fellow convicts conducted mock parole board hearings, coaching and mentoring Sirhan and helping him answer possible questions the 2021 parole board might put to him in the hope he might elicit more sympathy from parole board members. The team of inmates included Joel Baptiste, a former leading figure in the Aryan Brotherhood, in for life for murder; Suge Knight, the founder of Death Row Records, serving twenty-eight years for manslaughter; Mexican mafia leader Arturo Guzman; Roque Martinez, a top boss in the notorious crime syndicate Nuestra Familia; Cameron Morris, a former member of the Crips; and Michael Goodwin, convicted of the killing of Mickey Thompson and his wife in the couple's driveway. Sirhan's problem, they concluded, was that he had an inability to accept responsibility "for that which he knew that he had done." Baptiste said his 'crew put the word out' that Sirhan was not to be touched. The group agreed that once Sirhan felt physical safety, opening up would become easier.[525]

On taking office, Los Angeles District Attorney George Gascón had issued a directive that his office's 'default policy' regarding parole hearings was not to attend or take any position on parole for inmates. It was later acknowledged that Sirhan's upcoming 2021 parole hearing was also aided by a recent California law that required the parole board to consider things like age, health, and childhood trauma as mitigating factors—things it had not considered before.[526]

On August 27, 2021, in his sixteenth appearance before the parole board, Sirhan told commissioners that he had attended self-help programs and meditated regularly. He cried during the hearing when he was asked how he felt about the Middle East. He promised to "[drop] it from my conscience." Sirhan added, "Senator Kennedy was the hope of the world…and I harmed all of them and it pains me to experience that, the knowledge for such a horrible deed, *if I did in fact do that...* [emphasis added] I'm still responsible for being there and probably causing this whole incident, *through my own gun or other guns* [emphasis added]."[527]

Despite Sirhan's insistence that he may not have been guilty after all, the parole board's two-person panel voted to grant him parole after finding that he no longer posed a threat to society. They duly noted Sirhan's "lack of taking complete responsibility," then legalistically assigned greater, mitigating weight to Sirhan's advanced age, and, per the 2018 California law, his youth at the time of the offense. He had served fifty-three years in prison. The successful parole of Sirhan nearly 'tore' the Kennedy family apart after two of Kennedy's sons, Robert F. Kennedy Jr. and Douglas Kennedy, supported Sirhan's parole plea, according to an unnamed close friend of the family.[528]

Robert Kennedy's widow, Ethel, was adamant that her husband's killer should not be released. "Our family and our country suffered an unspeakable loss due to the inhumanity of one man. We believe in the gentleness that spared his life, but in taming his act of violence, he should not have the opportunity to terrorize again. He should not be paroled," she said.[529]

Six of her children—Joseph P. Kennedy II, Courtney Kennedy, Kerry Kennedy, Christopher G. Kennedy, Maxwell T. Kennedy, and Rory Kennedy— also opposed parole for Sirhan, and urged the full parole board or Governor Gavin Newsom to reverse the recommendation. They filed a statement with the parole board on August 27, 2021, opposing Sirhan's release.

Rory Kennedy said Sirhan had already been shown compassion when his death sentence was changed to life in prison. She wrote a guest essay in the *New York Times* saying that Sirhan did not deserve parole, citing his lack of remorse and unwillingness to accept responsibility. "It is a high-minded notion, after all, the belief that everyone—*everyone* deserves a chance for rehabilitation and, after having served enough time in prison, even parole."[530]

Maxwell Taylor Kennedy said:

> My father, Sen. Robert F. Kennedy, was murdered in June 1968 by Sirhan Sirhan in full view of many witnesses, including my mother, some of my father's closest friends and a number of journalists and photographers. There is no question that Sirhan killed my father... Justice is not served by releasing a confessed political assassin, a first-degree murderer, who is serving a life sentence for his role in a crime against America.

He pointed out that the new parole process introduced by Los Angeles' District Attorney Gascón was flawed in that no prosecutor was allowed to appear at the hearing, "for the first time ever to give voice to the views of the families... In assassinating my father, Sirhan committed a crime against America. He must not be released."[531]

Robert Kennedy's oldest son, Joseph P. Kennedy, was equally angered at the board's decision, declaring:

> Two commissioners of the 18-member California Parole Board made a grievous error last Friday in recommending the release of the man who murdered my father... The prisoner killed my father because of his support of Israel. The man was tried, convicted and sentenced to death. Yet he now may walk free, no doubt to the cheers of those who share his views. Let there be no mistake, the prisoner's release will be celebrated by those who believe that political disagreements can be solved by a gun.[532]

On January 13, 2022, California Governor Gavin Newsom denied Sirhan's parole. He wrote an op-ed in the *Los Angeles Times* stating that even though the state parole board had recommended Sirhan for parole, the severity of the crime and Sirhan's "current refusal to accept responsibility for it" led Newsom to deny the request. His decision was also based on his conclusions that,

> Kennedy's assassination not only changed the course of this nation and robbed the world of a promising young leader; it also left his 11 children without a father and his wife without a husband... Kennedy's family bears his loss every day. Millions of Americans lost a unifier in a time of national turmoil and grief, just nine weeks after the assassination of the Rev. Martin Luther King, Jr., and four-and-a-half years after the murder of Kennedy's brother, President John F. Kennedy.[533]

In response to Newsom's decision, Kerry Kennedy said, "[Sirhan] is a man who has shown no remorse, who has shown no ability to take responsibility for his crime and he is a current danger to the people of California and to our country."[534]

On March 1, 2023, at his seventeenth parole board appearance, Sirhan once again attempted to portray his act of assassination as some kind of crime that could be excused.

> "Remember... if I may give an illustration...the judge, and the courts... absolved that Armenian [assassin] because of the diminished capacity and the stresses...and injustices that he had suffered at the hands [of the Turks]...because of his...Christian faith and his Armenian ancestry. So, things happen. And, again, it could have happened with a...with a Jew against Hitler.

Sirhan told the commissioners his mind was in a "different world than to concentrate or to think about Robert Kennedy". What amazed him, he said, was the accusation he was lying in wait for Kennedy in order to kill him. "That is an untrue," he said, "because I didn't even know that he was going to come into that section until the girl pulled me into that pantry area."[535]

Instead of citing the conspiracy theories that purportedly proved his innocence, Sirhan told the board it was his 'youth' that was responsible. "Perhaps with my youth," he said, "I was more, much, much more impulsive and reckless. And that's a part of being young, I suppose. But I'm not so now. You know, without acting, without thinking through, without thinking of the consequences, without, you know, without being reasonable." When he was asked to give an example of his 'recklessness', Sirhan answered, "When I, when I drove to that... hotel, I believe, I was...there was no traffic on the high...on the freeway. And I believe I drove a little bit faster than I should have. I remember that. But it being reckless, reckless."

During the parole hearing, the only time Sirhan was moved to emotion, the only time he broke down in tears, was not over the death of Kennedy, but the plight of Palestinians. His parole was denied because he continued "to lack insight into what caused him to shoot the senator and then-presidential candidate." The board recommended Sirhan "do more work to better understand what makes a person a political assassin."[536]

12

THE ABUSE OF HISTORY

"Sirhan believed his crime was legitimate and he was intensely proud of his act. He believed he was the Arab equivalent of a CIA executioner." Robert Blair Kaiser

"God's own country becomes stranger and stranger. Everything, even lunacy, is mass-produced here, but somehow they manage to return to normality." Albert Einstein in a letter about his adopted country (America), to his son

In a 2006 interview with his hometown newspaper, Sirhan's last remaining brother Munir did his best to whitewash all the known and established facts about his brother Sirhan. He said that since the last time he saw his brother after his mother "passed away and our other two brothers have passed...he's still hopeful that something will come through to vindicate him. He's not a Muslim; [he's] always been a Christian, a devout Christian. But I've heard the California authorities have listed him as second on their list of terrorists, next to Osama bin Laden, even though he's not a Muslim."[537]

That same year, Munir was also interviewed for a television documentary about the Robert Kennedy assassination. He was used by the documentary-maker to create the myth that Sirhan was a non-violent devout Christian. "From the start," Munir said, "I doubted the charges because Sirhan couldn't hurt a fly." Viewers were left unaware of Sirhan's atheism, his belief in the occult and his frequent and angry anti-American outbursts.

The documentary viewers and the newspaper readers were also left ignorant of the overwhelming evidence which pointed to Sirhan's pathological hatred of Jews and the assassin's stated desire to eliminate US leaders, including Robert Kennedy, who had given their support to Israel. "It was horrifying to go through this. It was unbelievable," Munir said. "He had never said anything about Kennedy either way.

He wasn't capable of it, running at someone and shooting them. Now he's spent nearly his entire life in prison, and he's the only family I have left. But I still have hope the truth will come out, and I know he prays for that."

Munir also recalled that Sirhan, who was five years older, attempted to be a typical American teenager by studying hard at John Muir High School and maintaining a paper route before attending Pasadena City College. He said Sirhan used to study languages a lot "because he had a dream of becoming a United Nations interpreter, hoping to bring peace to the world at a time when Israeli-Arab tensions were at full boil amid the era of the Six-Day War." Munir insisted the Sirhan family were a "normal, happy, God-fearing family." In reality, Munir's brother was a disturbed young man who had a doting and bigoted mother and a distant, rigid and punitive father. [538]

The newspaper readers and TV viewers were also left unaware of Sirhan's strong belief in violent solutions to social and economic problems. Sirhan admired the Black Panthers (who used violence to forward their agenda), believing they were just like him: underdogs within American society. He hated Kennedy supporters Rosey Grier and Rafer Johnson, deriding their 'Uncle Tom' ways. The militants, he said, had not bought Kennedy's image.[539] According to Munir, Sirhan also became enamoured with the Black Muslims, who "were like him culturally." Sirhan attended the Black Muslim Temple in Central Los Angeles until being told he could not join the organization because he was not black.[540]

There is also evidence that Sirhan embraced communist ideology, despite the protestations of conspiracy writers who say otherwise. According to Lisa Pease, "When [Michael McCowan] looked at a collection of books Sirhan owned he jumped to the conclusion that Sirhan was a communist."[541] But Sirhan did indeed embrace the communist creed, as shown by his notebooks and the statements he made to his friend, Walter Crowe. He became fascinated with revolutionary politics and had been intensely interested in Fidel Castro's book, *History Will Absolve Me*.[542]

It was Sirhan's lawyers who, more than anyone else, kept Sirhan's false hopes of his being granted a new trial alive. Sirhan's attorney, Lawrence Teeter, denied Sirhan was anti-Jewish or that the assassin was aware of Robert Kennedy's support for military aid to Israel. He blamed the CIA. William Pepper promoted the idea that Sirhan was innocent and also claimed the assassination was carried out by the CIA, without any credible evidence whatsoever to support his claims. This was one of the reasons why Sirhan's parole was rejected time and time again. His lawyers had pressed him to claim innocence, which led to the inevitable conclusion he had not come to terms with the seriousness of his criminal act.

However, it is the conspiracy authors, the QAnon-type cabal of conspiracy followers, who are primarily responsible for promoting a false history of the assassination by deliberately providing an alternative interpretation of reality and skewering the evidence in the case to suit a conspiracy agenda. Sirhan's defenders deliberately or ignorantly fed the media with false biographies of the assassin, which is nothing less than an abuse of history.

Unfortunately, the conspiracists have been aided and abetted by gullible mainstream media journalists who became experts in their own mind and in that of others as well. Many were ignorant of the mountains of evidence in the case assembled by the FBI and the LAPD, as well as private investigators like Dan Moldea. The media has thus contributed to the public confusion about the assassination.* This is called 'lazy journalism', which happens when journalists do not do their homework or check the accuracy of the information they find. Often, their reportage does not come under close editorial scrutiny.

In recent decades it was authors Philip Melanson, William Klaber, Lisa Pease, William Turner, Jon Christian, Tim Tate and CNN journalist Brad Johnson who persuaded the public of Sirhan's lack of motive and his purported lack of political interest or having held any type of extremist thought. Philip Melanson wrote, "To say that Sirhan shot RFK for political reasons asks us to believe something quite improbable—that Sirhan, a man without any history of violent acts, political fanaticism or interest in the impact of RFK's candidacy on the Middle East, suddenly became so obsessed with RFK's support of Israel that he committed murder." [543]

In their 1997 book *Shadow Play*, Melanson and his co-author William Klaber wrote

> Nothing in Sirhan's youth appears to lead to the most pivotal moment of his life...a review of Sirhan's interviews with his doctors and lawyers reveals that he is noteworthy for his lack of hatred for his victim... In the dozens of police interviews conducted with virtually everyone

* The most egregious article was written by the *Washington Post*'s Tom Jackman who utilized Lisa Pease's recent book, *A Lie Too Big To Fail* (2018), to present the notion that Sirhan may have been a hypnotized 'patsy.' If Lisa Pease's book had been published in 1979, it would have been laughed out of town. The only reason it got any traction from Jackman's 2019 article was because details of the story had faded from popular memory.

> who had contact with Sirhan during the year prior to the assassination, there emerged not a single instance of Sirhan having commented on Kennedy's support of Israel, on jet bombers, or on anything relating Kennedy to Jews, Israelis or the Middle East.[544]

As readers will have discovered, those claims are completely asinine.

It was Melanson who selected a part of the Los Angeles Police Department Summary Report to ostensibly show that Sirhan was not interested in politics. According to Melanson, "[The] LAPD's Summary Report indicates that he was a member of the Organization of Arab Students at PCC. The head of the group, Kanan Hamzek [*sic*], told LAPD that Sirhan seemed very interested in schoolwork but did not seem interested in politics. Another leader described the group as just 'a social organization' for Arab students—a far cry from 'radical Arab affairs'. Melanson, however, omits the most important point of Hamzeh's remarks to police investigators: "At that time Sirhan did not appear to be interested in politics. *But Hamzeh felt that Sirhan could easily have been influenced by any Arab nationalist cause since he had intense feelings against the Israelis* [emphasis added]."[545]

In their 2006 book *The Assassination of Robert F. Kennedy – The Conspiracy and Cover-Up*, William Turner and Jon Christian wrote, "There was virtually nothing in Sirhan's background to indicate that he normally viewed Robert Kennedy as a malevolent figure..." because he was "... a Palestinian merely by birth, not by political conviction."[546]

In her 2018 book, Lisa Pease cites acquaintances of Sirhan who described him as polite and non-violent. "The FBI and LAPD were… puzzled," she writes, "as they had trouble finding people who could testify to the kind of rage that's usually associated with killers…nearly everyone described Sirhan as polite, respectful and friendly, [and] had explicitly told them that 'Sirhan did not appear to be particularly aware of any political party, was not interested in groups or being a leader and was not openly fanatical about politics'."[547]

Tim Tate and Brad Johnson, in their book 2018 book *The Assassination of Robert F. Kennedy,* attempted to remove any kind of motive by referencing Sirhan's friend Ivan Garcia, who told LAPD's Special Unit Senator detectives that Sirhan had not been "particularly fanatical about politics." The authors wrote:

> The more police delved into his background, the more baffled they became. None of the people he'd worked with could recall him showing any interest in politics. Ivan Valladres Garcia, his closest friend, could barely believe this 'extremely polite, sensitive and thoughtful' young

> man could possibly have shot Kennedy—whom he'd never even mentioned. What could have been his motivation to shoot Bobby? Not only did he appear non-political, he'd never been in trouble before, bar two minor traffic offences.[548]

As readers will have discovered, the quoted statement made by Garcia, who in reality was not a 'close friend' of Sirhan's, cannot be understood in the correct context without reference to Garcia's mother, who told police investigators that Garcia and Sirhan never discussed politics. And, as readers will also have discovered, the conspiracy authors have ignored the testimonies of dozens of Sirhan's close friends, acquittances and fellow workers, who have captured the real core of his personality, character and political ideology.

Tate and Johnson's book also includes a completely distorted and false re-telling of RFK assassination witness Everett Buckner's story of seeing a girl at the shooting range he managed in order to bolster the false claim that Sirhan had been aided and abetted by fellow conspirators. Buckner was the range master at the gun club Sirhan had attended on the day of the assassination. He told police he had observed a woman talking to Sirhan and heard her say, "Get away from me…someone will recognise us." However, the authors failed to inform their readers that Buckner had retracted his conspiracy story after police officers confronted him with the woman, Claudia Williams, whose name was omitted from Tate and Johnson's book. Williams' only connection with Sirhan resided in the fact he had offered to show her how to shoot her new pistol while her husband had gone rifle shooting at a nearby range.

Dan Moldea, in his book *The Killing of Robert Kennedy*, was the first writer to recognise that, given the size and scope of this famous case, it was inevitable mistakes would be made. Many ideas about the assassination originated with a misunderstanding of the ballistics evidence and a botched investigation by the LAPD. He also recognized how controversies about the assassination began with human error, including misplacing files, misidentifying purported bullet holes in the kitchen pantry by police officers. He also discovered that some FBI agents and LAPD police officers involved in investigating the crime scene were not trained in ballistics and there had been an innocent mix up between Sirhan's gun and a 'test' gun which led to much conspiratorial speculation. Additionally, destroyed files, mistakes in the collection and collating of LAPD crime scene evidence and witness confusion also led to a false history of the assassination being propagated. This is perhaps the major reason why conspiracy advocates were able to plant so much doubt in the minds of the American public and translate any mistakes in the investigation into conspiratorial shenanigans.[549]

Many other purported tales of conspiratorial intrigue were solved long ago: a 'girl in a polka dot dress' who allegedly controlled Sirhan; allegations that multiple teams of CIA-controlled assassins were skulking around the Los Angeles Ambassador Hotel; allegations that Sirhan was never close enough to RFK to fire the fatal shot; allegations of Sirhan firing 'blanks'; and accusations about a security guard's purported involvement in the assassination. All have been addressed and debunked over the years, yet the media have still characterized them as 'mysteries.' (See Appendix)

One of the most disturbing outcomes of Sirhan's quest for freedom has been the intervention in the case by Robert Kennedy's son, Robert Kennedy Jr., in 2019. He claimed Sirhan was innocent of killing his father and that Thane Eugene Cesar, the security guard who accompanied Robert Kennedy through the pantry of the Ambassador Hotel on the night of the shooting, was the real assassin. He made the allegations about Cesar shortly after the former security guard died in 2019, saying he was hired by the CIA to kill Kennedy without providing any evidence to support his claim.* Kennedy Jr. met Sirhan at the Richard J. Donovan Prison in San Diego. After they shook hands, Sirhan expressed "the shame he felt for being associated with his father's assassination." Kennedy Jr. replied, "I know you didn't kill my father," later characterizing the assassin as a "sweet man."[550]

"Cesar waited in the pantry as my father spoke in the ballroom," RFK Jr. told a reporter, "then grabbed my father by the elbow and guided him toward Sirhan." He also claimed that it was Cesar who fired the fatal shot with a .22 pistol. "Cesar was a bigot who hated the Kennedys for their advocacy of Civil Rights for Blacks," he said. Kennedy Jr. also believed Sirhan's claim he could not remember shooting RFK.**[551]

---

* In a written statement, a CIA spokesperson said: "The notion that the CIA was involved in the deaths of either John F. Kennedy or Robert F. Kennedy is absolutely false." Outside The Beltway, Stephen L. Taylor, June 27, 2023, Yet Another Example of the Weakness of US Parties, https://www.outsidethebeltway.com/yet-another-example-of-the-weakness-of-us-parties/

** RFK Jr. has repeatedly stated that Dr Thomas Noguchi's autopsy was "perfect," yet Noguchi admitted making a crucial mistake in his examination of Kennedy's body. The bullets from Sirhan's gun had six grooves. At the time of the autopsy, Noguchi, after removing a bullet from Kennedy's sixth cervical vertebra, noted that the bullet had five grooves. As Nuguchi stated, this was done immediately after he removed the bullet, while wearing surgical gloves and away from the operating table where lighting was poor. Dr Noguchi admits not being a ballistics expert and that his examination was only

Kennedy Jr. was emulating a favorite tactic of conspiracy authors: pointing the finger of guilt at another suspect. And it is helpful if the alleged perpetrator of the crime is dead as this will naturally help their case. As conspiracists know too well, dead people cannot sue for libel and slander. Cesar did not sue any of the authors who named him because his lawyer told him it was futile in suing people who did not have any money.

Every conspiracy book about the assassination has used only one source to make the claim that Cesar was the shooter: Don Schulman, a runner for Los Angeles TV station KNXT. Tim Tate and Brad Johnson et al utilised this single purported witness to build their Sirhan-is-innocent tale. However, the authors failed to provide a full account of Schulman's claims and it left their readers ignorant of his full account of what he allegedly witnessed.

In the mid-1970s Thomas Kranz, Los Angeles County Board of Supervisors special counsel, who had been appointed to independently re-investigate the assassination, independent of LAPD and FBI involvement, interviewed Schulman. He told Kranz he was "tremendously confused" and that the words he used to describe the shooting to reporters in 1968 in the aftermath of the shooting were the result of "confusion." Schulman reported that he meant to tell reporters, "Kennedy had been hit three times, he had seen an arm fire, he had seen the security guards with guns, but he had never seen a security guard fire and hit Robert Kennedy."[552] To further add suspicion to Schulman's initial reports, Robert Blair Kaiser stated that the news runner had not even been in the pantry area at the time of the shooting. Kaiser quoted KNXT-TV employees, Frank Raciti and Dick Gaither, as saying that Schulman had been standing with them inside the Embassy Room.

Conspiracists propose that Cesar, who owned a .22 pistol, used it that night to kill Kennedy. However, there is no evidence to support this. In reality, he carried his official weapon, a .38 pistol, which he handed over to his supervisor to be checked when he arrived at the Ambassador.[553] Cesar had been standing to the right rear of Kennedy and holding his elbow as they moved through the pantry when the senator was hit four times; the fourth shot entered his jacket but did not wound him. One shot hit Kennedy in the head, just behind his right ear. The other two bullets that wounded Kennedy entered near

---

cursory. Noguchi admitted this mistake in 1971 and 1974. *Kranz Report. Complaint Filed by Attorney Godfrey and Theodore Charach*, 23.

his right armpit as the senator was raising his hands to cover his head. Kennedy was protecting himself from a 'lunging' Sirhan. Two or three men collapsed on Cesar, knocking him to the floor. Security guard Fred Murphy helped him to stand up after the shots were fired. Cesar only drew his gun, holding it at a 45-degree angle, when he stood up after falling to the floor when the first shots ended.

Conspiracists claim Cesar was the person responsible for the 'head shot' and that Sirhan was, at best, either a second shooter or a simple distraction firing 'blanks.' However, not one person observed Cesar fire his gun. Not one person out of seventy-seven people in the pantry saw Cesar place his gun anywhere near Kennedy's body.

Conspiracists claim Sirhan was never closer to Kennedy than at least 5 or 6 feet away when the shots were fired. However, proof that Sirhan shot Kennedy at point blank range resides in the fact that the retrieved bullet that hit Kennedy under his armpit, lodging in his neck, was matched to Sirhan's gun to the exclusion of all other guns. This entry wound was matched with Kennedy's jacket, which showed 'tattooing,' meaning it was a 'point blank' shot.

Three bullets struck Kennedy, while the fourth bullet passed harmlessly through the shoulder of his jacket. The head wound and all bullet entry points on his jacket show 'tattooing,' which is proof that he was shot at very close range for all four shots. A 'Walker Acid Test' had been conducted on Senator Kennedy's suit coat in the area of the entrance wounds. This test indicated that the muzzle of the weapon was held *at a distance of one to six inches from the Senator's coat* (emphasis added) at the time he was shot.[554]

There were at least three witnesses who saw Kennedy turning his head just as the shots were fired. Any estimates of muzzle distance or the angle of Sirhan's gun were based on the position of the gun either before the shooting began or at the time of the first shot and, as witnesses have testified, the arc of Sirhan's gun was travelling downwards as the shots were fired. While each statement initially places Sirhan in front of Kennedy, they vary in describing the direction and distance between Kennedy and Sirhan and, additionally, eyewitness statements paint a chaotic picture, which would undoubtedly make it difficult for them to gauge the exact locations of Sirhan and Kennedy at any millisecond of time.

Five people who were close to Kennedy saw Sirhan, and Sirhan alone, shoot him from a point-blank distance. Vincent DiPierro had an unobstructed view of the shooting from his position some five feet behind Kennedy, and said it was true that Sirhan was standing about three feet from the senator. However, he said that when he fired the shots, Sirhan's arm was extended and the assassin lunged forward, bringing the muzzle of his Ivor-Johnson revolver to within several inches of the right side of Kennedy's head. The gun, he said, was fired at "almost point-blank range." Juan Romero, who shook hands with the senator only seconds before Kennedy was shot, said he saw the gunman reaching toward the senator and then observed the senator place his hands to his face. Boris Yaro was standing four or five feet from Kennedy when he was shot and saw Sirhan 'lunging' at Kennedy. Kennedy backed away with his arms raised toward his head as Sirhan held his gun "extended and high" and "charged" toward Kennedy, firing the gun. Edward Minasian said that while Kennedy was shaking hands, he saw Sirhan reach around Karl Uecker, who was leading Kennedy by the arm, to shoot the senator.[555] Yet it is the statement of witness Frank Burns that best describes Sirhan's positioning when the point-blank range shots to Kennedy were fired. Burns saw Kennedy throwing up his hands toward his head as the senator was "twisting to his left and falling back." Burns saw Sirhan coming closer to Kennedy and then, "pursuing [Kennedy's] body so that the arc of the gun was coming down to the floor as the body was going down." *[556]

For the 'Cesar-did-it' fantasy to work, the security guard would have had to put his gun very close to Kennedy's head at the same time Sirhan was firing rapidly in his direction, which would have also involved a considerable chance of being shot. And why would a murderer who was under threat of execution if caught, hang on to the purported murder weapon (Cesar's .22 pistol, which he left at home) for three months before he rid himself of it? Conspiracists allege that

---

* As the Kranz Report stated, "The ballistics examination and test results conducted by the ballistics panel in 1975 proved that for a second gunman to have shot any of [the Kennedy, Weisel, and Goldstein bullets], the second gunman would have had to have shot a weapon with the exact same imperfections, same muzzle defects, same leaded barrel conditions and same individual characteristics as the weapon used by Sirhan. Additionally, this second gunman would have had to use the same type of ammunition, firing at approximately the exact same moment as the Sirhan weapon was being fired." Assuming for the sake of argument that the second gunman was standing directly behind Senator Kennedy and slightly to the right, of the three bullets recovered from Kennedy, Goldstein and Weisel, all were identified by five of the seven experts as having come from one gun, with the other two experts testifying under oath that they found no evidence these three bullets had come from a second gun. Therefore, assuming there was a second gunman, he would have had to have fired into a north-west-north position to hit Senator Kennedy from the right, rear, and then conversely and almost simultaneously, this second gunman would have had to have made a substantial turn to his left and fired directly behind the senator, into a western direction, striking victims Goldstein and Weisel.

Cesar used his own .22 pistol for the shooting instead of his regulation .38 gun. He sold his .22 pistol in September 1968, months after the assassination. It begs the question; what kind of conspirators would commit such a blunder?

Additionally, Cesar's positioning around the Ambassador Hotel was controlled by William Gardner, the head of the hotel's security team and Fred Murphy, who had been supervising the Ace guards. That night, Cesar was ordered to move to a number of positions around the hotel to assist with crowd control. His last order was to position himself in the pantry/rear of stage area. This means that for Cesar to rendezvous with Sirhan to commit the assassination, Gardner and Murphy would also have had to be part of the purported conspiracy.

In response to Kennedy Jr.'s preposterous allegations about Cesar, Dan Moldea said, "I think [RFK Jr.] has been misled, conned, and corrupted by the conspiracy crowd to believe this garbage that the man that murdered his father is innocent."[557] There are other numerous points of reference which render a purported conspiracy to kill Robert Kennedy a complete fantasy:

- Sirhan did not have car insurance. He admitted he was speeding on his way to the Ambassador Hotel. Why would conspirators overlook the fact he had no insurance for his car when it could have led to the collapse of the purported conspiracy immediately if he was stopped by police?
- Sirhan was an immigrant and it was illegal to purchase a weapon. Why would conspirators risk choosing an innocent patsy who could have been arrested at any time on this charge? Sirhan had violated three California laws by merely possessing the pistol. Had police officers and security guards on duty that night at the Ambassador stopped and searched Sirhan, he would have been arrested. Conspiracy advocates allege that Sirhan had been used as a patsy by a highly powerful group of conspirators, yet they supposedly chose a man who had been risking the whole conspiratorial venture in using an illegal weapon at a police range earlier that day.
- In the hours before the assassination, Sirhan voiced his disapproval of Robert Kennedy to witnesses Enrique Rabago and Humphrey Cordero. Additionally, those who promote the conspiracy line never question the ludicrous nature of this purported plot. If plotters had successfully hypnotized and then programmed him to forget, they would assuredly have been equally successful in making sure he did not do anything to bring attention to himself before the shooting: "Remember Sirhan, don't drink and don't tell anyone of your disdain for Senator Kennedy,

otherwise you may be ejected from the hotel and our plot will fail." And why would conspirators choose such a patsy when Sirhan could have been stopped and searched if the two men had informed security of Sirhan's anti-Kennedy sentiments? Had these men reported Sirhan to the hotel's security, the alleged plot would have collapsed.

- Additionally, the notion of a hypnotic assassin is, by its very nature, an erratic tool. Not even true believers in the robotic assassin notion could possibly be sure Sirhan would not suddenly remember who hypnotized him, then secure an immunity deal with the Los Angeles District Attorney to avoid the death penalty.
- When Sirhan was arrested, he was taken to a police station where he refused to tell police officers his name. Unfortunately, conspiracists never ask why, if Sirhan had been a hypnotized subject programmed to forget, he did not ask police officers, "Why have I been arrested?"

Another favorite trick used by the conspiracists is to blame faceless organizations such as the Pentagon, the FBI and the CIA or accuse former employees of the CIA who are dead and cannot respond to their irresponsible allegations. This had been the accusation of choice of Sirhan's lawyers, William Pepper and Lawrence Teeter.

However, when the media covered Pepper's role in defending Sirhan, journalists had apparently forgotten the blunders he made when defending another famous assassin, James Earl Ray. Pepper tried to prove an ex-soldier killed Martin Luther King Jr. and named him in the belief he was dead. However, the ex-soldier was still alive and confronted the lawyer during a television interview arranged by CBS. It should have led to Pepper's eternal disgrace but given the nature of how conspiracy mongers always double down in the face of incriminating facts against them, Pepper quickly and disingenuously provided a mea culpa—he had simply named the wrong soldier. The next time he used the bogus excuse that another person killed King, he made sure he was dead before he irresponsibly libelled him. Shelby County Assistant District Attorney John Campbell said he had "spent four years on Mr Pepper's [Martin Luther King assassination] theories… After you've watched them change [so frequently] you just don't want to hear any more of them. It's so bizarre that it's hard to take it seriously anymore. It's a tragedy. This should be taken seriously, but it's become almost comical."[558]

Sirhan defenders refuse to acknowledge how he used his 'amnesia' to get himself off the hook when it came to the most important part of his story—premeditation. Any witness who testified to Sirhan's premeditation was branded a 'liar.' As Dan Moldea discovered during his three interviews with the assassin, Sirhan was forthcoming and mostly truthful in his answers, except when it came to "means, motive and opportunity."

Sirhan showed the manipulative side of his character when he confessed to one of his jailers, Deputy Sheriff I. B. Mills, that he was so smart he "knew what the bastard [prosecution psychiatrist Seymour Pollack] wanted to know." "I just play him along," Sirhan said. "You know, he's a Goddamn Jew, a God-damn blood sucking Jew, don't you? What I can't understand is how the American people can just sit around and let the bastards grow in power. The bastards are all in the highest positions."[559]

The idea that Sirhan suffered from amnesia is clearly invented, as police officers discovered. Proof that he knew why he had been arrested resided in the fact he told police officers after his arrest that he did not want to speak about the crime because they "would hold it over me." However, even if Sirhan did indeed experience a memory lapse, his amnesia was not necessarily the result of hypnosis or drunkenness. In North America and Europe, some criminals convicted of a violent crime—26 percent of men who have been convicted of manslaughter or murder—frequently claim they cannot recall the crime. Some studies indicate that anywhere from 25 to 65 percent of violent criminals say they do not remember committing manslaughter or murder. With regard to actual amnesia as opposed to feigned amnesia, studies have shown that "amnesia is not uncommon in the case of violent crime and in particular homicide where it can occur in 30–40 percent of cases. A related state is 'psychogenic amnesia' which is associated with stress."[560]The psychological term is 'blocking,' which happens when an emotionally traumatising event causes such distress that the ego literally blocks it from rising to conscious awareness.

Some research shows that intense stress can cause failure to recall anything learned in a given situation. Experts have concluded that the combination of stress hormones in the brain that occurs during intense trauma results in post-incident amnesia in which, immediately after a critical incident, the majority of information will not be remembered. The greater the trauma, the more likely a subject is to experience post-incident amnesia.[561] Keith Ashcroft, head of the Centre for Forensic Psychopathology in Manchester, England, agrees and has concluded that "there are certain psychological defences which stop people remembering things, and one of those is trauma."[562]Russell Vorpagel, an FBI profiler, also supports the notion that traumatic episodes can lead to amnesia, believing that forgetting "is a way of subconsciously lying to your conscience."[563]

This view is supported by Sirhan trial prosecution psychiatrist Seymour Pollack, who interviewed Sirhan and concluded that if true, Sirhan's claimed amnesia could be "... a retrograde amnesia rather than a deliberate lie. Retrograde amnesia is a form of amnesia that develops after an event, when a person cannot bear to face knowledge of what has happened."

However, Sirhan's claims that he had been suffering an amnesiac state and could not remember writing in his notebooks or shooting Kennedy is debunked by his own words.

During his 1985 parole hearing he said, "I obviously had those thoughts, [*set down in his notebooks*] but I just cannot, in all sincerity, remember them."[564] Yet he clearly could remember them at the time of his trial. When Sirhan was asked by prosecutor Lynn Compton if he was "charged up, you were mad, and you were writing something down about eliminating or killing him, right?" Sirhan answered, "At the time, yes."[565] With reference to the entries in his notebooks that referred to his anti-American beliefs, he was asked by the trial prosecutor, "Yet you don't deny that at some point in your career you felt very strongly about the overthrow of the United States Government?" Sirhan replied, "As I said, at that time, Sir." The prosecutor responded, "At the time you wrote the material down?" Sirhan said, "Yes, Sir, when I wrote it down and only at that time, Sir. I don't remember entertaining it after or before. I don't even remember that itself right then."[566]

Sirhan's memory was not impaired when his own trial lawyer questioned him about his notebooks. "Do you have any idea that you wrote that on the same day that you saw this [*Campaign Biography of Robert Kennedy*] on television? You were so mad that you almost immediately went and wrote this down in your book?" Grant Cooper asked. Sirhan replied, "Well, within a short time... Because I couldn't believe it. He [Kennedy] was...the last straw." Cooper then asked Sirhan if he thought at the time that Kennedy "should be dead?" "I didn't like him at all," Sirhan said. "So, whatever in hell happened to him, I didn't give a damn."

"Well, obviously you felt that you were the one to stop him," Cooper replied.

"Yes, I did," Sirhan said.[567]

Sirhan had discovered that Kennedy was due to give a speech at the Ambassador on the Sunday night before Tuesday's primary election day. When Robert Kaiser asked Sirhan if he had been at the Ambassador Hotel that night, Sirhan said, "I stayed home, Sir, that day." When Kaiser reminded Sirhan that there may exist movie footage of the hotel on the night in question, he "frowned" and said, "I don't think I was at the Ambassador that day." This claim by Sirhan revealed a conscious effort to hide the fact that he had been stalking Kennedy. He explained that everything was "hazy." It was a typical refrain he would come to use repeatedly whenever he wanted to avoid incriminating evidence that showed motive, means and opportunity. He finally confessed to his lawyer he really had been at the Ambassador that day.[568]

Sirhan brushed up on his knowledge of psychology to ready himself for his trial, asking a deputy sheriff to order him a book, *Psychology You Can Use.* By his own admission Sirhan practiced self-hypnotism using literature supplied by the Rosicrucians. Sirhan got the "chills" following his arrest and exhibited similar symptoms at the end of hypnosis sessions with a defense-appointed psychiatrist. However, the prosecution psychiatrist also attempted to hypnotize Sirhan but was unable to elicit the assassin's full co-operation. He said Sirhan had been feigning. Additionally, conspiracists refuse to recognize that Sirhan was known to enter trance-like states even when he was a child (see Chapter 1). He had also read about killer Perry Smith's 'trance-like' behavior, had watched movies like the *Manchurian Candidate* and read extensively about hypnotic subjects and how they behaved. But rather than accept the true facts about Sirhan's purported hypnotic state, conspiracists chose to believe the fabulists.

Conspiracy writers also ignore the wealth of evidence that shows how Sirhan had been gaming the system. He had faked his outbursts in court during his trial, telling his brother Adel he had planned them all along. At one point he asked Michael McCowan if he should "flip" as a way of demonstrating he was clever at fooling the court. He would "prove" that the outbursts were part of a clever plan.[569]

Sirhan read a lot about famous crimes, including the Boston Strangler, a murderer who used the diminished responsibility/ disassociated state defense. He was interested in the Jack Kirschke case and of how defense lawyers were able to argue for reduced sentences on the basis that the crimes were committed when the perpetrator was 'emotionally charged,' even attending trials in Los Angeles with his brother Munir. Sirhan at first denied this and then admitted he had indeed attended trials, but only to "learn about the legal process." He also read about how Perry Smith's lawyers argued for 'diminished responsibility'/ 'disassociated state.'

The story of the assassination of Senator Robert Kennedy is a typical example of how people become set in their beliefs in the face of overwhelming evidence that proves them wrong. It is my belief, after researching this case since its inception in 1968, that the real mystery is not whether Sirhan alone fired the shots, but what went on in the mind of the assassin, and what motivated him. Sirhan wanted to rescue his failed life by acting in defense of a purported 'noble cause' and becoming a 'hero' to his fellow Palestinians. He once pointed a finger at Robert Blair Kaiser's forehead, made a popping sound, and said, "That's all that rules the world. Lee Harvey Oswald ruled the world for that moment that trigger was pulled."[570]

There is also no doubt in my mind that Sirhan was indoctrinated in hating Jews by his parents, his schoolteachers in Jerusalem, and was inspired to act by the propaganda espoused by Arab extremist political groups. In fact, it is this kind of indoctrination that still exists to this day.[571] In both Gaza and the West Bank, printed educational textbooks present Jews as despicable, worthless and sinister figures, utterly depersonalised and debased.[572]

Sirhan had already harbored thoughts of murder when he began to consider the possibility of killing his former employer, ranch boss Bert C. Altfillisch. As his indignation grew, it became more compelling that he had to do something to make someone pay for the position American society placed him in. In this state of mind Sirhan's actions become logical. The majority of murders are committed this way; most murders are crimes of passion. At the time the murder is committed, nothing else seems of comparable importance than the murder, but afterwards the perpetrator looks back on it as a kind of insanity. It is possible Sirhan had been suffering from catathymia, a state in which mental processes are under the control of the emotions and in some cases involves a steady build-up of anger and frustration leading to a violent explosion.

Additionally, Sirhan was extremely frustrated by the fact that he lived in a society in which many individuals, who he considered to be 'intellectually inferior,' treated him with what he perceived to be a lack of respect. He was angry, frustrated and bitter about his 'second-class citizenship.' He craved recognition, believing his intellectual skills should have made him a 'somebody.'

There is little doubt that Sirhan was, at the very least, in some form of deranged state, most likely fueled by his anger at the nationwide celebrations for the anniversary of the Six-Day War. His trancelike state was likely caused by his alcohol intake and his intense concentration (the result of his hypnotic self-improvement exercises) rather than any efforts by conspirators to hypnotize him. Sirhan confessed he had been drunk and it is likely his memory was impaired, but not expunged, by the Tom Collins drinks he had consumed earlier in the evening.

Sirhan was also attempting to redress the grievances he had built up inside him against the United States which, in his mind, had treated him badly and had relegated him to the bottom of the heap. He was reinforced in his beliefs by those radical groups that propagated violent action as a way to change society. In effect, he had been emotionally inoculated by the moral self-justification that the promoters of revolutionary violence had espoused. Sirhan's decision to strike out in a purposeful way, to act as a hero to his people, was his way of heeding the call to radical action. And he chose the last vestiges of his self-esteem, his identity as a Palestinian Arab, to accomplish that mission.

Sirhan tried to explain his motives when arrested when he cried out, "I can explain" and "I did it for my country," but America did not listen or failed to understand. Most could not see Kennedy's murder for what it was, and instead blamed America's ills.

Sirhan's murder of Robert Kennedy was embraced, condoned, and applauded throughout the Arab world. Many American congressmen and other officials said they suspected Kennedy's murder was a political one motivated by Arab fanaticism and indicated that instructions had been issued at "top levels of Government to help spare the Arabs, especially the State of Jordan, from any outburst of American public opinion against Arab peoples," believing any criticism would only advantage terrorists in the Middle East. The government, they said, also feared stirring up trouble with Jordan, who they needed to secure a settlement following the Six-Day War.

The press in some Arab countries had no such compunction, saying Kennedy was made to pay for US pro-Israel policies. Some "regret" was voiced over the assassination. Jordan's Ambassador to the United Nations, Muhammad el-Farrah, expressed the Jordanian government's "strong condemnation" of "the criminal act committed against an outstanding American and a leading public servant." However, that was not the main thrust of the Arab response. The Beirut newspaper *Al Kifah* said "Jews were behind it." Some Palestinians expressed the belief that Sirhan had been a "hired killer" and an agent in a Zionist plot to discredit the Arabs.[573] There are some mitigating circumstances of why the media generally ignored the Palestinian terrorist connection. Palestinian terrorism was in its infancy during the time of pre-Munich Olympics massacre hijacking days. Americans were in collective denial about the growing Arab anger about America's total support for Israel amongst Palestinians and Arab states.

For the next five decades, the idea that Sirhan's act held no real political underpinning continued to be the standard. Robert Kennedy biographers referred to Sirhan as "a disturbed Jordanian immigrant," (Joseph Palermo, *In His Own Right: The Political Odyssey of Senator Robert F. Kennedy*), "a mentally unstable, unemployed drifter," (Evan Thomas, *Robert Kennedy: His Life*) and "a twenty-four-year-old Jordanian." (Nellie Bly, *The Kennedy Men: Three Generations of Sex, Scandal and Secrets*). Other RFK biographers like Arthur Schlesinger Jr., William Vanden Heuval and Milton Gwirtzman, similarly failed to address the issue of Sirhan's politics.

After Sirhan had been subdued in the pantry of the Ambassador Hotel, he said he "did it for my country. I love my country." Jesse Unruh, leader of Kennedy's campaign in California, said Sirhan told him the same thing in a police car on the way to the police station. These words were not reported by most of the American press (including *The New York Times*, the *Christian Science Monitor, LIFE* and *TIME*), although they were initially mentioned by *The Associated Press* and *United Press*. Many were confused as it was reported Sirhan was an immigrant from Jordan, and it was understood that America had a friendly relationship with that country. They were unaware Sirhan had been speaking about being a 'Palestinian.'

The truth of the matter is that Robert Kennedy's assassin was reared on a relentless diet of anti-Semitic hatred from an early age, and it was that indoctrination that led to the murder of one of the most promising politicians of the twentieth century. It was the first major act of Palestinian terrorism targeting the United States. As Michael Fischbach wrote:

> The June 1968 assassination of Senator Robert F. Kennedy at the hands of Sirhan Sirhan, a Palestinian refugee from the 1948 Arab-Israeli War, has long been viewed by the American public as an example of the inchoate violence that stalked the country during the 1960s. That is no accident. Various parties succeeded in depoliticizing the assassination and sidelining the Middle Eastern dimensions of the crime despite the efforts of others to highlight the political background for Sirhan's action.[574]

To this day, the media continues to avoid calling the assassination of Robert Kennedy an act of terrorism, which suggests that mainstream US news media outlets are clearly sympathetic to the Palestinian cause. Some are proudly so, and many journalists avoid saying anything that makes the Palestinians look bad (apart from the *New York Jewish Week).* On July 4, 2013, the popular MSNBC program *Morning Joe* featured a special five-minute segment, narrated by veteran anchor Tom Brokaw, about the fiftieth anniversary of the JFK assassination. Robert

Kennedy's assassination was referenced, but no mention was made of Sirhan. Mainstream publications like the *Huffington Post* characterized Sirhan as "a 24-year-old Palestinian whose motives have never been determined."[575] Additionally, a documentary made for Sky TV (UK), *1968*, which was broadcast on the fiftieth anniversary of Robert Kennedy's assassination, correctly described Sirhan as a Palestinian, but then proceeded to answer the question of why he was assassinated by alluding to J. Edgar Hoover's hatred for Kennedy, Kennedy's pledge to end the war in Vietnam and that "a lot of people" did not want him to be president.[576]

Although Robert Kennedy Jr. has been duped by the false histories of his father's assassination, his siblings have not followed suit. In October 2023, Rory, Kerry, Joseph and Kathleen wrote in a statement, "Bobby might share the same name as our father, but he does not share the same values, vision or judgment..."[577]

Sirhan could have targeted any of the leading presidential candidates that year to publicize, through a violent act, the cause of the Palestinians. Hubert Humphrey, Eugene McCarthy, Richard Nixon and Nelson Rockefeller all supported military aid to Israel and believed in the continuing American Israeli alliance. So why did Sirhan choose RFK?

In the years between 1963 and 1968, American political culture had been dominated by the idea of a 'Kennedy Dynasty' and myths surrounding JFK's assassination. Year after year books, movies, television documentaries and political news stories gave a cult-like status to Lee Harvey Oswald, JFK's assassin. The assassin even appeared on the cover of *TIME* magazine in 1964. Sirhan, like Oswald, wanted to be noticed and wanted to be a somebody after having lived a life of failure. Killing any of the other candidates would certainly have given him status throughout the Arab world, but his true target had an even greater symbolism attached to it. Sirhan would become the 'Second Kennedy Assassin.'

He knew that killing Kennedy would give him a greater world exposure that the other candidates could not provide. It was no accident that Sirhan set his sights on the candidate who was the brother of the martyred president. It was also no accident that Sirhan chose the candidate who was tipped by the media to become the next president, thus giving the young Palestinian international exposure and instant fame. Carmen Falzone asked Sirhan if he was so angry because the US supported Israel, why did he not kill the president?

Sirhan answered, "Don't you understand? I did kill the president. Kennedy would have been president. And if he was that pro-Israel when he wasn't president, imagine how he would be as president. So, I decided to change history."[578]

However, although Sirhan had always relished the thought that his fellow Palestinians considered him to be a 'hero,' he eventually decided his path to freedom would have to be in persuading the courts and parole boards he was simply a 'patsy' controlled by others. Bolstered by the support from Robert Kennedy Jr., Sirhan continues to promote the false idea that he was a tool in the hands of conspirators.

APPENDIX

THE ROBERT KENNEDY ASSASINATION MYTHS

Myth 1 – Thane Eugene Cesar was the real assassin of Robert Kennedy

See:
The Killing of Robert F. Kennedy: An Investigation of Motive, Means, and Opportunity, Dan Moldea, Paperback, March 1, 2018

Boston Globe, Bobby Kennedy's son thinks he was killed by a second shooter. Is there anything to it?
Nik DeCosta-Klipa, May 31, 2013 https://www.boston.com/news/history/2018/05/31/rfk-assassination-conspiracy-theory-second-shooter/

Washington Decoded, A Lie On Every Page – A Review of *A Lie Too Big to Fail: The Real History of the Assassination of Robert F. Kennedy*
Lisa Pease, March 11, 2019 https://www.washingtondecoded.com/site/2019/03/pease.html#more

If RFK Jr. Lies About His Own Father's Murder, Then He will Lie About Anything – Trump's blessing in disguise does another crazy interview Dan Moldea, March 24, 2024 https://mobology.substack.com/p/if-rfk-jr-lies-about-his-own-fathers?utm_source=post-email-title&publication_id=1728335&post_id=142431478&utm_campaign=email-post-title&isFreemail=true&r=12bwq5&triedRedirect=true

Myth 2 – Sirhan could not have caused the fatal shot because the gunpowder burns prove it was a close-range shot, and eyewitness statements place him too far away from the senator in order to cause such wounds. Sirhan was never less than three feet away from the senator, so was unable to fire the point-blank fatal shot to RFK's head.

See:

Casetext, Sirhan v. Galaza, "Case No. CV 00–05686 BRO AJWx. 2015-01-05" *Sirhan v. Galaza*, 76 F. Supp. 3d 1073, (C.D. Cal. 2015) https://casetext.com/case/sirhan-v-galaza-2

Report and Recommendations of Magistrate Judge, Judge Andrew J. Wistrich https://www.leagle.com/decision/infdco20150106770 15/48

The murder of Senator Robert Kennedy *https://www.moldea.com/RFKcase.html*

Dan Moldea, *The Killing of Robert F. Kennedy*, 312-313, 326 Murder of Robert Kennedy: an interview with investigative journalist Dan Moldea https://www.youtube.com/watch?v=3_neFc5NKJ4

The Robert Kennedy Assassination – The Final Truth Mel Ayton, March 19, 2021 http://crimemagazine.com/robert-kennedy-assassination-—-final-truth

Myth 3 – More bullets were fired in the pantry than Sirhan's pistol could hold.

See:

The Forgotten Terrorist by Mel Ayton, Appendix B – Analyses of "The Pruszynski Tape" by acoustics expert Philip Harrison, Page 295

Cision PR Web, RFK Assassination: Audio Expert Using Modern Technology Concludes 8 Shots Were Fired at Senator Kennedy, Negating "Second Shooter" Claims, https://www.prweb.com/releases/rfk-assassination-audio-expert-using-modern-technology-concludes-8-shots-were-fired-at-senator-kennedy-negating-second-shooter-claims-820021737.html

History News Network, How the Discovery Channel Duped the American Public About the RFK Assassination Acoustics Debate http://hnn.us/articles/44466.html

The Robert Kennedy Assassination – The Acoustics Evidence Steve Barber https://historynewsnetwork.org/article/36915

According to the FBI files, most of the estimated seventy-seven witnesses in the pantry could not remember how many shots had been fired and described the gunshots in terms of "a number of shots", "a series of firecrackers", "several shots" or "a number of shots in rapid succession." However, of those seventy-seven who ventured an opinion about how many shots had been fired, all but a few put the number of shots at eight or less, including: Dolores Beilenson, Ira Goldstein (one of the shooting victims), Irwin Stroll (another shooting victim), Harold Edward Hughes, Pete Hamill, Ralph Elmore, Joseph A. LaHive, Richard Aubry, David Saul Barrett, Richard L. Cohen, David M. Esquith, Jacqueline Sullivan, James Cummings, Paul Green Houston, Richard Edward Drew, Bob Funk, Roosevelt Grier, Robert Anthony Toigo, Barbara Rubin, Freddy Plimpton, Lon Bruce Rubin, Dun Gifford, Charles Bailey, Jimmy Breslin, Stanley Kawalac, Robert Ray Breshears, Thomas Perez, Uno Timanson, Gabor Kadar and Rafer Johnson.

Kristi Witker observed people "running in all directions" and heard "two very distinct series of pop-pop-pop . . . pop-pop-pop-pop-pop. Three pops, then five, eight in all." She saw the "gunman standing, pointing the gun and firing."

Barbara Rubin heard "three shots followed by five quick shots."

Vincent DiPierro heard "eight shots,"

Harold Edward Hughes heard "…two series of shots, possibly three or four in each…"

Freddy Plimpton heard "five shots in rapid succession and two or three scattered shots after that."

Harold L Burba heard "three shots fairly close, followed by several more."

Bill Eppridge, who took photos of the mortally wounded senator, thought he "had better count the shots." He counted a total of "six shots."

Ira Goldstein, a shooting victim, heard "seven shots." Later, he recounted the sound and rhythm of the shots.

Irwin Stroll, another shooting victim, heard "six firecracker noises."

Pete Hamill heard "five shots fired in rapid succession."

Ralph Elmore heard "four sounds in rapid succession."
Joseph A. LaHive heard "six or seven shots."
David Saul Barrett heard "a loud pop, it sounded just like a breaking balloon, there was a short pause and then three more pops in rapid succession..."
Richard L. Cohen heard "a total of five shots."
David M. Esquith heard "five (popping) noises."
Jacqueline Sullivan heard "pop, pop, pop, pop."
James Cummings heard "three gunshots with about a second interval between each shot and then a series of shots."
Paul Green Houston heard "a rapid series of muffled pops, perhaps six."
Richard Edward Drew heard "two shots then a half second pause, and then three more shots."
Roosevelt Grier heard "two or three sounds which resembled the sounds of firecrackers."
Dolores Beilenson, wife of state senator Anthony C. Beilenson, heard "three popping noises."
Lon Bruce Rubin heard "six shots."
Dun Gifford heard "one shot, a short delay, then heard five more shots."
Charles Bailey heard "five shots."
Jimmy Breslin heard "one shot [then] three or four more."
Stanley Kawalac heard "four distinct shots."
Robert Ray Breshears heard "four shots."
Thomas Perez heard "seven shots in about three seconds."
Uno Timanson heard "three or four shots."
Rafer Johnson "couldn't count them... but I know it was like four or five."
Gloria Farr heard "four rapid and distinct cracks."
Gabor Kadar heard "five rapid explosions."
Dr Stanley Abo "mentally counted them. [I] counted seven."
Larry Irvin Findly heard "a sound like two balloons bursting then several more bursts."
Angelo DiPierro heard "two shots ring out." A few seconds later he heard "several shots... in rapid fire."
Niwa Yoshio, who worked in the kitchen, heard "five pops."

Myth 4 – Sirhan was an alleged hypnotised assassin.
See:
National Geographic Channel, CIA Secret Experiments, March 10, 2008 https://www.imdb.com/title/tt1142353/

JFK Assassination.net, The JFK and RFK Assassinations and the Bogus Manchurian Candidate Theories Mel Ayton https://www.jfk-assassination.net/Manchurian.htm

History News Network, Who Killed RFK? Sirhan Sirhan Did It Mel Ayton, 4 June 2018 https://historynewsnetwork.org/article/169208

The promotion of the idea Sirhan had been a CIA hypnotized assassin is not supported by historical fact. The historical record shows that the CIA made two attempts to produce a 'Manchurian Candidate Assassin'. The first involved a hypnotist hired by the agency to hypnotize a suspected Mexican double agent. The hypnotist's job was to coax the subject to murder a Soviet KGB agent. Eventually, the hypnotist, code-named 'Mindbender', decided the idea was unrealistic and decided not to continue. The second attempt occurred in 1966 when the CIA hired a hypnotist to coax a Cuban exile to return to his homeland and assassinate Fidel Castro. The hypnotist tried to coerce three subjects into committing the act—all attempts failed. (John Marks, The Search for the Manchurian Candidate, 1991, W.W. Norton and Co., 110 and 154)

In May 1968 the Israeli intelligence services were advised by a Swedish-born navy intelligence psychologist, Binyamin Shalit, of the possibility that a hypnotized killer could be used to assassinate Yasser Arafat, the PLO leader. Shalit said a Palestinian prisoner with the "right characteristics to undergo brainwashing and hypnotism" could be sent across the border to Jordan, join Fatah forces there and attempt to kill Arafat.

Sharit's plan was approved by the Israeli government. The Palestinian selected by Sharit was a 28-year-old, "solidly built…swarthy man… not particularly bright, easily influenced, and seemingly not entirely committed to Yasser Arafat's leadership". However, Rafi Sutton, the Israeli intelligence operative who was to oversee the plan, said it was a "foolish, crazy idea". After two months of so-called 'brainwashing' the Palestinian was sent to Jordan in December 1968. Although Shalit insisted the assassin was in an 'optimal hypnotic state' the plan ended in failure when the 'hypnotic killer' turned himself into the Katameh (Jordan police). He told the police officers that Israeli agents had tried to brainwash him into killing Arafat and showed them the pistol he was given. When he was handed over to Fatah, he made a "passionate speech in support of Yasser Arafat". (*Rise and Kill First – The Secret History of Israel's Targeted Assassinations*, Ronen Bergman, Random House, NY, 2018)

Among the many myths about hypnosis are the following: • a subject is asleep when hypnotized. • a subject is unconscious when hypnotized. • hypnosis involves domination and manipulation by the hypnotist. • a hypnotist can make people act outside their own moral principles. • people can be hypnotized over the telephone. • people can be awakened only by the hypnotist who has total power over the subject. • hypnosis can cause psychosis. • hypnosis can make a subject tell the truth.

According to psychologist Dr Graham Wagstaff, an expert in hypnosis: "On the basis of such research... hypnotic subjects do not lose consciousness, control of their behavior, or their normal scruples, and are no more likely to engage in self-repugnant or anti-social activities than equivalently motivated non-hypnotic subjects."

The definition of hypnosis provided by the American Psychological Association clearly rejects the notion of the hypnotic automaton, stating: "Contrary to some depictions of hypnosis in books, movies or television, people who have been hypnotized do not lose control over their behavior." Notably also, in a further recent survey of ten experts on forensic hypnosis conducted by Vingoe (1995), all rejected the view that "during hypnosis the control a person normally has over him or herself is in the hands of the hypnotist." A similar view is expressed by the editors of the contributors to what is probably the most important academic volume on hypnosis to be published this decade, *Theories of Hypnosis*, edited by Lynn and Rhue, who conclude: "Since the 'golden age' of hypnotism (the 1880s and 1890s), the view of the hypnotized subject as a passive automaton under the sway of a powerful hypnotist has faded in popularity. In fact, this rather extreme position is not endorsed by any of the theorists whose ideas are represented in this book."

Researcher and author Robin Waterfield, who has studied the subject over many years, believes the scientific community has established that "Hypnotism is not a truth serum; it cannot make you unwittingly reveal all the skeletons in your cupboard, your deepest and darkest sexual fantasies, your youthful dreams and misdemeanours. You can even lie when hypnotized, either deliberately or unconsciously in the sense that you might be recovering pseudo-memories." Waterfield also discovered that "...it is difficult to tell if a subject is fully hypnotized. There have been a number of cases where a hypnotized subject in a criminal case has lied to direct police away from the subject's culpability.... Self-defense mechanisms, therefore, are not undermined by hypnosis which renders the application unreliable in helping to discover the veracity of the subject's thoughts. Experts therefore are clear in their belief that a hypnotized subject, including defendants in criminal trials, may lie, confabulate or fantasize if there is motivation to do so."

Most experts agree that you cannot be hypnotized without your consent. Under hypnosis the hypnotist is merely a 'facilitator' guiding the subject's own efforts. It is also true that a hypnotized subject can break out of a trance at any time he or she chooses. But while in a trance the subject is in an advanced state of suggestibility—a suggestibility which does not negate the subject's own values, principles and personal morals. The will is lowered but not removed. Furthermore, subjects undergoing hypnosis do not wake up, because they have never been asleep to begin with. The subject consciously knows that he or she has been doing under a hypnotic trance. The relaxed feelings they experience usually gives a diminished awareness of the outside world and a focusing on their inner feelings and thoughts and a fixation on the words of the hypnotist who suggests the direction the subject's thoughts will take.

As far as post-hypnotic suggestion is concerned the majority of experts believe that a subject *always* has the choice whether or not to comply. When people appear in stage shows they are acting out foolishly because their inhibitions are lowered. More serious cases of criminals hiring hypnotists to assist in their criminal enterprises simply do not exist. Experiments which have, at the outset, proven that a hypnotized subject has obeyed a command to kill have been proven to be flawed.

Sirhan's lawyer hired psychologist Daniel Brown to examine Sirhan, who concluded that "Mr Sirhan did not act under his own volition and knowledge at the time of the assassination and is not responsible for actions coerced and / or carried out by others." Sirhan was, Brown said, a true "Manchurian Candidate," hypno-programmed into carrying out a violent political act without knowing it." Readers will no doubt be unaware of Dr Daniel Brown's highly controversial and unproven studies in 'repressed memory,' all rejected by The Royal College of Psychiatrists in Britain, The British Psychological Society and, in the US, The American Psychological Association.

Additionally, the existence of repressed memory recovery has not been accepted by mainstream psychology. According to the American Psychological Association, it is impossible to distinguish repressed memories from false ones without corroborating evidence, nor are they unequivocally proven to exist, and some experts in the field of human memory feel that no credible scientific support exists for the notions of repressed/recovered memories. The mechanism(s) by which both of these phenomena happen are not well understood and, at this point, it is impossible, without other corroborative evidence, to distinguish a true memory from a false one. (Memories of Childhood Abuse, evidence – *Pezdek, K; Hodge, D. (July–August 1999).* "Planting false childhood memories: The role of event plausibility")

Porter S; et al. (2001). "Memory for murder. A psychological perspective on dissociative amnesia in legal contexts". Int J Law Psychiatry. 24 (1): 23–42.
doi:10.1016/S0160-2527(00)00066,)
http://www.apa.org/topics/trauma/memories.aspx?item=1
https://www.sciencedirect.com/science/article/pii/S0160252700000662?via%3Dihub
https://thepsychologist.bps.org.uk/volume-30/july-2017/false-memories-childhood-abuse
http://skepdic.com/repress.html http://www.fmsfonline.org/?ginterest=RepressedMemories

Myth 5 – Sirhan did not have any strong political opinions.

See:

The Guardian, Shot Heard Round The World Stephen Kinzer https://www.theguardian.com/commentisfree/2008/jun/13/israelandthepalestinians.usa

Haaretz, Why Sirhan Sirhan, a Jerusalem-born Palestinian, Shot Bobby Kennedy Nettanel Slyomovics https://www.haaretz.com/us-news/2018-05-24/ty-article-magazine/.premium/palestinian-terrorist-or-american-psycho-what-motivated-rfks-killer/0000017f-ef3c-d0f7-a9ff-effd0dfd0000

Heritage, Jewish News Agency, The Terrorists Whose Names Must Not Be Mentioned Stephen Flatow, July 20, 2018 https://www.heritagefl.com/story/2018/07/20/opinions/the-terrorists-whose-names-must-not-be-mentioned/10119.html

Washington Examiner, Will Bobby Kennedy's killer go free? Jeff Jacoby, September 23, 2021 https://www.washingtonexaminer.com/politics/will-bobby-kennedys-killer-go-free?fbclid=IwAR0FYXKUi4U21PNkYrn6V6Mk4iXmCXOE_G-hEiGeioW7kX1GLil4WsRlPJA

Perspectives on Terrorism Vol. 11, No. 5, Review: *The Forgotten Terrorist: Sirhan Sirhan and the Assassination of Robert F. Kennedy* Mel Ayton Review by Joshua Sinai, October 2017, p.52 Published by: Terrorism Research Initiative. https://www.jstor.org/stable/26297933?refreqid=excelsior%3A562a91ea4a8734fbb8681fcdf6d4cf49&seq=1#metadata_info_tab_contents

Israel Behind The News, Sirhan Was An Unaffiliated Terrorist Mel Ayton, 3 September 2021 https://israelbehindthenews.com/2021/09/03/sirhan-was-an-unaffiliated-terrorist/

Myth 6 – A woman wearing a polka dot dress assisted Sirhan to assassinate Robert Kennedy.

See:

History News Network, The Assassination of Robert F. Kennedy and the Girl In The Polka Dot Dress Mel Ayton https://historynewsnetwork.org/article/38496

Crime Magazine, The Robert Kennedy Assassination – The Final Truth by Mel Ayton, http://crimemagazine.com/robert-kennedy-assassination---final-truth

Myth 7 – The ballistics evidence proves the bullets that killed Kennedy were not fired from Sirhan's gun.

See:

The Killing of Robert F. Kennedy: An Investigation of Motive, Means, and Opportunity Dan Moldea, 2018 See: Chapters 8, 17, 23, 26
The Report of Thomas F. Kranz on the Assassination of Senator Robert F. Kennedy, March 1977, https://archivesspace.lib.umassd.edu/repositories/3/archival_objects/12179

Myth 8 – Multiple teams of CIA-controlled assassins skulking around the Los Angeles Ambassador Hotel.

See:

History News Network, Did The CIA Kill Bobby Kennedy? The BBC's Blunder Mel Ayton https://historynewsnetwork.org/article/32193

Myth 9 – The bullets introduced at trial as the Kennedy neck bullet and the Goldstein bullet were substitutes for the actual bullets.

See:

Sirhan Bishara Sirhan, Petitioner v. George Galaza, Warden, et al, Respondent. United States District Court, C.D. California., Signed January 5, 2015. Relevant Sections - Ballistics evidence. Bullets Second revolver, https://casetext.com/case/sirhan-v-galaza-2

PODCASTS

History on the Net, The Forgotten Assassin – Sirhan Sirhan and the Killing of Robert F. Kennedy © 2000-2023, Salem Media. December 14, 2023 https://www.historyonthenet.com/forgotten-assassin-sirhan-sirhan-killing-robert-f-kennedy

Inside The War Room - Mel Ayton on Sirhan Sirhan September 10, 2021 https://dispatchesfromthewarroom.substack.com/p/52-mel-ayton-on-sirhan-sirhan-815#details and https://podcasts.apple.com/us/podcast/inside-the-war-room/id1566250068?i=1000534952321

Ava Maria Radio, Kresta In The Afternoon - Rearview Mirror: Why did Sirhan Sirhan Kill RFK? (2 segments) June 6, 2016 https://avemariaradio.net/oldsite/audio-archive/kresta-afternoon-june-6-2016-hour-2/

The Peter Boyles Show – RFK – All These Years Later June 26, 2019 https://omny.fm/shows/peter-boyles-show/rfk-all-these-years-later-jun-26-2019-hr-2?in_playlist=peter-boyles-show!podcast and https://www.melayton.com/the-forgotten-terrorist

The Peter Boyles Show, Mel Ayton and Dan Moldea Interview, 2018 https://www.melayton.com/the-forgotten-terrorist

History Unplugged – Interview With Mel Ayton - The Forgotten Assassin – Sirhan Sirhan and the Killing of Robert F. Kennedy https://www.parthenonpodcast.com/history-unplugged-podcast/the-forgotten-assassin-sirhan-sirhan-and-the-killing-of-robert-f-kennedy and https://www.spreaker.com/user/10740198/mel-ayton-spreaker

Lori Spencer, Kennedy Americans, Who Killed Bobby Kennedy? https://www.youtube.com/playlist?list=PLXBcSYiYQxldlHGAjTPLcdyXmDNa2Ny0W

SELECT BIBLIOGRAPHY

Court Documents

Trial of Sirhan Bishara Sirhan https://www.maryferrell.org/php/showlist.php?docset=1659

People v. Sirhan, 1972, 7 Cal.3d 710, 497 P.2d 1121, 102 Cal rprt. 385-Cal.06/16/1972. https://law.justia.com/cases/california/supreme-court/3d/7/710.html

Report and Recommendations of Magistrate Judge, Judge Andrew J. Wistrich: On August 26, 2013, Judge Wistrich filed a sixty-seven-page Report and Recommendation, https://casetext.com/case/sirhan-v-galaza

Government Reports

California State Archives. The Los Angeles Police Department Records Of The Robert F. Kennedy Assassination Investigation. The 1969 Final Report (10 volume Edition used by LAPD to indicate expurgated portions of the 1969 Report) Approximately 1,500 pages. Courtesy of Nancy Zimmelman, Archivist, California State Archives, Reference Desk, 1020 O Street, Sacramento, CA 95814. https://www.sos.ca.gov/archives/collections/rfk, https://archives.cdn.sos.ca.gov/collections/rfk/guide.pdf

Report consisting of the Los Angeles County Board of Supervisors Independent Investigation by Special Counsel Thomas F. Kranz. (Kranz Report) 1977, https://archivesspace.lib.umassd.edu/repositories/3/archival_objects/12179 and https://findingaids.lib.msu.edu/repositories/2/archival_objects/111282

Inventory of the Los Angeles County Sheriff's Department Records - Sirhan Sirhan Case Jail Logs, Online Archive of California, California State Archives, Collection Number: File 96-03-17 https://oac.cdlib.org/findaid/ark:/13030/kt2j49r8f6/dsc/#c01-1.3.7.2

FBI Records: "Robert F Kennedy Assassination - (Summary)". 138 pages. Sirhan's Notebooks, FBI Files, RFK-LA-56-156-SUB X-01-VOLS.05, 06, 15, https://vault.fbi.gov/Robert%20F%20Kennedy%20%28Assassination%29%20/Robert%20F%20Kennedy%20%28Assassination%29%20Part%201%20of%203/view

FBI Files, Sirhan's Notebooks RFK-LA-56-156-SUB X-01-VOL.05,06, 15, https://www.maryferrell.org/showDoc.html?docId=99658#relPageId=19

Mary Ferrell Foundation Robert F. Kennedy Assassination Archives

Special Unit Senator LAPD Collection

Microfilmed records from the LAPD's Special Unit Senator investigation, plus records from later investigations.

FBI Los Angeles Field Office Files

FBI files from the Los Angeles Field Office on the RFK assassination.

Appeal of Sirhan Bishara Sirhan

Documents related to appeals of Sirhan's conviction in his 1969 trial for killing Robert Kennedy.

Request to the Los Angeles Grand Jury

1992 request for grand jury investigation, with exhibits, based on revelations in LAPD files released a few years earlier.

Petition for Writ of Habeas Corpus

The late attorney Lawrence Teeter's petition for a new trial for Sirhan Sirhan, with exhibits.

Sirhan Sirhan Court Documents

Court documents related to Sirhan Sirhan's appeals. William Pepper and co-counsel Laurie Dusek became Sirhan's attorneys following Larry Teeter's death in 2005.

Sirhan Sirhan Parole Hearings

Transcripts of parole hearings since 1985 for Sirhan Sirhan.

Miscellaneous RFK Assassination Documents

Various short documents not part of the collections listed above.

https://www.maryferrell.org/pages/RFK_Assassination_Documents.html

Medical and Ballistics Reports

Sturdivan, Larry M., *Report on RFK's wounds* prepared for Mel Ayton. February 27, 2006, published in *The Forgotten Terrorist* by Mel Ayton (University of Nebraska Press/ Potomac Books, 2019)

Larry Sturdivan is an acclaimed and recognized expert on wound ballistics. He has a Bachelor of Science in physics from Oklahoma State University and a Master of Science in statistics from the University of Delaware. He worked at the US Army's Ballistics Research Laboratory, Aberdeen Proving Ground, Maryland, from 1964 through 1972, and then at the Edgewood Research, Development, and Engineering Center, Aberdeen Proving Ground, from 1972 through 1995. In 1964 he observed ballistics tests conducted at the Biophysics Laboratory of Edgewood Arsenal in support of the Warren Commission's investigation into President John F. Kennedy's assassination. He has held positions from bench-level research to management and was the associate technical director for technology at Edgewood. He wrote the majority of the casualty criteria for bullets, fragments, etc. used by the United States and the North Atlantic Treaty Organization (NATO) and has had contracts to update them. In 1978, as a senior researcher, he was made the US Army's contact in helping the House Select Committee on Assassinations (HSCA) as it reinvestigated the JFK assassination. He was a consultant in mathematical and statistical modelling for LMS Scientific Applications and has written a book entitled *The JFK Myths: A Scientific Investigation of the Kennedy Assassination*, which was published in 2005.

Journal of Neurosurgery, 'The Assassination of Robert F. Kennedy: an analysis of the senator's injuries and neurosurgical care' by Jordan M. Komisarow MD, Theodore Pappas MD, Megan Llewellyn MSMI, and Shivanand P. Lad MD, PhD, 19 Jun 2018, Vol: 130: Issue 5, https://doi.org/10.3171/2018.4.JNS18294

The Robert Kennedy Autopsy, Dr Thomas Noguchi https://vault.fbi.gov/Robert%20F%20Kennedy%20%28Assassination%29%20/Robert%20F%20Kennedy%20%28Assassination%29%20Part%201%20of%203

Books

Baddely, A.D., *Human Memory: Theory and Practice*, Allyn and Bacon, 1997

Baden, Michael, *Unnatural Death: Confessions of a Forensic Pathologist*, London: Sphere Books, 1989.

Baker, Robert Allen, *They Call It Hypnosis*, Buffalo, Prometheus Books, 1990

Black, Ian, *Enemies and Neighbours*, Penguin Books, 2017

Bly, Nellie, *The Kennedy Men: Three Generations of Sex, Scandal and Secrets*, Kensington Books, 1996

Brog, David, *Reclaiming Israel's History*, Regnery, 2017

Capote, Truman, *In Cold Blood*, London: Penguin Books, 1967

Dershowitz, Alan, *The Case for Israel*, John Wiley and Sons Inc, 2003

Elon, Amos, *A Blood-Dimmed Tide*, Columbia University Press, 1998Gates, Daryl F., *Chief: My Life in the LAPD*, New York: Bantam Books, 1993

Houghton, Robert A., *Special Unit Senator: The Investigation of the Assassination of Senator Robert F. Kennedy*, Random House, 1970

Jansen, Godfrey H., *Why Robert Kennedy Was Killed: The Story of Two Victims*, Third Press, 1970

Kaiser, Robert Blair, *RFK Must Die*, E. P. Dutton, 1970

________________*RFK Must Die: A History of the Robert Kennedy Assassination and Its Aftermath*, Second Edition, 2008

Karsh, Efraim, Arafat's War: The Man and His Battle for Israeli Conquest, Grove Press, 2003

Klaber, William, and Melanson, Philip H., *Shadow Play: The Murder of Robert F. Kennedy, the Trial of Sirhan Sirhan and the Failure of American Justice*, St. Martin's Press, 1997

Klagsbrun, Francine and Whitney, David C., *Assassination: Robert F. Kennedy, 1925-1968*, Cowles, 1968

Marks, John, The Search for the Manchurian Candidate: The CIA and Mind Control, Norton, 1979

Mehdi, Mohammed Taki, *Kennedy and Sirhan: Why?*, New World Press, 1968

Melanson, Philip H., *The Robert F. Kennedy Assassination: New Revelations on the Conspiracy and Cover-up*, Shapolsky, 1991

________________*Who Killed Robert Kennedy?*, Odonian Press, 1993

Moldea, Dan E., The Killing of Robert F. Kennedy: An Investigation of Motive, Means, and *Opportunity*, Norton, 1995

Noguchi, Thomas T., *Coroner to the Stars*, Corgi, 1983

Palermo, Joseph, *In His Own Right: The Political Odyssey of Senator Robert F. Kennedy*, Columbia University Press, 2001

Parkin, Alan J. *Memory and Amnesia*, Psychology Press, 1997

Pease, Lisa, *A Lie Too Big to Fail: The Real History of the Assassination of Robert F. Kennedy*, Feral House, 2019

Pease, Lisa, and James DiEugenio, eds., *The Assassinations: Probe Magazine on JFK, MLK, RFK and Malcolm X*, Feral House, 2003

Pennock Pamela E., *The Rise of the Arab American Left – Activists, Allies, and Their Fight against Imperialism and Racism, 1960s – 1980s*, The University of North Carolina Press, 2017

Schacter, Daniel L., *Searching For Memory: The Brain, The Mind, the Past*, Basic Books, 1997

Seigenthaler, John., *A Search for Justice*, Aurora Publishers, 1971

Shihab, Aziz, *Sirhan.*, Naylor Co. 1969

Thomas, Evan, *Robert Kennedy: His Life*, Simon and Schuster, 2000

Turner, William W. and John G. Christian., *The Assassination of Robert F. Kennedy: A Searching Look at the Conspiracy and Cover-up 1968-1978*, New York: Thunders Mouth Press, 1993

Turner, William, *Rearview Mirror: Looking Back At the FBI, The CIA And Other Tales*, Penmarin Books. 2001

Waterfield, Robin, *Hidden Depths: The Story of Hypnosis*, Macmillan, 2002

Witcover, Jules, *The Last Campaign of Robert Kennedy*, Ace Publishing Corporation, 1969

Vorpagel, Russell, *Profiles in Murder: An FBI Legend Dissects Killers and their Crimes*, Dell, 1998

Dan Moldea Archives

Youtube, Moldea on the murder of Robert Kennedy: "Sirhan did it alone." https://www.youtube.com/watch?v=40jnhrA9kR8

Moldea.com, "DiEugenio's The Curious Case of Dan Moldea," www.moldea.com

Michael McCowan https://www.moldea.com/McCowanLetter.html

Intermezzo: RFK Jr On RFK'Ss Murder, A QAnon-like pro-Sirhan Cult is Born by Dan Moldea, September 8, 2023 https://mobology.substack.com/p/intermezzo-rfk-jr-on-rfks-murder?utm_source=substack&utm_medium=email

RFK Jr On RFK's Murder, False Facts and Half-Baked Opinions by Dan Moldea Parts 1 and 2, June 22, 2023 https://mobology.substack.com/p/rfk-jr-on-rfks-murder-false-facts https://www.youtube.com/watch?v=40jnhrA9kR8

RFK Jr. on his father's murder: A fantasy June 28, 2023 https://mobology.substack.com/p/rfk-jr-on-his-fathers-murder-a-fantasy

Gavin Newsom discusses RFK Jr. on *Meet the Press* today, September 10, 2023 https://mobology.substack.com/p/gavin-newsom-discusses-rfk-jr-on?utm_source=substack&utm_medium=email

"Politifact names RFK Jr's "campaign of conspiracy theories" as the biggest lie of 2023 by Dan E. Moldea, December 21, 2023 https://mobology.substack.com/p/politifact-names-rfk-jrs-campaign?utm_source=post-email-title&publication_id=1728335&post_id=140100301&utm_campaign=email-post-title&isFreemail=true&r=12bwq5&utm_medium=email

Other Archives

Bay Area Television Archive at San Francisco State University https://diva.sfsu.edu/collections/sfbatv/bundles/238810

Soundcloud, Sirhan Interview with Jack Perkins, May 22, 1969 https://soundcloud.com/user-282716576/sirhan-interview-with-jack-perkins-23-5-69

Sneed, Larry A. Live ABC Radio, CBS Radio and NBC radio news broadcasts supplied by kind permission of JFK assassination author and Kennedy researcher.

Journals

The Middle East Journal, 'Sirhan Sirhan and the Assassination of Robert F. Kennedy: Palestinian Rage and the Depoliticization of a Tragedy' by Michael R. Fischbach
Middle East Institute, Volume 76, Number 2, Summer 2022, https://muse.jhu.edu/view_citations?type=article&id=865502

The Middle East Forum https://www.meforum.org/topics/31/palestinians

Middle East Forum, Obama's Connection to Sirhan Sirhan Daniel Pipes, November 2, 2008 https://www.danielpipes.org/blog/2008/11/obamas-connection-to-sirhan-sirhan#continued

Modern Arab Propaganda Has Incorporated Nazi Propaganda Joseph E. Katz (Middle Eastern Political and Religious History Analyst Brooklyn, New York) www.eretzyisroel.org http://www.eretzyisroel.org/~samuel/nazi.html#2

'Assassination in Khartoum' by David A. Korn, Bloomington: Indiana University Press, 1993, Reviewed by Daniel Pipes, *American Spectator*, February 1994, https://www.danielpipes.org/608/assassination-in-khartoum

'Palestine, Sirhan Sirhan and Robert F. Kennedy's assassination' by Sherifa Zuhur, June 5, 2018 https://www.aljazeera.com/opinions/2018/6/5/palestine-sirhan-sirhan-and-robert-f-kennedys-assassination

Anti-Defamation League, Anti-Israeli Activism On US campuses, 10.12.2022, https://www.adl.org/resources/report/anti-israel-activism-us-campuses-2021-2022

Jewish Virtual Library, Anti-Semitism In Palestinian School Textbooks, EU Study Confirms Incitement in Palestinian Textbooks, 2021 https://www.jewishvirtuallibrary.org/eu-study-confirms-incitement-in-palestinian-textbooks

The Tablet, How Robert Kennedy's Assassination Foreshadowed the Rise of Palestinian Terrorism Ron Capshaw, June 6, 2018 https://www.tabletmag.com/sections/news/articles/how-robert-kennedys-assassination-foreshadowed-the-rise-of-palestinian-terrorism?fbclid=IwAR3AfmHrxGh8YQoF_hXND6P8I8cVYDSO4Z9Cffl5uILUytlibkLSbG_59wY

Heritage, *Florida Jewish News*, The Terrorists Whose Names Must Not be Mentioned Stephen Flatow, July 20, 2018 https://www.heritagefl.com/story/2018/07/20/opinions/the-terrorists-whose-names-must-not-be-mentioned/10119.html

Carroll, Robert Todd, The Sceptic's Dictionary – Hypnosis, www.skeptic.com.

Coe, W.C. and K. Ryken, "Hypnosis and Risks to Human Subjects," *American Psychologist*, August 1979. Vol:10 No: 6 https://psycnet.apa.org/record/1979-32919-001

Author Correspondence

James W. Kenney, Letter to the author, September 25, 2003

Graham Wagstaff, Letter to the author, March 15, 2003

Dr. Eyzel Cardena, Society for Clinical and Experimental Hypnosis, Letter to the author, January 21, 2004

NOTES

1 History News Network, 'How Hollywood has been Fooled By Robert F Kennedy Assassination Conspiracy Theorists', Mel Ayton, March 13, 2019, http://hnn.us/article/171610 and *The Washington Post*, 'Kennedy, King and Malcolm X Relatives and Scholars Seek New Seek New Assassination Probes', https://www.washingtonpost.com/history/2019/01/25/kennedy-king-malcolm-x-relatives-scholars-seek-new-assassination-probes/

2 See: *Kennedy Assassination,* John McAdams, 'The JFK and RFK Assassinations and the Bogus 'Manchurian Candidate' Theories', Mel Ayton, https://www.jfk-assassination.net/Manchurian.htm

3 Most recently here: https://historynewsnetwork.org/article/169208 and here: https://www.moldea.com/RFKcase.html

4 *Pasadena Weekly*, November 16, 2006, https://pasadenaweekly.com/the-real-manchurian-candidate/

5 Jansen, Godfrey H., *Why Robert Kennedy Was Killed: The Story of Two Victims*, Third Press, 1970, New York, 82

6 Jansen, 82

7 RFK LAPD Microfilm, Volume 113 (Sirhan Family Files), Current Section: Life in These United States, https://www.maryferrell.org/showDoc.html?docId=99852#relPageId=331&search=Monroe_Arms

8 RFK LAPD Microfilm, Volume 62 (Interviews, I-1223 thru I-1359), Current Section: Lillenas, Mrs. Haldor, July 22, 1968, FBI Office, Salem Oregon, June 9, 1968, LA 56-15-6-424) (FBI Interview with Mrs Haldor Lillenas (Lola), Mission, Kansas, June 10, 1968 LA 56-156- 406 https://www.maryferrell.org/showDoc.html?docId=99757#relPageId=330&search=lola_lillenas

9 RFK LAPD Microfilm, Volume 62 (Interviews, I-1223 thru I-1359), Current Section: Lillenas FBI Interview with Mrs Haldor Lillenas (Lola), Mission, Kansas, June, 10 1968 LA 56-156- 406, https://www.maryferrell.org/php/showlist.php?docset=1686 and RFK Assassination: L.A.F.O. No. 56-156: Volume 2 (Ser. 251-500) (Evangeline Lillenas, daughter), https://www.maryferrell.org/showDoc.html?docId=99631#relPageId=230&search=haldor_lillenas

10 Letter From Haldor Lillenas to District Director Immigration and Naturalisation Service, Los Angeles, August 31, 1957, https://www.maryferrell.org/search.html?q=haldor%20lillenas
11 Jansen, 39
12 Jansen, 40-41
13 Jansen, 40
14 Jansen, 116
15 Trial of Sirhan Bishara Sirhan, Volume 8, 2019-2313, January 30 - February 1969, Current Section: Mary Sirhan, https://www.maryferrell.org/showDoc.html?docId=99502#relPageId=136
RFK LAPD Microfilm, Volume 98 (Transcripts of Recorded Interviews) Current Section: Interview of Mary Sirhan, June 19, 1968 https://www.maryferrell.org/showDoc.html?docId=99841#relPageId=65
16 Jansen, 78
17 RFK LAPD Microfilm, Volume 75 (SUS Final Report) Current Section: Early Years in Jerusalem https://www.maryferrell.org/showDoc.html?docId=99761#relPageId=303
18 Black, Ian, *Enemies and Neighbours*, Penguin Books 2017, 105
19 Black, 105
20 Jansen, 53
21 Jansen, 53
22 Jansen, 53
23 Kaiser, Robert Blair, *RFK Must Die*, New York: E. P. Dutton, 1970, 305
24 Trial of Sirhan Bishara Sirhan, Volume 16, 4422-4720, 26 February - 3 March 1969, https://www.maryferrell.org/showDoc.html?docId=99531#relPageId=281
25 Dershowitz, Alan, *The Case for Israel*, John Wiley and Sons Inc, 2003, 54.
26 Trial of Sirhan Bishara Sirhan, Volume 16, 4422-4720, 26 February - 3 March 1969, https://www.maryferrell.org/showDoc.html?docId=99531#relPageId=263
27 Sirhan Sirhan Parole Hearings, https://www.maryferrell.org/php/showlist.php?docset=1958
28 Kaiser, 204 and Trial Testimony https://www.maryferrell.org/php/showlist.php?docset=1659
29 Jansen, 66
30 Jansen, 72
31 RFK Assassination: L.A.F.O. #56-156: Sub File Y, Volume 1, https://www.maryferrell.org/showDoc.html?docId=118223#relPageId=59&search=Ziad_Hashimeh
32 Kaiser, 205
33 RFK Assassination: L.A.F.O. Files-Sub H, Volume 4 https://www.maryferrell.org/showDoc.html?docId=99647#relPageId=259&search=Zaid_hashimeh

34 Trial of Sirhan Bishara Sirhan, Volume 17, 4721-5026, March 3 – 4, 1969 Current Section: Direct Examination https://www.maryferrell.org/showDoc.html?docId=99532#relPageId=115

35 Jansen, 56

36 Black, 118

37 Dershowitz, 8

38 RFK LAPD Microfilm, Volume 75 (SUS Final Report), 341 https://www.maryferrell.org/showDoc.html?docId=99761#relPageId=306&search=Joseph_Tabello

39 Black, 129

40 PBS, Column: 'How I told Sirhan Sirhan's father that his son killed Bobby Kennedy', Terence Smith, June 6, 2018 https://www.pbs.org/newshour/world/column-how-i-told-sirhan-sirhans-father-that-his-son-killed-robert-f-kennedy

41 Levin, Andrea 'On Camera – Jenning's Jerusalem Jihad', December 31, 1996, www.world.std.com

42 FBI, Denver, Colorado, Assassination of Senator Robert F. Kennedy, Los Angeles, California, June 5, 1968; June 18, 1968, Sub X 01, Vol: 4, 53, https://www.maryferrell.org/php/showlist.php?docset=1686

43 Report, incitement, antisemitism still prevalent in UNRWA classrooms by Ash Obel, March 15, 2023, https://www.timesofisrael.com/report-finds-incitement-antisemitism-still-prevalent-in-unrwa-classrooms/ And so it is even today. UN Relief and Works agencies still use educational materials designed for Palestinian children which teaches Palestinian children throughout the West Bank, Gaza Strip and elsewhere, regularly calling for the murder of Jews, and creating teaching materials that glorify terrorism, encourage martyrdom, demonize Israelis, and incite antisemitism. Seventh graders are instructed to describe Israeli soldiers as 'Satan's Aid' and a textbook chapter implores Muslims to "liberate" the Al-Aqsa Mosque. Children are asked to listen to a poem with the following line: "Give me a Kalashnikov, an [M-] 14, an axe and a knife." The *Algemeiner*, 'This is Not Normal': Antisemitism in Palestinian School Curriculum Persists as Problem Despite Global Outrage, Experts Say, https://mcusercontent.com/cda888712516195d04c9534ec/images/d6fd97b9-79c1-4d1b-aa4e-c488661c4f5f.png

44 Jansen, 78

45 Jansen, 80

46 Dokimos, A., 'The Testimony of a Palestinian Muslim Turned Christian in Israel,' www.dokimos.org/shepherdsvoice, 1

47 Mehdi, Mohammed Taki, *Kennedy and Sirhan: Why?*, New World Press, 1968, 88

48 Black,130

49 Jansen, 76

50 RFK LAPD Microfilm, Volume 75 (SUS Final Report) Current Section: Early Years in Jerusalem https://www.maryferrell.org/showDoc.html?docId=99761#relPageId=306&search=Joseph_Tabello

51 Brog, David, Reclaiming Israel's History, Regenery, 2017, 114

52 Kaiser, 418

53 Jansen, 83

54 RFK LAPD Microfilm, Volume 75, SUS Final Report Current Section: Chronicle of Sirhan's Family in The United States https://www.maryferrell.org/showDoc.html?docId=99761#relPageId=312

55 *LIFE* Magazine, 'The Notebook That Read "Robert Kennedy Must Be Killed"', June 1968, 30

56 Kaiser, 276

57 Kaiser, 166

58 Department of State, Letter dated December 2, 1968 from Assistant Legal Advisor Robert H. Neuman to Los Angeles Police Chief Robert Houghton, LAPD files https://www.maryferrell.org/php/showlist.php?docset=1689

59 RFK LAPD Microfilm, Volume 98 (Transcripts of Recorded Interviews) Current Section: Interview of Mary Sirhan, 19 Jun 1968 https://www.maryferrell.org/showDoc.html?docId=99841#relPageId=65

60 Houghton, Robert A., *Special Unit Senator: The Investigation of the Assassination of Senator Robert F. Kennedy*, Random House, 1970, 162 (Lillenas died of a heart attack whilst vacationing in Aspen, Colorado in 1959.)

61 RFK LAPD Microfilm, Volume 75 SUS Final Report Current Section: Chronicle of Sirhan's Family in The United States, page 346, https://www.maryferrell.org/showDoc.html?docId=99761#relPageId=312.
At the time of the Robert Kennedy assassination, he lived at El Bateh, Ramallah, Israel. He died in 1987. *New York Times*. Reuters Bishara Sirhan, Assassin's Father December 9, 1987 http://www.nytimes.com/1987/12/09/obituaries/bishara-sirhan-assassin-s-father.html

62 *Assassination of Robert F. Kennedy 1925-1968 by the Editors of United Press International and Cowles*, edited by Francine Klagsbrun and David C. Whitney, Cowles, 1968, 113

63 Jansen, 105

64 SUS Final Report Religious Background RFK LAPD Microfilm, Volume 75 (SUS Final Report) https://www.maryferrell.org/showDoc.html?docId=99761#relPageId=311 https://www.maryferrell.org/showDoc.html?docId=99761#relPageId=259

65 Jansen, 116, RFK LAPD Microfilm, Volume 75 (SUS Final Report) Current Section: Religious Background, 389 https://www.maryferrell.org/showDoc.html?docId=99761#relPageId=354

66 RFK LAPD Microfilm, Volume 75, SUS Final Report, Current Section: Religious Background, 389 https://www.maryferrell.org/showDoc.html?docId=99761#relPageId=354

67 FBI Interviews, Interview with J. Edward Burn, Lancaster, California Los Angeles-56-New, June 7, 1968, RFK LAPD Microfilm, Volume 115 (Sirhan Family Files), Current Section: Religious Background, https://www.maryferrell.org/showDoc.html?docId=99854#relPageId=383&search=J_Edward%20Burn

68 RFK LAPD Microfilm, Volume 75 (SUS Final Report), Current Section: Religious Background https://www.maryferrell.org/showDoc.html?docId=99761#relPageId=357

69 FBI Files, Interview with (Redacted) June 10, 1968 https://www.maryferrell.org/php/showlist.php?docset=1686

70 Interview with Linda Kamakian, 8-9-68, FILE I-170, RFK LAPD Microfilm, Volume 52 (Interviews, I-135 thru I-298) Current Section: Kamakian, Linda, August 9, 1968 https://www.maryferrell.org/showDoc.html?docId=99738#relPageId=118

71 Houghton, 114

72 Jansen, 138.

73 RFK LAPD Microfilm, Volume 75 SUS Final Report Current Section: Chronicle of Sirhan's Family in The United States, 349, https://www.maryferrell.org/showDoc.html?docId=99761#relPageId=312

74 RFK LAPD Microfilm, Volume 52 (Interviews, I-135 thru I-298), Current Section: Abbott, Fredrick, November 4, 1968 and Linda H Abbott, 11-4-68 FILE I-168, https://www.maryferrell.org/showDoc.html?docId=99738#relPageId=112

75 FBI Interview with Mary Sirhan, June 18, 1968, Los Angeles 56-156, RFK LAPD Microfilm, Volume 98 (Transcripts of Recorded Interviews) Current Section: Interview of Mary Sirhan, June 19, 1968 https://www.maryferrell.org/showDoc.html?docId=99841#relPageId=65

76 Jansen, 76

77 RFK LAPD Microfilm, Volume 51 (Interviews, I-70 thru I-134), Current Section: Eustace, Ann, August 1, 1968 https://www.maryferrell.org/showDoc.html?docId=99737#relPageId=321&search=Ann_Mary%20Eustace

78 RFK LAPD Microfilm, Volume 74, Interviews, I-4725 thru I-4837, SUS Final Report, Current Section: The Assassin https://www.maryferrell.org/showDoc.html?docId=99760#relPageId=343

79 LAPD Summary Report, 49, RFK LAPD Microfilm, Volume 75 (SUS Final Report) Current Section: Chronicle of Sirhan's Family in The United States https://www.maryferrell.org/showDoc.html?docId=99761#relPageId=312

80 Kaiser, 255

81 Jansen, 116
82 Kaiser, 103
83 RFK LAPD Microfilm, Volume 100 (Transcripts of Recorded Interviews) Current Section: Interview of Saidallah Sirhan, June 18, 1968 https://www.maryferrell.org/showDoc.html?docId=99843#relPageId=49 RFK LAPD Microfilm, Volume 75 (SUS Final Report) Current Section: Chronicle of Sirhan's Family in The United States https://www.maryferrell.org/showDoc.html?docId=99761#relPageId=312
84 RFK LAPD Microfilm, Volume 75 (SUS Final Report) Current Section: Chronicle of Sirhan's Family in The United States, 350 https://www.maryferrell.org/showDoc.html?docId=99761#relPageId=312
85 FBI Interview with Saidallah Bishara Sirhan, June 18, 1968, Los Angeles 56-156 RFK LAPD Microfilm, Volume 100 (Transcripts of Recorded Interviews) Current Section: Interview of Saidallah Sirhan, June 18, 1968 https://www.maryferrell.org/showDoc.html?docId=99843#relPageId=49
86 RFK LAPD Microfilm, Volume 100 (Transcripts of Recorded Interviews) Current Section: Interview of Saidallah Sirhan, June 18, 1968 https://www.maryferrell.org/showDoc.html?docId=99843#relPageId=49
87 Kaiser, 198
88 LAPD Summary Report, 379
89 Kaiser, 198
90 RFK LAPD Microfilm, Volume 75 (SUS Final Report) Current Section: Chronicle of Sirhan's Family in The United States https://www.maryferrell.org/showDoc.html?docId=99761#relPageId=315
91 LAPD Interview with Linda Massri, July 4, 1968, Summary Report 694
92 RFK LAPD Microfilm, Volume 50 (Legal Files, Interviews, I-1 thru I-72) Current Section: Alex, Abraham, June 6, 1968
RFK LAPD Microfilm, Volume 75 (SUS Final Report) Current Section: Chronicle of Sirhan's Family in The United States, 350 https://www.maryferrell.org/showDoc.html?docId=99761#relPageId=312
93 RFK Assassination: L.A.F.O. #56-156: Sub File X-3, Volume 10 Current Section: Appendix - W.E.B. Du Bois Clubs of America (DCA) https://www.maryferrell.org/showDoc.html?docId=99662#relPageId=127&search=Robert_E%20Ritchey
94 Jansen, 140, RFK LAPD Microfilm, Volume 75 (SUS Final Report) Current Section: Chronicle of Sirhan's Family in The United States, 348 https://www.maryferrell.org/showDoc.html?docId=99761#relPageId=314
95 RFK LAPD Microfilm, Volume 75 (SUS Final Report) Current Section: Chronicle of Sirhan's Family in The United States, 350 https://www.maryferrell.org/showDoc.html?docId=99761#relPageId=312
96 Kaiser, 364

97 RFK LAPD Microfilm, Volume 100 (Transcripts of Recorded Interviews) Current Section: Interview of Saidallah Sirhan, June 18, 1968 https://www.maryferrell.org/showDoc.html?docId=99843#relPageId=49

98 RFK LAPD Microfilm, Volume 94 (Transcripts of Recorded Interviews) Current Section: Interview of Adel Bishara Sirhan, June 5, 1968 https://www.maryferrell.org/showDoc.html?docId=99837#relPageId=182

99 RFK LAPD Microfilm, Volume 99 (Transcripts of Recorded Interviews) Current Section: Interview of Patricia Alice Strathmann, July 16, 1968 https://www.maryferrell.org/showDoc.html?docId=99842#relPageId=352&search=patricia_strathman

100 RFK LAPD Microfilm, Volume 94 (Transcripts of Recorded Interviews) Current Section: Interview of Adel Bishara Sirhan, June 5, 1968, https://www.maryferrell.org/showDoc.html?docId=99837#relPageId=182

101 RFK LAPD Microfilm, Volume 94 (Transcripts of Recorded Interviews) Current Section: Interview of Adel Bishara Sirhan, June 5, 1968 https://www.maryferrell.org/showDoc.html?docId=99837#relPageId=182

102 Jansen, 118

103 RFK LAPD Microfilm, Volume 76 (SUS Final Report) Current Section: Investigations Involving the Fez Restaurant https://www.maryferrell.org/showDoc.html?docId=99762#relPageId=98&search=The_Fez

104 RFK Assassination: LAFO, #56-156: Sub File X-4, Volume 13 Current Section: D. Additional Investigation Relating to Sirhan Family https://www.maryferrell.org/showDoc.html?docId=99665#relPageId=161&search=Myleen_Kaye%20(Eileen%20Murphy)

105 RFK LAPD Microfilm, Volume 76 (SUS Final Report) Current Section: Investigations Involving the Fez Restaurant https://www.maryferrell.org/showDoc.html?docId=99762#relPageId=98&search=The_Fez

106 RFK Assassination: L.A.F.O. #56-156: Sub File X-4, Volume 13, Current Section: D. Additional Investigation Relating to Sirhan Family https://www.maryferrell.org/showDoc.html?docId=99665#relPageId=173&search=Ali_Kalla

107 Jansen, 13.

108 *The Washington Post*, 'Sirhan', Cynthia Gorney, August 20, 1979 https://www.washingtonpost.com/archive/lifestyle/1979/08/20/sirhan/75cd41f0-e570-4bc4-ac93-83f251eec765/

109 Houghton, 162

110 FBI Files, Interview with Terence A. Fell, June 7, 1968, San Francisco, California File: SE 62, https://www.maryferrell.org/showDoc.

html?docId=99665#relPageId=223&search=Terence_Fell,%20 Sirhan, RFK Assassination: L.A.F.O. #56-156: Sub File X-1, Volume 13, Current Section: C. Associates and Acquaintances, Terence Fell https://www.maryferrell.org/showDoc.html?docId=99665#relPageId=223&search=Robert_comfort

111 RFK LAPD Microfilm, Volume 75 (SUS Final Report) Current Section: School History in United States, https://www.maryferrell.org/showDoc.html?docId=99761#relPageId=325&search=Nina_Tihomirov

112 RFK LAPD Microfilm, Volume 51 (Interviews 1 – 14937), LAPD Sgt Strong, Interview with O'Hanian, I 1831, July 25, 1968, https://www.maryferrell.org/showDoc.html?docId=99753#relPageId=137

113 RFK LAPD Microfilm, Volume 85 (SUS Final Report, 3rd copy) Current Section: Chapter IV. The Assassin https://www.maryferrell.org/showDoc.html?docId=99771#relPageId=350

114 Kaiser, 404, RFK LAPD Microfilm, Volume 75 (SUS Final Report) Current Section: School History in United States https://www.maryferrell.org/showDoc.html?docId=99761#relPageId=325&search=Nina_Tihomirov

115 RFK LAPD Microfilm, Volume 50 (Legal Files, Interviews, I-1 thru I-72) Current Section: Beran, Edward, August 14, 1968 https://www.maryferrell.org/showDoc.html?docId=99736#relPageId=152&search=Edward_Beran

116 RFK LAPD Microfilm, Volume 88 (SUS Final Report, 3rd copy, News Media Files) Current Section: Volume VIII https://www.maryferrell.org/showDoc.html?docId=99831#relPageId=184&search=Samuel_Soghomonian

117 RFK LAPD Microfilm, Volume 75 (SUS Final Report) Current Section: School History in United States https://www.maryferrell.org/showDoc.html?docId=99761#relPageId=320&search=Samuel_Soghomonian

118 RFK LAPD Microfilm, Volume 75 (SUS Final Report) Current Section: School History in United States https://www.maryferrell.org/showDoc.html?docId=99761#relPageId=321&search=Samuel_Soghomonian.

119 RFK LAPD Microfilm, Volume 85 (SUS Final Report, 3rd copy) Current Section: Chapter IV. The Assassin https://www.maryferrell.org/showDoc.html?docId=99771#relPageId=349

120 RFK LAPD Microfilm, Volume 85 (SUS Final Report, 3rd copy) Current Section: Chapter IV. The Assassin https://www.maryferrell.org/showDoc.html?docId=99771#relPageId=354

121 RFK LAPD Microfilm, Volume 85 (SUS Final Report, 3rd copy), Current Section: Chapter IV. The Assassin https://www.maryferrell.org/showDoc.html?docId=99771#relPageId=355

122 RFK LAPD Microfilm, Volume 52 (Interviews, I-135 thru I-298) Current Section: Haggerty, Michael P., June 19, 1968 California State Archives, CSA - K83 I-227, June 19, 1968. Taped Interviews, Michael Haggarty, https://www.maryferrell.org/showDoc.html?docId=99738#relPageId=255&search=Michael_Haggerty

123 Kaiser, 364

124 FBI Kensalt Files, LA56-156 FBI Interview of David Overholt Stevens https://www.maryferrell.org/showDoc.html?docId=99663#relPageId=125&search=David_Overholt%20Stevens

125 Kaiser, 199

126 Kaiser, 170

127 'Sirhan', Gorney, August 20, 1979 https://www.washingtonpost.com/archive/lifestyle/1979/08/20/sirhan/75cd41f0-e570-4bc4-ac93-83f251eec765/

128 Kaiser, 200

129 Kaiser, 168

130 Kaiser, 169

131 RFK LAPD Microfilm, Volume 75 (SUS Final Report) Current Section: School History in United States https://www.maryferrell.org/showDoc.html?docId=99761#relPageId=325&search=Nina_Tihomirov

132 FBI Files, RFK Assassination: L.A.F.O. #56-156: Sub File X-5, Volume 17 Current Section: B. Employment https://www.maryferrell.org/showDoc.html?docId=99671#relPageId=155

133 Kaiser, 281

134 RFK LAPD Microfilm, Volume 72 (Interviews, I-4256 thru I-4537) Current Section: Beehan, T. Edward, October 17, 1968 https://www.maryferrell.org/showDoc.html?docId=99748#relPageId=80&search=Beehan

135 Jansen, 126

136 FBI Files, Summary, SAC Los Angeles to Director, June 10, 1968 LA 56-156 and RFK LAPD Microfilm, Vol 23 (Card Index, WH-ZU) Current Section: Young, Keith A. https://www.maryferrell.org/showDoc.html?docId=99706#relPageId=215&search=Keith_Young

137 RFK Assassination: L.A.F.O. #56-156: Sub File X-4, Volume 13 Current Section: C. Associates and Acquaintances https://www.maryferrell.org/showDoc.html?docId=99665#relPageId=205&search=Ivan_Garcia

138 RFK LAPD Microfilm, Volume 75 (SUS Final Report) Current Section: School History in United States https://www.maryferrell.org/showDoc.html?docId=99761#relPageId=324&search=Nina_Tihomirov

139 Kaiser, 199-200

140 Kaiser, 199
141 Kaiser, 278-279
142 LAPD Summary Report, 383, RFK LAPD Microfilm, Volume 75 (SUS Final Report) Current Section: Social Activities, https://www.maryferrell.org/showDoc.html?docId=99761#relPageId=348&search=Gwendalee_Gum
143 FBI Files, RFK Assassination: L.A.F.O. #56-156: Sub File X-4, Volume 13 Current Section: C. Associates and Acquaintances, https://www.maryferrell.org/showDoc.html?docId=99665#relPageId=210&search=Robert_Comfort
144 RFK LAPD Microfilm, Volume 98 (Transcripts of Recorded Interviews) Current Section: Interview of Mary Sirhan, June 19, 1968 https://www.maryferrell.org/showDoc.html?docId=99841#relPageId=65
145 FBI Files, RFK Assassination: L.A.F.O. #56-156: Sub File X-4, Volume 13 Current Section: C. Associates and Acquaintances, https://www.maryferrell.org/showDoc.html?docId=99665#relPageId=210&search=Robert_Comfort
146 RFK LAPD Microfilm, Volume 52 (Interviews, I-135 thru I-298) Current Section: Flaster, Morris, June 17, 1968 https://www.maryferrell.org/showDoc.html?docId=99738#relPageId=193&search=Morris_Flaster
147 FBI Files, Interview with Bruce E. Fulton, June 14, 1968, Los Angeles 56-156 File # BH 44-1772, RFK Assassination: L.A.F.O. No. 56-156: Volume 4 (Ser. 751-950) https://www.maryferrell.org/showDoc.html?docId=99633#relPageId=325&search=Bruce_Edward%20Fulton
148 RFK LAPD Microfilm, Volume 75 Current Section: School History in United States https://www.maryferrell.org/showDoc.html?docId=99761#relPageId=325&search=Nina_Tihomirov
149 RFK LAPD Microfilm, Volume 99 (Transcripts of Recorded Interviews) Current Section: Interview of Patricia Alice Strathman, July 16, 1968 Interview with Patricia Alice Strathman by Officer Poteete, July 16, 1968, File I-3018, https://www.maryferrell.org/showDoc.html?docId=99842#relPageId=332
150 RFK LAPD Microfilm, Volume 49 (Tape Summaries, Vehicle Reports, Legal Files, Index to "W" File) Current Section: Strathman, John Henry, July 24, 1968 https://www.maryferrell.org/showDoc.html?docId=99735#relPageId=78
151 SUS Transcript. RFK LAPD Microfilm, Volume 49 (Tape Summaries, Vehicle Reports, Legal Files, Index to "W" File) Current Section: Strathman, John Henry, July 24, 1968 https://www.maryferrell.org/showDoc.html?docId=99735#relPageId=78
152 Houghton, 181
153 Klagsbrun, Francine and Whitney, David C., *Assassination: Robert F. Kennedy, 1925-1968*, Cowles, New York, 1968, 110

154 RFK LAPD Microfilm, Volume 49 (Tape Summaries, Vehicle Reports, Legal Files, Index to "W" File) https://www.maryferrell.org/showDoc.html?docId=99735#relPageId=85, RFK LAPD Microfilm, Volume 99 (Transcripts of Recorded Interviews) Current Section: Interview of Patricia Alice Strathman, Interview with Patricia Alice Strathman by Officer Poteete, July 16, 1968, File I-3018https://www.maryferrell.org/showDoc.html?docId=99842#relPageId=332

155 RFK LAPD Microfilm, Volume 49 (Tape Summaries, Vehicle Reports, Legal Files, Index to "W" File) https://www.maryferrell.org/showDoc.html?docId=99735#relPageId=85, RFK LAPD Microfilm, Volume 99 (Transcripts of Recorded Interviews) Current Section: Interview with Patricia Alice Strathman by Officer Poteete, July 16, 1968, File I-3018 https://www.maryferrell.org/showDoc.html?docId=99842#relPageId=332

156 RFK LAPD Microfilm, Volume 78 (SUS Final Report) Current Section: Appendix X. Interview Summaries (continued) https://www.maryferrell.org/showDoc.html?docId=99764#relPageId=47&search=Margaret_Lojeski

157 FBI Files, Airtel To LA From San Francisco, Interview with Assistant Professor Lowell J Bean, June 21, 1968 https://www.maryferrell.org/showDoc.html?docId=99853#relPageId=1&search=Lowell_J%20Bean,

158 RFK LAPD Microfilm, Volume 75 (SUS Final Report) Current Section: Investigations of Possible Conspiracies https://www.maryferrell.org/showDoc.html?docId=99761#relPageId=20&search=Hamzeh

159 RFK LAPD Microfilm, Volume 52 (Interviews, I-135 thru I-298) Current Section: Fell, Terry, June 17, 1968 https://www.maryferrell.org/showDoc.html?docId=99738#relPageId=247

160 RFK Assassination: L.A.F.O. #56-156: Sub File X-5, Volume 18 Current Section: Miscellaneous https://www.maryferrell.org/showDoc.html?docId=99672#relPageId=84&search=Fawwaz_H.%20Zedan

161 RFK LAPD Microfilm, Volume 76 (SUS Final Report) Current Section: Arab Student Groups https://www.maryferrell.org/showDoc.html?docId=99762#relPageId=110

162 RFK LAPD Microfilm, Volume 75 (SUS Final Report) https://www.maryferrell.org/showDoc.html?docId=99761#relPageId=20&search=Hamzeh

163 RFK Assassination: L.A.F.O. #56-156: Sub File X-3, Volume 10, Current Section: C. Associates and Acquaintances, FBI Interview with Faz'l Inayat Khan, June 20, 1968 https://www.maryferrell.org/showDoc.html?docId=99662#relPageId=208

164 RFK LAPD Microfilm, Volume 76 (SUS Final Report) 402-403 pollical background Current Section: Political Background https://www.maryferrell.org/showDoc.html?docId=99762#relPageId=12

RFK Assassination: L.A.F.O. #56-156: Sub File X-3, Volume 10, Current Section: C. Associates and Acquaintances, FBI Interview with Faizullah Khan, Los Angeles 56-156, June 24, 1968 https://www.maryferrell.org/showDoc.html?docId=99662#relPageId=208&search=Inayat_Khan

165 SUS Final Report, 370

166 RFK LAPD Microfilm, Volume 76 (SUS Final Report) Current Section: Political Background, Mohan Goel https://www.maryferrell.org/showDoc.html?docId=99762#relPageId=8

167 RFK LAPD Microfilm, Volume 75 (SUS Final Report) Current Section: School History in United States https://www.maryferrell.org/showDoc.html?docId=99761#relPageId=324&search=Nina_Tihomirov

168 Kaiser, 199

169 Kaiser, 219

170 Trial of Sirhan Bishara Sirhan, Volume 17, 4721-5026, March 3 - 4 1969 Current Section: Direct Examination https://www.maryferrell.org/showDoc.html?docId=99532#relPageId=115

171 Jansen, 126

172 Kaiser, 281

173 Kaiser, 227

174 Houghton, 231

175 Kaiser, 202

176 FBI Kensalt Files, Interviews, June 7, 1968, Inglewood, Ca LA 56-156 and June 8, 1968, Corona, Ca LA-56-156

177 ABC Television, RFK's Assassination: 50 Years Later, https://www.youtube.com/watch?v=71CSYAe18WE

178 RFK LAPD Microfilm, Volume 79 (SUS Final Report, and 2nd copy) Current Section: Theosophical Society Investigation, Walter Rathke, https://www.maryferrell.org/showDoc.html?docId=99765#relPageId=61&search=Walter_Thomas%20Rathke,

179 Kaiser, 286, 292, 343

180 Kaiser, 286, 292, 343, RFK LAPD Microfilm, Volume 76 (SUS Final Report) Current Section: The Rosicrucian Order https://www.maryferrell.org/showDoc.html?docId=99762#relPageId=1

181 RFK LAPD Microfilm, Volume 76 (SUS Final Report) Current Section: The Rosicrucian Order https://www.maryferrell.org/showDoc.html?docId=99762#relPageId=1

182 Kaiser, 292

183 RFK LAPD Microfilm, Volume 74 (Interviews, I-4725 thru I-4837), SUS Final Report https://www.maryferrell.org/showDoc.html?docId=99760#relPageId=347

184 RFK LAPD Microfilm, Volume 82 (SUS Final Report, 2nd copy) Current Section: Final Reports (Van

Antwerp https://www.maryferrell.org/showDoc.html?docId=99769#relPageId=41&search=Edward_Van%20Antwerp, RFK LAPD Microfilm, Volume 78 (SUS Final Report) Current Section: Appendix X. Continuation of Summaries (Genevieve Taylor) https://www.maryferrell.org/showDoc.html?docId=99764#relPageId=186&search=Edward_Van%20Antwerp

185 RFK LAPD Microfilm, Volume 68 (Interviews, I-2995 thru I-3509) Current Section: Van Antwerp, Edward Shirley, February 2, 1969, https://www.maryferrell.org/showDoc.html?docId=99744#relPageId=15&search=Van_Antwerp

186 RFK LAPD Microfilm, Volume 55 (Interviews, I-704 thru I-878) Current Section: Taylor, Genevieve, December 18, 1968 https://www.maryferrell.org/showDoc.html?docId=99750#relPageId=318&search=Edward_Van%20Antwerp

RFK LAPD Microfilm, Volume 78 (SUS Final Report) Current Section: Appendix X. Continuation of Summaries https://www.maryferrell.org/showDoc.html?docId=99764#relPageId=186&search=Van_Antwerp

187 RFK LAPD Microfilm, Volume 102 (Case Preparation Files - Interviews) Current Section: Interview John Abonyi, December 19, 1968 https://www.maryferrell.org/showDoc.html?docId=99845#relPageId=325&search=John_ABONYI

188 Kaiser, 206

189 Los Angeles County Sheriff's Department, Sirhan Sirhan Case File 1968-1969 (hereafter SSCF68-69), Operational Log Sheriff's Logs, July 15, 1968, Officer I.B. Mills https://oac.cdlib.org/findaid/ark:/13030/kt2j49r8f6/ https://oac.cdlib.org/findaid/ark:/13030/kt2j49r8f6/entire_text/

190 LAPD Summary Report, 385, Kaiser, 207, RFK LAPD Microfilm, Volume 49 (Tape Summaries, Vehicle Reports, Legal Files, Index to "W" File) Current Section: Welch, Terry Mickey, June 29, 1968 https://www.maryferrell.org/showDoc.html?docId=99735#relPageId=124

191 FBI File # Los Angeles 56-156 June 8, 1968, Interview with (Redacted) at Norco, California Norco, California on at File # Los Angeles 56-156 Date dictated June 7, 1968, 456-156.

192 FBI Files, Interviews, June 7, 1968, Inglewood, Ca LA 56-156 and June 8, 1968, Corona, Ca LA-56156, https://www.maryferrell.org/php/showlist.php?docset=1686

193 Houghton, 192

194 Kaiser, 282

195 Kaiser, 282

196 RFK Assassination: L.A.F.O. #56-156: Sub File X-4, Volume 13 Current Section: C. Associates and Acquaintances Bruce Edward Fulton https://www.maryferrell.org/showDoc.html?docId=99665#relPageId=219&search=bruce_Edward%20fulton

197 Kaiser, 283

198 FBI, Norco, CA. Los Angeles 56 -156, June 8, 1968, 41

199 RFK LAPD Microfilm, Volume 73 (Interviews, I-4538 thru I-4751) Current Section: Moreno, Joseph Saldina, December 19, 1968 https://www.maryferrell.org/showDoc.html?docId=99759#relPageId=121

200 Kaiser, 207, RFK LAPD Microfilm, Volume 74 (Interviews, I-4725 thru I-4837, SUS Final Rep https://www.maryferrell.org/showDoc.html?docId=99760#relPageId=347

201 RFK LAPD Microfilm, Volume 48 (Progress Reports, Tape Summaries) Current Section: Heinemann, Lawrence, July 24, 1968 https://www.maryferrell.org/showDoc.html?docId=99734#relPageId=252&search=Larry_Heinnemann

202 Kaiser, 208

203 RFK LAPD Microfilm, Volume 57 (interviews, I-1517 thru I-1755) Current Section: Kramer, Patricia, July 25, 1968 https://www.maryferrell.org/showDoc.html?docId=99752#relPageId=335&search=Patricia_Kramer

204 RFK LAPD Microfilm, Volume 48 (Progress Reports, Tape Summaries) Current Section: Heinemann, Lawrence, July 24, 1968 https://www.maryferrell.org/showDoc.html?docId=99734#relPageId=252&search=Larry_Heinnemann

205 FBI Files, Norco, CA. Los Angeles 56 -156, June 8, 1968

206 Appeal of Sirhan Bishara Sirhan, Respondent's Brief, Current Section: A. Appellant's Background and the Events of June 1968 Millard Sheets https://www.maryferrell.org/showDoc.html?docId=99558#relPageId=57&search=Millard_Sheets, Houghton, 188.

207 RFK Assassination: L.A.F.O. #56-156: Sub File X-4, Volume 13 Current Section: C. Associates and Acquaintances https://www.maryferrell.org/showDoc.html?docId=99665#relPageId=205&search=Ivan_Garcia

208 RFK Assassination: L.A.F.O. #56-156: Sub File X-1, Volume 3 Current Section: D. Associates and Acquaintances, FBI File # Los Angeles 56-156 Date 6/8/68 Interview with (Redacted) at Norco, California6/6/68 Norco, California on at File # Los Angeles 56-156 Date dictated 6/7/68, 456-156. https://www.maryferrell.org/showDoc.html?docId=99656#relPageId=85&search=FBI,_NORCO

209 RFK LAPD Microfilm, Volume 68 (Interviews, I-2995 thru I-3509) Current Section: Wheeler, Robert Lynn, August 16, 1968 https://www.maryferrell.org/showDoc.html?docId=99744#relPageId=134&search=Robert_Lynn%20Wheeler,

210 Houghton, 191

211 Jansen, 129

212 Houghton, 191

213 Jansen, 129

214 Kaiser, 213

215 Kaiser, 198

216 RFK LAPD Microfilm, Volume 96 (Transcripts of Recorded Interviews, Grand Jury Transcripts), Current Section: Interview of Walter Crowe, July 8, 1968 https://www.maryferrell.org/showDoc.html?docId=99839#relPageId=9 Kaiser, 200

217 RFK LAPD Microfilm, Volume 47 (Progress Reports) Current Section: LAPD/FBI/D.A. Reports, Notes and Letters https://www.maryferrell.org/showDoc.html?docId=99733#relPageId=79&search=INTERVIEW_WITH%20Walter%20Crowe. RFK LAPD Microfilm, Volume 46 (Medical Records, Phone Call Summaries, Progress Reports) Current Section: Facts on Kennedy Headquarters-Interviews of Khan, Wayne, Khoury, Crowe, Good, Hotel Guest, https://www.maryferrell.org/showDoc.html?docId=99732#relPageId=298

218 RFK LAPD Microfilm, Volume 60 (Interviews, I-2102 thru I-2199, I-1036 thru I-1083) Current Section: Divale, William T., August 6, 1968 https://www.maryferrell.org/showDoc.html?docId=99755#relPageId=25&search=DIVALE,_William%20T.%208-6-68%20WALTER%20S.%20CROWE%20%20INESTIGATION

219 RFK LAPD Microfilm, Volume 96 (Transcripts of Recorded Interviews, Grand Jury Transcripts) Current Section: Interview with Walter Crowe, July 8, 1968, Audio Tape *29303 I-18138 July 1968 https://www.maryferrell.org/showDoc.html?docId=99839#relPageId=9

220 Houghton, 165

221 RFK LAPD Microfilm, Volume 96 (Transcripts of Recorded Interviews, Grand Jury Transcripts) Current Section: Interview of Walter Crowe, July 8, 1968, https://www.maryferrell.org/showDoc.html?docId=99839#relPageId=55

222 RFK LAPD Microfilm, Volume 100 (Transcripts of Recorded Interviews), Current Section: Interview of Margaret C. Crowe and Walter Crowe, Sr., July 18, 1968 https://www.maryferrell.org/showDoc.html?docId=99843#relPageId=190

223 Kaiser, 166

224 RFK LAPD Microfilm, Volume 96 (Transcripts of Recorded Interviews, Grand Jury Transcripts) Current Section: Interview of Walter Crowe, July 8, 1968 https://www.maryferrell.org/showDoc.html?docId=99839#relPageId=26

225 Karsh, Efraim, *Arafat's War: The Man and His Battle for Israeli Conquest*, New York: Grove Press, 2003, 36

226 Karmon, Dr Ely, 'Fatah and the Popular Front for the Liberation of Palestine,' http://www.ictconference.org/aarticles/c1847.php

227 Karsh, 38-46

228 Jansen, 188
229 Jansen, 151
230 Karsh, 38-46
231 RFK LAPD Microfilm, Volume 96 (Transcripts of Recorded Interviews, Grand Jury Transcripts), Current Section: Interview of Walter Crowe, July 8, 1968 https://www.maryferrell.org/showDoc.html?docId=99839#relPageId=9,
Interview with Walter Crowe, July 8, 1968, Tape *29303 I-1813, Walter M. Crowe was administered a polygraph examination on July 8, 1968, in the polygraph facilities of the LAPD Scientific Investigation Division
232 RFK LAPD Microfilm, Volume 96 (Transcripts of Recorded Interviews, Grand Jury Transcripts) Current Section: Interview of Walter Crowe, Tape *29303 I-1813, July 8, 1968 https://www.maryferrell.org/showDoc.html?docId=99839#relPageId=10
233 RFK LAPD Microfilm, Volume 96 (Transcripts of Recorded Interviews, Grand Jury Transcripts) Current Section: Interview of Walter Crowe, July 8, 1968 https://www.maryferrell.org/showDoc.html?docId=99839#relPageId=26
234 RFK Assassination: L.A.F.O. #56-156: Sub File X-4, Volume 13 Current Section: C. Associates and Acquaintances https://www.maryferrell.org/showDoc.html?docId=99665#relPageId=216&search=Robert_comfort
235 Joseph E. Katz, 'Modern Arab Propaganda Has Incorporated Nazi Propaganda,' October 22, 2003 www.eretzyisroel.org
236 Elon, Amos, *A Blood-Dimmed Tide*, Columbia University Press, 1998, 93
237 Katz, Joseph E. (Middle Eastern Political and Religious History Analyst Brooklyn, New York) Modern Arab Propaganda Has Incorporated Nazi Propaganda www.eretzyisroel.org, http://www.eretzyisroel.org/~samuel/nazi.html#2
238 Jansen, 150
239 Kaiser, 187
240 Kaiser, 188
241 Seigenthaler, John, *A Search for Justice*, Aurora Publishers, Nashville, 1971, 253
242 Kaiser, 277
243 Soundcloud Sirhan Interview with Jack Perkins, 22 May 1969, https://soundcloud.com/user-282716576/sirhan-interview-with-jack-perkins-23-5-69
244 Kaiser, 211
245 Parole Suitability Hearing, State of California Board of Parole Hearings, Sirhan Bishara Sirhan, CDC No: B21014, R.J. Donovan Correctional Facility, San Diego, California, March 1, 2023, John Garcia Presiding Commissioner, Vijay Desai Deputy Commissioner, 9

246 Trial of Sirhan Bishara Sirhan, Volume 17, 4721-5026, March 3 – 4 1969, Current Section: Direct Examination (continued) https://www.maryferrell.org/showDoc.html?docId=99532#relPageId=220
247 Trial of Sirhan Bishara Sirhan, Volume 17, 4721-5026, March 3 - 4 1969, Current Section: Direct Examination (continued) https://www.maryferrell.org/showDoc.html?docId=99532#relPageId=45
248 Kaiser, 97
249 Kaiser, 421
250 Seigenthaler, 258
251 Kaiser, 166, Seigenthaler, 295
252 Seigenthaler, 258
253 Kaiser, 253
254 RFK LAPD Microfilm, Volume 99 (Transcripts of Recorded Interviews) Current Section: Interview of Patricia Alice Strathmann, July 16, 1968https://www.maryferrell.org/showDoc.html?docId=99842#relPageId=332
255 Transcript RFK LAPD Microfilm, Volume 99 (Transcripts of Recorded Interviews) Current Section: Interview of Patricia Alice Strathmann, July, 16 1968 https://www.maryferrell.org/showDoc.html?docId=99842#relPageId=332
256 Interview Transcript RFK LAPD Microfilm, Volume 99 (Transcripts of Recorded Interviews) Current Section: Interview of Patricia Alice Strathmann, July 16, 1968 https://www.maryferrell.org/showDoc.html?docId=99842#relPageId=332
257 RFK LAPD Microfilm, Volume 49 (Tape Summaries, Vehicle Reports, Legal Files, Index to "W" File) Current Section: Strathmann, John Henry, July 24, 1968 https://www.maryferrell.org/showDoc.html?docId=99735#relPageId=78
258 RFK LAPD Microfilm, Volume 98 (Transcripts of Recorded Interviews) Current Section: Interview of Mary Sirhan, June 19, 1968 https://www.maryferrell.org/showDoc.html?docId=99841#relPageId=65
259 Kaiser, 209
260 RFK LAPD Microfilm, Volume 49 (Tape Summaries, Vehicle Reports, Legal Files, Index to "W" File) Current Section: Strathmann, John Henry, July 24, 1968 https://www.maryferrell.org/showDoc.html?docId=99735#relPageId=78
261 Transcript Interview Transcript RFK LAPD Microfilm, Volume 99 (Transcripts of Recorded Interviews) Current Section: Interview of Patricia Alice Strathmann, July 16, 1968 https://www.maryferrell.org/showDoc.html?docId=99842#relPageId=332
262 Transcript Interview Transcript RFK LAPD Microfilm, Volume 99 (Transcripts of Recorded Interviews) Current Section: Interview of

Patricia Alice Strathmann, July 16, 1968 https://www.maryferrell.org/showDoc.html?docId=99842#relPageId=332

263 Interview Transcript RFK LAPD Microfilm, Volume 99 (Transcripts of Recorded Interviews) Current Section: Interview of Patricia Alice Strathman, July 16, 1968 https://www.maryferrell.org/showDoc.html?docId=99842#relPageId=332

264 RFK LAPD Microfilm, Volume 68 (Interviews, I-2995 thru I-3509), Current Section: Rathke, Walter Tom, February 18, 1969 https://www.maryferrell.org/showDoc.html?docId=99744#relPageId=141

265 RFK LAPD Microfilm, Volume 76 (SUS Final Report) Current Section: The Rosicrucian Order https://www.maryferrell.org/showDoc.html?docId=99762#relPageId=1

266 RFK LAPD Microfilm, Volume 76 (SUS Final Report) Current Section: Political Background https://www.maryferrell.org/showDoc.html?docId=99762#relPageId=11&search=WALTER_T%20RATHKE

267 Kaiser, 514

268 Capote, Truman, *In Cold Blood*, Penguin Books, 1967, 289

269 RFK LAPD Microfilm, Volume 76 (SUS Final Report) Current Section: The Rosicrucian Order https://www.maryferrell.org/showDoc.html?docId=99762#relPageId=7&search=Henry_J.%20Ruthhardt

270 RFK LAPD Microfilm, Volume 98 (Transcripts of Recorded Interviews), Current Section: Interview of Mary Sirhan, June 19, 1968 https://www.maryferrell.org/showDoc.html?docId=99841#relPageId=65

271 Trial of Sirhan Bishara Sirhan, Volume 8, 2019-2313, January 30 February 5, 1969, Current Section: Direct Examination Sirhan Sirhan, https://www.maryferrell.org/showDoc.html?docId=99502#relPageId=131

272 RFK LAPD Microfilm, Volume 55 (Interviews, I-704 thru I-878) Current Section: Herrick, Jeanne S., June 28, 1968 https://www.maryferrell.org/showDoc.html?docId=99750#relPageId=305&search=Jeanne_Herrick

273 RFK Assassination: L.A.F.O. #56-156: Sub File X-4, Volume 13 Current Section: D. Additional Investigation Relating to Sirhan Family https://www.maryferrell.org/showDoc.html?docId=99665#relPageId=161&search=Myleen_Kaye%20(Eileen%20Murphy)

274 RFK LAPD Microfilm, Volume 95 (Transcripts of Recorded Interviews) Current Section: Statements of Munir B. Sirhan, William Price, and George Erhard, June 25, 1968 https://www.maryferrell.org/showDoc.html?docId=99838#relPageId=199&search=Munir_Sirhan

275 RFK LAPD Microfilm, Volume 52 (Interviews, I-135 thru I-298) Munir taped interview https://www.maryferrell.org/showDoc.html?docId=99837#relPageId=205

276 Kaiser, 426
277 Houghton, 183
278 Kaiser, 215
279 Kaiser, 214
280 Houghton, 195
281 RFK LAPD Microfilm, Volume 57 (interviews, I-1517 thru I-1755) Current Section: Weidner, John H. https://www.maryferrell.org/showDoc.html?docId=99752#relPageId=5
282 RFK LAPD Microfilm, Volume 57 (interviews, I-1517 thru I-1755) Current Section: Weidner, John H. https://www.maryferrell.org/showDoc.html?docId=99752#relPageId=3
Trial of Sirhan Bishara Sirhan, Volume 18, 5027-5328, 5 Mar 1969 - 6 Mar 1969 Current Section: Direct Examination (continued) https://www.maryferrell.org/showDoc.html?docId=99533#relPageId=18
283 RFK LAPD Microfilm, Volume 57 (interviews, I-1517 thru I-1755) Current Section: Weidner, John H. https://www.maryferrell.org/showDoc.html?docId=99752#relPageId=5
284 Jansen, 132
285 RFK LAPD Microfilm, Volume 49 (Tape Summaries, Vehicle Reports, Legal Files, Index to "W" File) Current Section: Court Summaries, Dec 9, 1968 through April 15, 1969 https://www.maryferrell.org/showDoc.html?docId=99735#relPageId=329&search=NAOMI_M.%20WEIDNER
286 Houghton, 196
287 Jansen, 135
288 Klagsbrun and Whitney, 40
289 Jansen, 134
290 RFK LAPD Microfilm, Volume 77 (SUS Final Report) Current Section: Summaries https://www.maryferrell.org/showDoc.html?docId=99763#relPageId=273&search=Elsie_BoBoy
291 RFK LAPD Microfilm, Volume 49 (Tape Summaries, Vehicle Reports, Legal Files, Index to "W" File) Current Section: Weidner, John A., June 26, 1968 https://www.maryferrell.org/showDoc.html?docId=99735#relPageId=119
292 FBI Files, Sirhan's Notebooks RFK-LA-56-156-SUB X-01-VOL.05,06, 15 https://www.maryferrell.org/showDoc.html?docId=99658#relPageId=19
293 RFK LAPD Microfilm, Volume 99 (Transcripts of Recorded Interviews), Current Section: Taped Conversation with Henry Peters, August 28, 1968 https://www.maryferrell.org/showDoc.html?docId=99842#relPageId=248&search=Henry_Peters
294 LAPD Interview Mrs Mary and Adel Sirhan, Background-Sirhan, August 8, 1968. RFK LAPD Microfilm, Volume 97 (Transcripts

of Recorded Interviews, Grand Jury Transcripts) Current Section: Interview of Mary Sirhan, Adel Sirhan and Sharif Sirhan, July 15, 1968 https://www.maryferrell.org/showDoc.html?docId=99840#relPageId=368

295 RFK LAPD Microfilm, Volume 99 (Transcripts of Recorded Interviews), Current Section: Taped Conversation with Henry Peters, August 28, 1968 https://www.maryferrell.org/showDoc.html?docId=99842#relPageId=248&search=Henry_Peters Complete statement recorded on Tape #29348 and in file at SUS

296 RFK LAPD Microfilm, Volume 60 (Interviews, I-2102 thru I-2199, I-1036 thru I-1083), Current Section: Heacock, Margaret, August 8, 1968 https://www.maryferrell.org/showDoc.html?docId=99755#relPageId=20&search=Maragert_heacock

297 RFK LAPD Microfilm, Volume 52 (Interviews, I-135 thru I-298) Current Section: Kamakian, Linda, August 9, 1968 FILE I-170, https://www.maryferrell.org/showDoc.html?docId=99738#relPageId=118

298 RFK LAPD Microfilm, Volume 98 (Transcripts of Recorded Interviews) Current Section: Interview of Mary Sirhan, June 19, 1968 https://www.maryferrell.org/showDoc.html?docId=99841#relPageId=65

299 RFK LAPD Microfilm, Volume 76 (SUS Final Report) Current Section: The Rosicrucian Order https://www.maryferrell.org/showDoc.html?docId=99762#relPageId=1

300 RFK LAPD Microfilm, Volume 58 (Interviews, I-1760 thru I-1925) Current Section: Hunt, Marilyn, July 19, 1968 https://www.maryferrell.org/showDoc.html?docId=99753#relPageId=10&search=Marilyn_Hunt

301 FBI Interview with Peter Selfe, June 9, 1968 https://www.maryferrell.org/showDoc.html?docId=99764#relPageId=155

302 LAPD Summary Report 384, RFK LAPD Microfilm, Volume 78 (SUS Final Report) Current Section: Appendix X. Continuation of Summaries https://www.maryferrell.org/showDoc.html?docId=99764#relPageId=130

303 RFK LAPD Microfilm, Volume 58 (Interviews, I-1760 thru I-1925) Current Section: O'Hanian, John aka "John the Jew," July 25, 1968 https://www.maryferrell.org/showDoc.html?docId=99753#relPageId=138

304 Jansen, 134

305 RFK LAPD Microfilm, Volume 57 (interviews, I-1517 thru I-1755), Current Section: Weidner, John H. https://www.maryferrell.org/showDoc.html?docId=99752#relPageId=3

306 Kaiser, 216

307 Kaiser, 217

308 Houghton, 248

309 Jansen, 139, RFK LAPD Microfilm, Volume 76 (SUS Final Report) Current Section: Investigations Involving the Fez Restaurant https://www.maryferrell.org/showDoc.html?docId=99762#relPageId=100

310 RFK LAPD Microfilm, Volume 76 (SUS Final Report) P400 Current Section: Political Background https://www.maryferrell.org/showDoc.html?docId=99762#relPageId=8

311 Soundcloud, Sirhan Interview with Jack Perkins, May 22, 1969 https://soundcloud.com/user-282716576/sirhan-interview-with-jack-perkins-23-5-69

312 Kaiser, 181

313 Kaiser, 228

314 RFK LAPD Microfilm, Volume 46 (Medical Records, Phone Call Summaries, Progress Reports) Interview with Walter Crowe, July 8, 1968, Tape *29303 I-1813 Walter M. Crowe was administered a polygraph examination on July 8, 1968, in the polygraph facilities of the Scientific Investigation Division. https://www.maryferrell.org/showDoc.html?docId=99850#relPageId=150&search=INTERVIEW_WITH%20Walter%20Crowe

315 Kaiser, 425

316 Pennock, 125

317 Siegenthaler, 255

318 Trial of Sirhan Bishara Sirhan, Volume 17, 4721-5026, March 3 – 4, 1969 Current Section: Direct Examination (continued) https://www.maryferrell.org/showDoc.html?docId=99532#relPageId=252

319 Witcover, Jules, *85 Days: The Last Campaign of Robert Kennedy*, New York: Ace Publishing, 1969, 218

320 Trial of Sirhan Bishara Sirhan, Volume 17, 4721-5026, March 3 – 4, 1969 https://www.maryferrell.org/showDoc.html?docId=99532#relPageId=45

321 FBI Files, RFK Assassination: L.A.F.O. #56-156, Sub File X-1, Volume 4, Current Section: Interviews of Members of Sirhan Family, https://www.maryferrell.org/showDoc.html?docId=99657#relPageId=52

322 Trial of Sirhan Bishara Sirhan, Volume 26, 7398-7712, March 28 - April 2, 1969 Current Section: Direct Examination, https://www.maryferrell.org/showDoc.html?docId=99541#relPageId=167

323 RFK LAPD Microfilm, Volume 52 (Interviews, I-135 thru I-298) Current Section: Haggerty, Michael P., June 19, 1968 California State Archives, CSA - K83 I-227. Taped Interviews, Michael Haggartyhttps://www.maryferrell.org/showDoc.html?docId=99738#relPageId=255&search=Michael_Haggerty

324 RFK Assassination: L.A.F.O. #56-156: Sub File X-4, Volume 15 Current Section: Physical Evidence, https://www.maryferrell.org/showDoc.html?docId=99667#relPageId=202&search=Joseph_Sheehan

325 'Israel Salutes America: 70 who counted in 70', July 25, 2018, https://www.thejewishstar.com/stories/israel-salutes-america-70-who-counted-in-70,15829

326 Sirhan's Notebooks, RFK Assassination: L.A.F.O. #56-156: Sub File X-1, Volumes 5-6 https://www.maryferrell.org/showDoc.html?docId=99658#relPageId=16

327 Houghton 246, RFK LAPD Microfilm, Volume 76 (SUS Final Report) Current Section: The Rosicrucian Order, https://www.maryferrell.org/showDoc.html?docId=99762#relPageId=1

328 Jansen, 195

329 RFK LAPD Microfilm, Volume 53 (Interviews, I-298 thru I-460) Current Section: Hume, Bert, June, 17, 1968 https://www.maryferrell.org/showDoc.html?docId=99739#relPageId=83&search=Bert_Blume

330 RFK LAPD Microfilm, Volume 52 (Interviews, I-135 thru I-298)Current Section: Redding, Paul, June 26, 1968 https://www.maryferrell.org/showDoc.html?docId=99738#relPageId=190&search=Susan_Redding and https://www.maryferrell.org/showDoc.html?docId=99699#relPageId=283&search=Susan_Redding

331 Kranz Report, 12

332 Parole Suitability Hearing Sirhan Parole Hearing, Board of Parole Hearings, John Gracia, Vijay Desai, Deputy Commissioner, Presiding Commissioner, March 1, 2023

333 Parole Suitability Hearing Sirhan Parole Hearing, Board of Parole Hearings, John Gracia, Vijay Desai, Deputy Commissioner, Presiding Commissioner, March 1, 2023

334 RFK LAPD Microfilm, Volume 51 (Interviews, I-70 thru I-134) Current Section: Buckner, Everett, July 2, 1968 https://www.maryferrell.org/showDoc.html?docId=99737#relPageId=175

335 RFK LAPD Microfilm, Volume 60 (Interviews, I-2102 thru I-2199, I-1036 thru I-1083) Current Section: Saccoman, Michael Anthony, July 2, 1968 https://www.maryferrell.org/showDoc.html?docId=99755#relPageId=344&search=MICHAEL_SOCCOMAN

336 RFK LAPD Microfilm, Volume 76 (SUS Final Report) Current Section: San Gabriel Valley Gun Club Investigation https://www.maryferrell.org/showDoc.html?docId=99762#relPageId=134&search=Fawwaz_H.%20Zedan

337 RFK LAPD Microfilm, Volume 51 (Interviews, I-70 thru I-134) Current Section: Mistri, Gaymoard,July 11, 1968 https://www.maryferrell.org/showDoc.html?docId=99737#relPageId=206

338 Trial of Sirhan Bishara Sirhan, Volume 17, 4721-5026, March 3 – 4, 1969 Current Section: Direct Examination (resumed) Sirhan https://www.maryferrell.org/showDoc.html?docId=99532#relPageId=211

339 LA County DA Thomas F Kranz, March 1977, Second Section, 6

340 Kranz part 1, 12/13

341 Moldea, 300
342 Sirhan parole Hearing, Presiding Commissioner Garcia, Sirhan Bishara Sirhan B-21014, March 1, 2023 Trial of Sirhan Bishara Sirhan, Volume 19, 5329-5604, March 6 - 1, 1969, Current Section: Direct Examination https://www.maryferrell.org/showDoc.html?docId=99534#relPageId=141&search=Hans_Peter%20Bidstrup
343 Kaiser, 436
344 RFK LAPD Microfilm, Volume 75 (SUS Final Report) Current Section: Sirhan's Activities the Night of June 4, 1968 https://www.maryferrell.org/showDoc.html?docId=99761#relPageId=260
345 RFK LAPD Microfilm, Volume 80 (SUS Final Report, 2nd copy) Current Section: Chapter IV. The Assassin https://www.maryferrell.org/showDoc.html?docId=99768#relPageId=63&search=Mary_Grohs,
346 RFK LAPD Microfilm, Vol 23 (Card Index, WH-ZU) Current Section: Worthey, Lonny L. https://www.maryferrell.org/showDoc.html?docId=99706#relPageId=162&search=Lonny_Worthy, https://www.maryferrell.org/showDoc.html?docId=99764#relPageId=234&search=Serous_A.%20Mashayeki FBI Kensalt Files, San Diego (44-394) to Los Angeles (56-136), June 28, 1968, 88, Sub E
347 FBI Files, FBI New York to Director, Los Angeles and Washington Field Offices, June 13, 1968, 56-156-A-261, https://www.maryferrell.org/php/showlist.php?docset=1686
348 RFK LAPD Microfilm, Volume 75 (SUS Final Report), Current Section: Sirhan's Activities the Night of June 4, 1968 https://www.maryferrell.org/showDoc.html?docId=99761#relPageId=259
349 Houghton, 279
350 LAPD Summary Report, 39
351 RFK LAPD Microfilm, Volume 94 (Transcripts of Recorded Interviews) Current Section: Interview of Thane Cesar,June 5, 1968 https://www.maryferrell.org/showDoc.html?docId=99837#relPageId=33
352 RFK LAPD Microfilm, Volume 52 (Interviews, I-135 thru I-298) Current Section: Harrington, Lorine, August 8, 1968 https://www.maryferrell.org/showDoc.html?docId=99738#relPageId=94&search=Munir_Sirhan
353 Trial of Sirhan Bishara Sirhan, Volume 12, 3223-3507, February 17 – 18, 1969, Current Section: Direct Examination. Jesus Perez https://www.maryferrell.org/showDoc.html?docId=99506#relPageId=152 Kaiser, 436-437
354 RFK LAPD Microfilm, Volume 85 (SUS Final Report, 3rd copy) Current Section: Chapter IV. The Assassin https://www.maryferrell.org/showDoc.html?docId=99771#relPageId=297
355 FBI interview of Henrietta Sterlitz, 2 October 1968 https://www.maryferrell.org/php/showlist.php?docset=1686

356 Trial of Sirhan Bishara Sirhan, Volume 12, 3223-3507, February 17 – 18, 1969, Current Section: Direct Examination Martin Patrusky https://www.maryferrell.org/showDoc.html?docId=99506#relPageId=161, https://www.maryferrell.org/showDoc.html?docId=99735#relPageId=366&search=Martin_Patrusky

357 FBI Interview with John William Lewis, June 28, 1968 https://www.maryferrell.org/php/showlist.php?docset=1686

358 RFK LAPD Microfilm, Volume 94 Transcripts of Recorded Interviews, Current Section: Interview of Thane Cesar, June 5, 1968 https://www.maryferrell.org/showDoc.html?docId=99735#relPageId=85

359 RFK LAPD Microfilm, Volume 49 (Tape Summaries, Vehicle Reports, Legal Files, Index to "W" File) Current Section: Caesar, Thane, June 5, 1968 https://www.maryferrell.org/showDoc.html?docId=99735#relPageId=85

360 RFK LAPD Microfilm, Volume 102 (Case Preparation Files - Interviews) Current Section: Interview Bill Barry, June 5, 1968 https://www.maryferrell.org/showDoc.html?docId=99845#relPageId=329&search=John_ABONYI

361 Steve Lopez, 'Ex-Busboy Will Never Forget Bobby Kennedy', *Los Angeles Times*, June 1, 2003, Ron Kessler, 'Experts Discount Second-Gun Theory', *Washington Post*, December 19, 1974

362 FBI Interview with Mrs Freddy Plimpton, July 1, 1968 https://www.maryferrell.org/php/showlist.php?docset=1686

363 Trial of Sirhan Bishara Sirhan, Volume 12, 3223-3507, February 17 - 18, 1969, Current Section: Direct Examination https://www.maryferrell.org/showDoc.html?docId=99506#relPageId=181

364 Kaiser, 438

365 RFK LAPD Microfilm, Volume 49 (Tape Summaries, Vehicle Reports, Legal Files, Index to "W" File) Current Section: Caesar, Thane, June 5, 1968 https://www.maryferrell.org/showDoc.html?docId=99735#relPageId=85 and RFK LAPD Microfilm, Volume 94 (Transcripts of Recorded Interviews), Current Section: Interview of Thane Cesar, June 5, 1968 https://www.maryferrell.org/showDoc.html?docId=99837#relPageId=33

366 RFK LAPD Microfilm, Volume 94 (Transcripts of Recorded Interviews), CSA-K134 I-310, June 14, 1968 https://www.maryferrell.org/showDoc.html?docId=99837#relPageId=1&tab=toc

367 Larry Sturdivan, Letter to the Author, November 28, 2006

368 KABC reporter Carl George, Interview with Dr Marcus McBroom, June 5, 1968, Larry Sneed Audio Tape Archives

369 RFK LAPD Microfilm, Volume 76 (SUS Final Report) Current Section: State of Mind - Interviews with Police After Arrest https://www.maryferrell.org/showDoc.html?docId=99762#relPageId=273

370 FBI interviews with Geraldine Agnes McCarthy, June 24, 1968 and Winnie Theresa Marshall, June 27, 1968

371 FBI Files – RFK LA 56 - 156 - 1968-1978, Statements by pantry and hotel witnesses are from the FBI Files, https://www.maryferrell.org/php/showlist.php?docset=1686

372 FBI interview with Albert Victor Ellis, June 20, 1968https://www.maryferrell.org/php/showlist.php?docset=1686

373 FBI interview with Laurie Gail Porter, June 14, 1968 https://www.maryferrell.org/php/showlist.php?docset=1686 .

374 FBI interview with Harry Benson, October 31, 1968 https://www.maryferrell.org/php/showlist.php?docset=1686

375 RFK LAPD Microfilm, Volume 76 (SUS Final Report) Current Section: State of Mind - Interviews with Police After Arrest, 623 https://www.maryferrell.org/showDoc.html?docId=99762#relPageId=273

376 Kaiser, 186

377 RFK LAPD Microfilm, Volume 76 (SUS Final Report), Current Section: State of Mind - Interviews with Police After Arrest https://www.maryferrell.org/showDoc.html?docId=99762#relPageId=273

378 RFK LAPD Microfilm, Volume 76 (SUS Final Report), Current Section: State of Mind - Interviews with Police After Arrest https://www.maryferrell.org/showDoc.html?docId=99762#relPageId=273

379 Kaiser, 93

380 Kaiser, 86, Trial of Sirhan Bishara Sirhan, Volume 15, 4120-4421, February 24 - 26, 1969 Current Section: Direct Examination Lt Jordan, LAPD, https://www.maryferrell.org/showDoc.html?docId=99530#relPageId=291

381 Newsweek, 'Sirhan: Tragedy of the Absurd', March 24, 1969, 22

382 RFK LAPD Microfilm, Volume 76 (SUS Final Report) Current Section: The Rosicrucian Order https://www.maryferrell.org/showDoc.html?docId=99762#relPageId=1

383 Kaiser, 342

384 Kaiser, 70

385 Kaiser, 70, Trial of Sirhan Bishara Sirhan, Volume 1, A1-A86, 1-210, June 7 1968 - January 6 1969, Trial of Sirhan Bishara Sirhan, Volume 31, 8823-9065, April 14 - May 21,1969

386 Kaiser, 2008 edition, 56

387 Kaiser, 265

388 NBC News, reporter John Dancy, Interview with John Weidner, June 5, 1968. Larry Sneed audio archives

389 RFK LAPD Microfilm, Volume 46 (Medical Records, Phone Call Summaries, Progress Reports) Current Section: Facts on Kennedy Headquarters-Interviews of Khan, Wayne, Khoury, Crowe, Good, Hotel Guest,

390 RFK LAPD Microfilm, Volume 46 (Medical Records, Phone Call Summaries, Progress Reports) Interview with Walter Crowe, July 8, 1968, Tape *29303 I-1813 Walter M. Crowe was administered a polygraph examination on July 8, 1968, in the polygraph facilities of the Scientific Investigation Division. https://www.maryferrell.org/showDoc.html?docId=99850#relPageId=150&search=INTERVIEW_WITH%20Walter%20Crowe

391 Kaiser, 240

392 Kaiser, 217

393 Kaiser, 515

394 Seigenthaler, 297

395 'Justice Department Keeps Watch on Arab Students Group As Sirhan Probe Continues' *Jewish Telegraph Agency*, June 24, 1968 https://www.jta.org/archive/justice-department-keeps-watch-on-arab-students-group-as-sirhan-probe-continues

396 'Sirhan Trial – It Stirs Deep and Conflicting Emotions,' Lacey Fosburgh, *New York Times*, January 19, 1969

397 'Sirhan Trial Seen Plodding Along in World of Own,' Douglas E Kneeland, *New York Times*, February 2, 1969

398 Jansen, 221

399 Klagsbrun and Whitney, 70

400 'Palestine Liberation Organization Portrays Sirhan As Commando Hero,' *Jewish Telegraphic Agency*, April 11, 1969, https://www.jta.org/archive/palestine-liberation-organization-portrays-sirhan-as-commando-hero

401 *TIME*, 'For Perspective and Determination', June 14, 1968, 9

402 Newsweek March 24, 1969, 'The Assassins: Who Did It – and Why', 24

403 'Rogers Backed But Judge Rejected Sirhan Guilty Plea For Life Term,' Frank Mankiewicz and Tom Braden, *Washington Post*, February 26, 1969 and 'Arab Press Plays Up Sirhan's Anti-Zionism' *New York Times*,, March 10, 1969

404 Pennock, Pamela E., *The Rise of the Arab American Left – Activists, Allies, and Their Fight against Imperialism and Racism, 1960s – 1980s*, The University of North Carolina Press, 2017, 122

405 Pennock, 140

406 RFK LAPD Microfilm, Volume 104 (Conspiracy Investigation Files) Current Section: The Fez Interviews https://www.maryferrell.org/showDoc.html?docId=99847#relPageId=245&search=Lou_Shelby

407 FBI Files, Interview of Phyllis Hazel Young, July 16, 1968, Los Angeles 56-156 https://vault.fbi.gov/Robert%20F%20Kennedy%20%28Assassination%29%20/Robert%20F%20Kennedy%20%28Assassination%29%20Part%201%20of%203/view

408 FBI Interview with Elsa Marie Butler, June 10, 1968, LA 56-156 https://vault.fbi.gov/Robert%20F%20Kennedy%20%28Assassination%29%20/

Robert%20F%20Kennedy%20%28Assassination%29%20Part%201%20of%203/view

409 FBI Files, Interview with (Redacted), Sherman Oaks, California, July 16, 1968, FBI Interview with Elsa Marie Butler, June 10, 1968, LA 56-156 https://vault.fbi.gov/Robert%20F%20Kennedy%20%28Assassination%29%20/Robert%20F%20Kennedy%20%28Assassination%29%20Part%201%20of%203/view

410 SUS Final Report, 484, RFK LAPD Microfilm, Volume 106 (Conspiracy Investigation Files) Current Section: Jerry Owen, https://www.maryferrell.org/showDoc.html?docId=99849#relPageId=380&search=Joyce_Stone

411 FBI Files, KENSALT Memo dated 6 June 1968, 56-156-1083, https://vault.fbi.gov/Robert%20F%20Kennedy%20%28Assassination%29%20/Robert%20F%20Kennedy%20%28Assassination%29%20Part%201%20of%203/view

412 RFK LAPD Microfilm, Volume 52 (Interviews, I-135 thru I-298) Current Section: Boujigian, Zareh Agop, August 28, 1968 https://www.maryferrell.org/showDoc.html?docId=99738#relPageId=240&search=Boujigian

413 Sirhan Sirhan Parole Hearing, June 26, 1985 https://www.maryferrell.org/showDoc.html?docId=146761

414 RFK Assassination: L.A.F.O. #56-156: Sub File X-4, Volume 13 Current Section: D. Additional Investigation Relating to Sirhan Family https://www.maryferrell.org/showDoc.html?docId=99665#relPageId=169&search=Ali_Kalla

415 RFK LAPD Microfilm, Volume 73 (Interviews, I-4538 thru I-4751), Current Section: Stephens, Merla, 12 Nov 1968 https://www.maryferrell.org/showDoc.html?docId=99759#relPageId=34&search=Ali_Kalla

416 'Sirhan's Father deeply shaken; "blackest day of my life"', *United Press International*, June 1968, https://www.upi.com/Archives/1968/06/06/Sirhans-father-deeply-shaken-blackest-day-of-my-life/7861527708424/

417 *LIFE*, June 1968, 30

418 Kaiser, 301

419 Kaiser, 422

420 Mehdi, 88

421 'Four Jordanian Lawyers Abandon Plan to Defend Sirhan in Trial for Kennedy Murder', *Jewish Telegraph Agency*, June 20, 1968 https://www.jta.org/archive/four-jordanian-lawyers-abandon-plan-to-defend-sirhan-in-trial-for-kennedy-murder

422 'Sirhan's Father In Amman: A Talk To "Ad Diffa" At Midnight', Text of *ad-Dilaa* article, June 17, 1968, Amman A-387 https://www.maryferrell.org/showDoc.html?docId=99631#relPageId=240&search=Bishara_Sirhan

423 'Bishara Sirhan, Assassin's Father', *New York Times*, December 9, 1987 https://www.maryferrell.org/showDoc.html?docId=99665#relPageId=138&search=Bishara_Sirhan,%20 Ad-diffa

424 'Sirhan's Father In Amman: A Talk To "Ad Diffa" At Midnight', Text of *ad-Dilaa* article, June 17, 1968, Amman A-387 https://www.maryferrell.org/showDoc.html?docId=99631#relPageId=240&search=Bishara_Sirhan

425 Online Archive of California, California State Archives, Collection Number: File 96-03-17 Inventory of the Los Angeles County Sheriff's Department Records - Sirhan Sirhan Case Jail Logs, June 15, 1968 https://oac.cdlib.org/findaid/ark:/13030/kt2j49r8f6/dsc/#c01-1.3.7.2

426 County of Los Angeles Sheriff's Department, Memo from Sheriff's Deputy Torres, badge Number 2319 to Inspector Carpenter, January 11, 1969, "Conversation overheard between Inmate and Dr Diamond" https://oac.cdlib.org/findaid/ark:/13030/kt2j49r8f6/dsc/#c01-1.3.7.2

427 Jail Logs, July 1, 1968 Entry by Harold Hoffman.

428 FBI Files, From Sac Los Angeles to FBI Director, Kensalt Summary, July 16, 1968 https://vault.fbi.gov/Robert%20F%20Kennedy%20%28Assassination%29%20/Robert%20F%20Kennedy%20%28Assassination%29%20Part%201%20of%203/view

429 FBI Files RFK LA 56-156, Sub X-05 Volume 17, 126, Interview held on July 30, 1968, August 8, 1968

430 'Robert Kennedy's Killer', Chris Miller, *Star News*. Los Angeles Sheriff's Museum, July 1, 2017.

431 Sheriff's Logs January 23, 1969

432 'Robert Kennedy's Killer', Chris Miller, *Star News*, Los Angeles Sheriff's Museum, July 1, 2017

433 Sheriff's Logs April 10, 1969, Online Archive of California, California State Archives, Collection Number: File 96-03-17 Inventory of the Los Angeles County Sheriff's Department Records - Sirhan Sirhan Case Jail Logs, https://oac.cdlib.org/findaid/ark:/13030/kt2j49r8f6/dsc/#c01-1.3.7.2

434 Kaiser, 169

435 Kaiser, 171

436 Letter from John M. Lawrence of Federated Americans Against Israeli Racism (FAIR) 57 West 10th Street, New York, NY to Sirhan B. Sirhan, June 7, 1968, Los Angeles County Sheriff's Department, File 3-26, General Subject Files-Organizing Committee for Clemency for Sirhan, June 1968 (hereafter GSF3-26); Sirhan received the letter on June 10, 1968

437 Copy of Letter to the Editor by John M. Lawrence to *Washington Post* sent Sirhan, June 25, 1968, GSF3-27

438 Copy of Letter to the Editor by John M. Lawrence to *Washington Post* sent Sirhan, June 25, 1968, GSF3-27

439 FBI Files, Subject Robert F. Kennedy Assassination, LA File: 56-156 Sub File X-3 Volume 9 https://vault.fbi.gov/Robert%20F%20Kennedy%20%28Assassination%29%20/Robert%20F%20Kennedy%20%28Assassination%29%20Part%201%20of%203/view

440 Letter from John M. Lawrence to Sirhan Sirhan, June 7, 1968, GSF3-26.

441 Letter from John M. Lawrence and Abdeen Jabara (attorney) to Sirhan, June 14, 1968, PDS1-32

442 Copies of "Insight," published by FAIR, April 1, 1968, (Vol. 1, No. 3), New York, N.Y., Los Angeles County Sheriff's Department, File 3-28, General Subject Files, June-November 1968, GSF3-28

443 Press Release from The Action Committee on American-Arab Relations, Secretary-General Dr. M. T. Mehdi, 441 Lexington Avenue, New York, New York, June 11, 1968, Los Angeles County Sheriff's Department Files-General Subject Files, 3-28; (LASDF-GSF3-28), June-November 1968 https://boomcalifornia.org/2018/06/05/the-killing-of-robert-f-kennedy/#_ednref27

444 Copy of Western Union Telegram, Sirhan B. Sirhan to FAIR, 57 West 10th Street, New York, NY, 2:30 P.M., June 13, 1968, PDS1-32. https://oac.cdlib.org/findaid/ark:/13030/kt2j49r8f6/dsc/#c01-1.3.7.2

445 Letter from Deputy T.I. Greene to Inspector R. Welch, June 14, 1968, Subject: "Sirhan Sirhan, Conversation" PDS1-32. https://oac.cdlib.org/findaid/ark:/13030/kt2j49r8f6/dsc/#c01-1.3.7.2

446 Online Archive of California, California State Archives Sheriff's logs, Memo by Deputy Dyson January 30, 1969, Collection Number: File 96-03-17 Inventory of the Los Angeles County Sheriff's Department Records - Sirhan Sirhan Case Jail Logs, https://oac.cdlib.org/findaid/ark:/13030/kt2j49r8f6/dsc/#c01-1.3.7.2

447 Sheriff's Logs, I.B. Mills January 23, 1969, https://oac.cdlib.org/findaid/ark:/13030/kt2j49r8f6/dsc/#c01-1.3.7.2

448 Sheriff's Logs, January 23, 1969, https://oac.cdlib.org/findaid/ark:/13030/kt2j49r8f6/dsc/#c01-1.3.7.2

449 Moldea.com, https://www.moldea.com/Sirhan-HeyPunk.html

450 Kaiser, 262

451 Trial of Sirhan Bishara Sirhan, Volume 31, 8823-9065, April 14 - May 21, 1969, Current Section: Thursday, April 17, 1969 https://www.maryferrell.org/showDoc.html?docId=99547#relPageId=29

452 Trial of Sirhan Bishara Sirhan, Transcript of the trial, January 6 – April 4, 1969 https://www.maryferrell.org/php/showlist.php?docset=1659

453 Trial of Sirhan Bishara Sirhan, Volume 27, 7713-8018, April 2 - 4, 1969 Current Section: Cross Examination (resumed),https://www.maryferrell.org/showDoc.html?docId=99542#relPageId=81

454 Sheriff's Logs April 2, 1969 https://oac.cdlib.org/findaid/ark:/13030/kt2j49r8f6/dsc/#c01-1.3.7.2

455 Jansen, 11

456 Trial of Sirhan Bishara Sirhan, Volume 31, 8823-9065, April 14 - May 21, 1969, Current Section: Thursday, April 17, 1969 https://www.maryferrell.org/showDoc.html?docId=99547#relPageId=29

457 LASD Retired, 'Protecting Sirhan Sirhan Robert Kennedy's Killer', Chris Miller, June 2017 https://lasdretired.org/wp-content/uploads/2020/05/Protecting-Sirhan-Sirhan-part-2.pdf

458 Kaiser 252, RFK LAPD Microfilm, Volume 75 (SUS Final Report) Current Section: Related Events Since the Assassination, 109 https://www.maryferrell.org/showDoc.html?docId=99761#relPageId=55

459 RFK LAPD Microfilm, Volume 75 (SUS Final Report) Page 110 Current Section: Related Events Since the Assassination https://www.maryferrell.org/showDoc.html?docId=99761#relPageId=55

460 RFK LAPD Microfilm, Volume 75 (SUS Final Report) Current Section: Related Events Since the Assassination, 112 https://www.maryferrell.org/showDoc.html?docId=99761#relPageId=55

461 Kaiser, 255

462 'Sirhan Brother Convicted of Threatening Mrs Meir', *New York Times*, June 14, 1973, 35, Kaiser, 256

463 RFK LAPD Microfilm, Volume 76 (SUS Final Report), Current Section: Investigations Involving the Fez Restaurant, https://www.maryferrell.org/showDoc.html?docId=99762#relPageId=98

464 'Defending Sirhan Sirhan', Dan Shine, 2018 https://bentley.umich.edu/news-events/magazine/defending-sirhan-sirhan/

465 Online Archive of California, California State Archives, Collection Number: File 96-03-17 Inventory of the Los Angeles County Sheriff's Department Records - Sirhan Sirhan Case Jail Logs, Deputy Torcaso (2741) to Inspector Welch/Lt Carpenter, June 2, 1969 https://oac.cdlib.org/findaid/ark:/13030/kt2j49r8f6/dsc/#c01-1.3.7.2

466 Bay Area Televion Archive, Interview with Mary Sirhan at San Quentin (1970) https://diva.sfsu.edu/collections/sfbatv/bundles/238798

467 Sirhan Sirhan Parole Hearing, May 23, 1989 https://www.maryferrell.org/showDoc.html?docId=146753

468 Gavin Newsom, Governor, State of California, Sirhan Sirhan, B-21014 First Degree Murder, Decision Date: January 13, 2022, https://www.gov.ca.gov/wp-content/uploads/2022/01/1.13.22-Sirhan-Reverse-Decision.pdf

469 Korn, David A., *Assassination in Khartoum*, Bloomington: Indiana University Press, 1993, Reviewed by Daniel Pipes in *American Spectator*, February 1994 https://www.danielpipes.org/608/assassination-in-khartoum and Sherifa Zuhur, *Palestine, Sirhan Sirhan and Robert*

F Kennedy's Assassination, June 5, 2018 https://www.aljazeera.com/opinions/2018/6/5/palestine-sirhan-sirhan-and-robert-f-kennedys-assassination

470 'The Terrorists whose Names Must Not Be Mentioned', Stephen Flatow, *Jewish News Syndicate*, July 10, 2018, https://www.jns.org/the-terrorists-whose-names-must-not-be-mentioned/

471 'Obama's Connection to Sirhan Sirhan', Daniel Pipes, Middle East Forum, November 2, 2008 https://www.danielpipes.org/blog/2008/11/obamas-connection-to-sirhan-sirhan#continued

472 Subsequent Parole Consideration Hearing State of California Board of Prison Terms Sirhan Sirhan CDC Number B-21014, California State Prison Corcoran, California, June 18, 1997 Steve Baker Presiding Commissioner, https://www.maryferrell.org/php/showlist.php?docset=1958

473 Sirhan Sirhan Parole Hearing June 18, 1997, Subsequent Parole Consideration Hearing State of California Board of Prison Terms Sirhan Sirhan CDC Number B-21014, California State Prison Corcoran, California, June 18, 1997 Steve Baker Presiding Commissioner https://www.maryferrell.org/showDoc.html?docId=146756#relPageId=1

474 'Sirhan DID shoot Bobby Kennedy….', Paul Callan, *The Mirror*, May 30, 2018 https://www.mirror.co.uk/news/world-news/sirhan-shoot-bobby-kennedy-held-12623836

475 Gavin Newsom, Governor, State of California, Sirhan Sirhan, B-21014 First Degree Murder, Decision Date: January 13, 2022 https://www.gov.ca.gov/wp-content/uploads/2022/01/1.13.22-Sirhan-Reverse-Decision.pdf

476 'Sirhan' Cynthia Gorney, *Washington Post*, August 20, 1979, 4 https://www.washingtonpost.com/archive/lifestyle/1979/08/20/sirhan/75cd41f0-e570-4bc4-ac93-83f251eec765/

477 'Sirhan Says Liquor, Anger Led To Killing', *Wilmington Morning Star*, September 27, 1980 https://news.google.com/newspapers?id=v-UVAAAAIBAJ&sjid=LBQEAAAAIBAJ&pg=5527%2C5825541

478 'Sirhan's family, 14 years later', Joan Goulding, *United Press International*, May 23, 1982 https://www.upi.com/Archives/1982/05/23/Sirhans-family-14-years-later/3665390974400/

479 Personality - Spotlight On Sirhan, April 25, 1982 https://www.upi.com/Archives/1982/04/25/Personality-Spotlight-on-Sirhan-Sirhan/9547388558800/,

480 Subsequent Parole Consideration Hearing State of California Board of Prison Terms Sirhan Sirhan CDC Number B-21014, California State Prison Corcoran, California, June 18, 1997 Steve Baker Presiding Commissioner, https://www.maryferrell.org/showDoc.html?docId=146756

481 Personality - Spotlight On Sirhan, April 25, 1982 https://www.upi.com/Archives/1982/04/25/Personality-Spotlight-on-Sirhan-Sirhan/9547388558800/,

482 'RFK would OK Parole, Sirhan says', Carol Oppenheim, *Chicago Tribune*, May 11, 1982, 9

483 'Panel in California cancels Sirhan's 1984 parole date', *New York Times*, May 22, 1982, 4.

484 Trial of Sirhan Bishara Sirhan, Volume 18, 5027-5328, March 5 - 6, 1969, Current Section: Cross Examination Sirhan by Compton https://www.maryferrell.org/showDoc.html?docId=99533#relPageId=222

485 Sirhan Sirhan, Parole Hearing June 26, 1989, Correctional Training Facility, Soledad https://www.maryferrell.org/showDoc.html?docId=146761

486 Sirhan Sirhan Parole Hearing March 27, 1986. Correctional Training Facility, Soledad https://www.maryferrell.org/php/showlist.php?docset=1958

487 Sirhan Sirhan Parole Hearing March 27, 1986. Correctional Training Facility, Soledad https://www.maryferrell.org/php/showlist.php?docset=1958

488 'Inside Sirhan Sirhan's 50-year quest for freedom after assassinating Robert F. Kennedy', *Times* staff, *Los Angeles Times*, August 27, 2021 https://www.latimes.com/california/story/2021-08-27/inside-sirhan-sirhans-50-year-quest-for-freedom-after-assassinating-robert-f-kennedy

489 RFK's assassination, June 2, 2008, 10:54 PM BST / Source: An msnbc.com Special Report, NBC News, Key figures associated with RFK's assassination and https://www.nbcnews.com/id/wbna24895033 https://www.maryferrell.org/showDoc.html?docId=146753

490 Sirhan Sirhan Parole Hearing May 28, 1987 https://www.maryferrell.org/showDoc.html?docId=146752

491 Subsequent Parole Consideration Hearing, State of California, Board of Prison Terms, Sirhan Sirhan, CDC Number B-21014, Correctional Training Facility, November 28, 1989 https://www.maryferrell.org/showDoc.html?docId=146753

492 Subsequent Parole Consideration Hearing, State of California, Board of Prison Terms, Sirhan Sirhan, CDC Number B-21014, Correctional Training Facility, November 28, 1989 https://www.maryferrell.org/showDoc.html?docId=146753

493 Subsequent Parole Consideration Hearing, State of California, Board of Prison Terms, Sirhan Sirhan, CDC Number B-21014, Correctional Training Facility, November 28, 1989 https://www.maryferrell.org/showDoc.html?docId=146753

494 Subsequent Parole Consideration Hearing, State of California, Board of Prison Terms, Sirhan Sirhan, CDC Number B-21014, Correctional Training Facility, November 28, 1989 https://www.maryferrell.org/showDoc.html?docId=146753

495 'Sirhan Sirhan Reveals Why He Killed Bobby Kennedy in 1989', *Inside Edition*, Interview by David Frost, https://www.youtube.com/watch?v=Ma_RpEcm7NY

496 Subsequent parole Consideration hearing, State of California, Board of Prison Terms, Sirhan Sirhan, CDC Number B-21014 Correctional Traing facility, November 28, 1989 https://www.maryferrell.org/showDoc.html?docId=146753

497 Sirhan Sirhan Parole Hearing June 26, 1990 https://www.maryferrell.org/showDoc.html?docId=146754

498 Sirhan Sirhan Parole Hearing June 26, 1990 https://www.maryferrell.org/showDoc.html?docId=146754

499 1994 Parole Hearing, Subsequent Parole Consideration Hearing, California State Prison- Corcoran, California, December 1, 1994, Mr Steve Baker, Presiding Commissioner https://www.maryferrell.org/showDoc.html?docId=146755

500 Sirhan Sirhan Parole Hearing December 1, 1994 https://www.maryferrell.org/showDoc.html?docId=146755

501 Moldea, Dan, *The Killing of Robert F. Kennedy – An Investigation of Means, Motive and Opportunity*, WW Norton and Co., 1995, 300

502 'The Real Manchurian Candidate', *Pasadena Weekly*, 16 November 2006, https://pasadenaweekly.com/the-real-manchurian-candidate/

503 Sirhan Sirhan Parole Hearing, June 18, 1997 https://www.maryferrell.org/showDoc.html?docId=146756

504 Sirhan Sirhan Parole Hearing March 22, 2001, Subsequent Parole Consideration Hearing State of California Board of Prison Terms, California State Prison – Corcoran, California, March 22, 2001 https://www.maryferrell.org/showDoc.html?docId=146757

505 Sirhan Sirhan Parole Hearing March 22, 2001, Subsequent Parole Consideration Hearing State of California Board of Prison Terms, California State Prison – Corcoran, California, March 22, 2001 https://www.maryferrell.org/showDoc.html?docId=146757

506 'The Real Manchurian Candidate', *Pasadena Weekly*, 16 November 2006, https://pasadenaweekly.com/the-real-manchurian-candidate/

507 Sirhan Sirhan Parole Hearing March 2, 2011 https://www.maryferrell.org/showDoc.html?docId=146760

508 Sirhan Sirhan Parole Hearing March 15, 2006 https://www.maryferrell.org/showDoc.html?docId=146759

509 2016 Parole Hearings, https://www.maryferrell.org/showDoc.html?docId=146888

510 Sirhan Sirhan Parole Hearing Mar 2, 20011 https://www.maryferrell.org/showDoc.html?docId=146760

511 Sirhan Sirhan Parole Hearing March 2, 20011 https://www.maryferrell.org/showDoc.html?docId=146760

512 'Convicted RFK assassin denied parole', Michael Martinez, CNN, March 3, 2011 http://edition.cnn.com/2011/CRIME/03/03/california.sirhan.parole.hearing/index.html

513 Moldea, 312-313, 326

514 'DiEugenio's The Curious Case of Dan Moldea,' www.moldea.com

515 'Handwritten notes by Robert F. Kennedy Assassin Sirhan Sirhan Shed New Light on Killer', *Los Angeles Times*, April 7, 2011, http://latimesblogs.latimes.com/lanow/2011/04/handwritten-notes-by-rfk-assassin-sirhan-sirhan-shed-new-light-on-killer.html

516 Kaiser, 388

517 Kaiser, 518

518 In The United States District Court For The Central District of California, Sirhan Bishara Sirhan, Petitioner v George Galaza, Warden, et all, Respondent CV-00-5686-CAS (AJW) Reply Brief Regarding Actual Innocence, Memorandum of Points and Authorities

519 See: Sirhan v. Galaza. Case No. CV 00–05686 BRO AJWx, 2015-01-05, SIRHAN B. Sirhan, Plaintiff, v. George GALAZA et al., Defendant. January 5, 2015 https://casetext.com/case/sirhan-v-galaza-2

520 Sirhan v. Galaza. Case No. CV 00–05686 BRO AJWx, January 5, 2015, Sirhan B. Sirhan, Plaintiff, v. George Galaza et al., Defendant https://casetext.com/case/sirhan-v-galaza-2

521 Gavin Newsom, Governor, State of California, Sirhan Sirhan, B-21014 First Degree Murder, Decision Date: January 13, 2022 https://www.gov.ca.gov/wp-content/uploads/2022/01/1.13.22-Sirhan-Reverse-Decision.pdf

522 Board of Parole Hearings CDC Number: B-21014 R.J. Donovan Correctional Facility at Rock Mountain, San Diego, California February 10, 2016, Brian Roberts, Presiding Commissioner, Keith Stanton, Deputy Commissioner. https://www.maryferrell.org/showDoc.html?docId=146888

523 'Bobby Kennedy's Assassin Sirhan Sirhan Is Stabbed In California Prison, The man who killed RFK in 1968 is in stable condition in a local hospital', Mary Pappenfuss, *Huffington Post*, August 31, 2019 https://www.huffingtonpost.co.uk/entry/sirhan-sirhan-sabbed-rft-bobby-kennedy-stabbing_n_5d6a1b50e4b0cdfe05706bcf, Kennedy assassin stabbed in prison — reports, August 31, 2019, https://www.dw.com/en/robert-f-kennedy-assassin-stabbed-in-prison-reports/a-50242120

524 Parole Suitability Hearing, State of California Board of Parole Hearings, Sirhan Bishara Sirhan, CDC No: B21014, R.J. Donovan Correctional Facility, San Diego, California, March 1, 2023, John Garcia Presiding Commissioner, Vijay Desai Deputy Commissioner, Indeterminate Sentence Parole Release Review, Sirhan Sirhan, B-21014 First Degree Murder, https://www.gov.ca.gov/wp-content/uploads/2022/01/1.13.22-Sirhan-Reverse-Decision.pdf

525 'How Sirhan was Mentored Through Parole by Suge Knight, Mafia leaders', Ryan Grim, *The Intercept*, September 8, 2021 https://theintercept.com/2021/09/08/sirhan-sirhan-parole-suge-knight/

526 'Board Says RFK Assassin Sirhan Changed Man; Grants Parole', Julie Watson and Brian Melley, *Associated Press*, August 27, 2021 https://apnews.com/article/middle-east-d5e12df9cc3c0241ab108bfc124dda1b

527 'Who is Sirhan Sirhan? His life before the RFK assassination', Justin Ray, *Los Angeles Times* https://www.latimes.com/california/newsletter/2021-08-30/sirhan-sirhan-robert-f-kennedy-essential-california

528 'Prison Fate Of Robert F. Kennedy's Assassin "Tore Family Apart" Before 78-Year-Old Inmate's Parole Was Denied' Aaron Johnson, Radar Online, March 2, 2023 https://radaronline.com/p/fate-of-robert-kennedy-assassin-tore-family-apart-before-parole-denied/

529 'RFK widow Ethel Kennedy says no to freeing killer Sirhan Sirhan', Carl Campanile, *New York Post*, September 7, 2021 https://nypost.com/2021/09/07/rfk-widow-ethel-kennedy-says-no-to-freeing-killer-sirhan-sirhan/?utm_source=sailthru&utm_medium=email&utm_campaign=news_alert&utm_content=20210907&utm_term=NYP%20-%20News%20Alerts&fbclid=IwAR1A7ojh2Ed_ZRmZBo-Qjqm0d3JUr84PRx8PIQDiyHHRcZq7krBE6NWUf2w

530 'Sirhan Sirhan, Robert F. Kennedy's killer, is recommended for parole', *Los Angeles Times*, August 27, 2021 https://www.latimes.com/california/story/2021-08-27/robert-f-kennedys-killer-faces-a-parole-board-today-the-l-a-d-a-will-not-oppose-his-release

531 'Op-Ed: In assassinating my father, Sirhan committed a crime against America. He must not be released', *Los Angeles Times*, August 28, 2021 https://www.latimes.com/opinion/story/2021-08-28/sirhan-robert-kennedy-assassination-parole

532 'RFK's oldest son condemns possible parole of Sirhan Sirhan,' *Los Angeles Times*, August 30, 2021 https://www.latimes.com/politics/story/2021-08-30/rfk-oldest-son-condemns-possible-parole-sirhan-sirhan

533 'Robert F. Kennedy's daughter Kerry says she is "deeply grateful" Gavin Newsom denied his killer Sirhan Sirhan's parole', *Mail Online*, January 14, 2022 https://www.dailymail.co.uk/news/article-10403327/Kerry-Kennedy-says-shes-deeply-grateful-Newsom-denying-Sirhan-Sirhan-parole.html

534 'Robert F. Kennedy's daughter Kerry says she is "deeply grateful" Gavin Newsom denied his killer Sirhan Sirhan's parole', *Mail Online*, January 14, 2022 https://www.dailymail.co.uk/news/article-10403327/Kerry-Kennedy-says-shes-deeply-grateful-Newsom-denying-Sirhan-Sirhan-parole.html

535 Parole Suitability Hearing, State of California Board of Parole Hearings, Sirhan Bishara Sirhan, CDC No: B21014, R.J. Donovan Correctional Facility, San Diego, California, March 1, 2023, John Garcia Presiding Commissioner, Vijay Desai Deputy Commissioner

536 Parole Suitability Hearing, State of California Board of Parole Hearings, Sirhan Bishara Sirhan, CDC No: B21014, R.J. Donovan Correctional Facility, San Diego, California, March 1, 2023, John Garcia Presiding Commissioner, Vijay Desai Deputy Commissioner https://populartimelines.com/timeline/Sirhan-Sirhan

537 'The Real Manchurian Candidate', *Pasadena Weekly*, November 16, 2006 https://www.pasadenaweekly.com/news/feature-stories/the-real-manchurian-candidate/article_b04b1bd9-09f5-596f-9f8e-e065ad25fedc.html

538 'The Real Manchurian Candidate', *Pasadena Weekly*, November 16, 2006 https://www.pasadenaweekly.com/news/feature-stories/the-real-manchurian-candidate/article_b04b1bd9-09f5-596f-9f8e-e065ad25fedc.html

539 Kaiser, 513

540 Kaiser, 214

541 Pease, Lisa, and James DiEugenio, eds., *The Assassinations: Probe Magazine on JFK, MLK, RFK and Malcolm X*, Los Angeles: Feral House, 2003, 629

542 Kaiser, 168

543 Melanson, Philip H., *The Robert F. Kennedy Assassination: New Revelations on the Conspiracy and Cover-up*, New York: Shapolsky, 1991, 68

544 William Klaber and Philip Melanson, *Shadow Play*, St Martin's Paperbacks, 1997, 180

545 LAPD Summary Report, 488

546 Turner, William and Christian, Jon, *The Assassination of Robert F. Kennedy – The Conspiracy and Cover-Up*, Carroll and Graf, 2006, 208

547 Pease, Lisa, *A Lie Too Big To Fail*, Feral House, 2018, 126-127

548 'Why the man who's spent 50 years in jail for killing Bobby Kennedy COULDN'T have done it', Tim Tate and Brad Johnson, Mail Online, May 25, 2018 https://www.dailymail.co.uk/news/article-5773147/Why-man-whos-spent-50-years-jail-killing-Bobby-Kennedy-it.html#ixzz5Gc00gyuX

549 Moldea.com, http://www.moldea.com/RFKcase.html

550 '"I KNOW You Didn't Kill My Father": Inside RFK Jr.'s Explosive 3-Hour Meeting', Radar Online, https://radaronline.com/p/rfk-jr-three-hour-meeting-bobby-kennedy-convicted-killer/

551 'Robert F Kennedy was assassinated by Thane Eugene Cesar, declares RFK Jr.', Chris Spargo, Mail Online, September 12, 2019 https://www.dailymail.co.uk/news/article-7456521/Robert-F-Kennedy-assassinated-Thane-Eugene-Cesar-Sirhan-Sirhan-says-RFK-Jr.html

552 LA County DA Thomas F Kranz, March 1977, Second LA County DA Thomas F Kranz, March 1977, Second Section, 6, Opinion, Commentary by Kranz On First Section and Conspiracy Theories,

Analysis, Investigations, Recommendations, Thane Eugene Cesar, Don Schulman, Ted Charach https://vault.fbi.gov/Robert%20F%20Kennedy%20%28Assassination%29%20/Robert%20F%20Kennedy%20%28Assassination%29%20Part%201%20of%203, Section, page 3

553 RFK LAPD Microfilm, Volume 94 (Transcripts of Recorded Interviews) Current Section: Interview of Thane Cesar, June 5, 1968 https://www.maryferrell.org/showDoc.html?docId=99837#relPageId=33

554 RFK LAPD Microfilm, Volume 76 (SUS Final Report) Page 652,Current Section: Analysis of the Murder Weapon and Bullets https://www.maryferrell.org/showDoc.html?docId=99762#relPageId=299&search=WALTER_T%20RATHKE See also: RFK LAPD Microfilm, Volume 103 (Case Preparation Files, Conspiracy Investigation Files), Current Section: Ballistics, https://www.maryferrell.org/showDoc.html?docId=99846#relPageId=105, 652, RFK LAPD Microfilm, Volume 77 (SUS Final Report), Current Section: Examination of Clothing https://www.maryferrell.org/showDoc.html?docId=99763#relPageId=48

555 FBI Interviews, DiPierro, Romero, Yaro, Minasian https://www.maryferrell.org/php/showlist.php?docset=1686

556 FBI Interview with Frank Burns, https://www.maryferrell.org/php/showlist.php?docset=1686

557 'Bobby Kennedy's son thinks he was killed by a second shooter. Is there anything to it?', Nik Decosta- Klipa, Boston.com, May 31, 2018 https://www.boston.com/news/history/2018/05/31/rfk-assassination-conspiracy-theory-second-shooter/?fbclid=IwAR3bTkhBxsiieWEHyTseOx03yEhs4j1XEDOAdTxrGlHWRtN0Uzk0c8tzE8c

558 *'Who Killed Martin Luther King?'*, Tony Stark, *The Guardian*, November 28, 1999 https://www.theguardian.com/theobserver/1999/nov/28/life1.lifemagazine1

559 Sheriff's Logs, January 28, 1969, Online Archive of California, California State Archives, Collection Number: File 96-03-17 Inventory of the Los Angeles County Sheriff's Department Records - Sirhan Sirhan Case Jail Logs, https://oac.cdlib.org/findaid/ark:/13030/kt2j49r8f6/dsc/#c01-1.3.7.2

560 Schacter, Daniel L., *Searching For Memory: The Brain, the Mind, the Past,* New York Basic Books 1997, 227

561 Scgacter, Daniel L., *Searching For Memory: The Brain, the Mind, the Past,* New York Basic Books 1997, 227

562 'Murder In Mind Weekly', Clint Witchall, *The Guardian*, April 15, 2004, 20

563 Vorpagel, Russell, *Profiles in Murder: An FBI Legend Dissects Killers and Their Crimes*, New York: Dell, 1998, 142

564 Sirhan Sirhan Parole Hearing, June 26, 1985, https://www.maryferrell.org/php/showlist.php?docset=1958

565 Trial of Sirhan Bishara Sirhan, Volume 18, 5027-5328, March 5 – 6, 1969 Current Section: Cross Examination Sirhan by Compton https://www.maryferrell.org/showDoc.html?docId=99533#relPageId=222

566 Trial of Sirhan Bishara Sirhan, Volume 18, 5027-5328, March 5 – 6, 1969 Current Section: Cross Examination Sirhan by Compton https://www.maryferrell.org/showDoc.html?docId=99533#relPageId=222

567 Kaiser, 251-252

568 Kaiser, 239

569 Kaiser, 469

570 Kaiser, 328

571 'Anti-Semitism In Palestinian School Textbooks, EU Study Confirms Incitement in Palestinian Textbooks', Jewish Virtual Library, 2021, https://www.jewishvirtuallibrary.org/eu-study-confirms-incitement-in-palestinian-textbooks

572 'New Palestinian curriculum shows no improvements, antisemitism remains, Palestinian children are still being taught to glorify martyrdom and jihad against Israel', Donna Rachel Edmunds, *Jewish Post*, September 22, 2020 https://www.jpost.com/middle-east/new-palestinian-curriculum-shows-no-improvements-antisemitism-remains-643152 'UN Teachers Call To Murder Jews, Reveals New Report,' March 14, 2023, https://unwatch.org/un-teachers-call-to-murder-jews-reveals-new-report/

573 'Administration Fears Assassination Could Hurt US Relations with Arab States', *Jewish Telegraphic Agency*, June 7, 1968 https://www.jta.org/archive/administration-fears-assassination-could-hurt-u-s-relations-with-arab-states

574 'Sirhan Sirhan and the Assassination of Robert F. Kennedy: Palestinian Rage and the Depoliticization of a Tragedy', Michael R. Fischbach, *The Middle East Journal*, Middle East Institute, Volume 76, Number 2, Summer 2022, https://muse.jhu.edu/view_citations?type=article&id=865502

575 'The Volokh Conspiracy, Speaking of the Kennedy Assassination', David Bernstein, November 23, 2013 https://volokh.com/2013/11/23/speaking-kennedy-assassination/

576 '1968 – A Year of War Turmoil and Beyond', 3DD production in association with Sky Arts, 2018

577 'RFK Jr's Family Bashes Him After Third Party Announcement', Nikki McCann Ramirez, *Rolling Stone*, October 9, 2023 https://www.rollingstone.com/politics/politics-news/robert-f-kennedy-jr-announces-2024-independent-run-1234849138/

578 'Sirhan', Cynthia Gorney, *Washington Post*, August 20, 1979, 4 https://www.washingtonpost.com/archive/lifestyle/1979/08/20/sirhan/75cd41f0-e570-4bc4-ac93-83f251eec765/

INDEX